Stagolee Shot Billy

Stagolee Shot Billy

Cecil Brown

Harvard University Press
Cambridge, Massachusetts, and London, England
2003

To Alan Dundes, with great admiration

Publication of this book has been supported through the generous
provisions of the Maurice and Lula Bradley Smith Memorial Fund

Library of Congress Cataloging-in-Publication Data
Brown, Cecil, 1943–
Stagolee shot Billy / Cecil Brown.
p. cm.
Includes bibliographical references and index.
ISBN 0-674-01056-6 (alk. paper)
1. Stagolee (Legendary character)
2. African Americans—Songs and music—History and criticism.
3. Ballads, English—United States—History and criticism.
4. Literature and folklore—United States.   5. African American criminals—Folklore.
6. African American men in literature.   7. African American men—Folklore.
8. Saint Louis (Mo.)—Folklore.   9. African Americans—Folklore.   I. Title.
PS478.B76 2003
813'.54—dc21   2002192241

Acknowledgments

Many people helped in the making of this book. It was Alan Dundes who first urged me to write a complete history of Stagolee. Further encouragement came from Charles Henry, Jan Mohammed, Olly Wilson, and Amin Sweeney.

Tom Luddy gave the manuscript to Greil Marcus, who in turn gave it to Lindsay Waters at Harvard University Press, and Lindsay's perseverance and patience brought the project to completion. Zachary Taylor helped me organize the chapters.

My ideas about Stagolee were refined in the course of valuable discussions with Al Young, Ishmael Reed, Mel Watkins, Steve Jamison, David Henderson, Quincy Troupe, Billy Woodberry, Phil Kaufman, Paul Wilner, Leon Litwack, Sterling Stuckey, George Lakov, Quincy Troupe, Big John Henry, Jürgen Streeck, Dr. Ingrid Krutzner, Susan Golden, and David Peebles.

A few individuals, though they departed this life some time ago and were not directly involved in the writing of the manuscript, nevertheless inspired me by their example. These were my father, Cecil Culphert Brown; my uncles Lindsey Waddell and Lofton Freeman; and my brother Donald Ray Brown.

Essential help came from John Waide at the archives of Saint Louis University, Mildred Rigs of the Saint Louis Public Library, and Randy Bloomgant of the Missouri Historical Society. Ellen Thomasson of the Missouri Historical Society kindly provided the photographs of Judge David Murphy and Nathaniel Craig Dryden. I am indebted to Russell David, whose dissertation on Stagolee furnished important details; and to Judy David, his widow, who generously shared items from his archives.

And I am deeply grateful to Randi Rucker for her patience, forbearance, and encouragement.

Contents

Introduction: The Tradition of Stagolee

There is . . . a culture of the Negro which is his and has been
addressed to him; a culture which has, for good or ill, helped to
clarify his consciousness and create emotional attitudes which
are conducive to action. This culture has stemmed mainly from
two sources: (1) the Negro church; and (2) the folklore of the
Negro people.

—RICHARD WRIGHT, 1957

What does the [Stagolee] song say exactly? . . . It says no man
gains immortality thru public acclaim.

—BOB DYLAN, 1993

While I was growing up on a tobacco farm in North
Carolina in the late 1950s and early 1960s, the most important legend to me was that of Stagolee. As chanted in the form of a "toast"
by my Uncle Lindsey, the narrative presented a young god of virility. In those days, to young black field hands sitting in the shade of
a tree at the end of the tobacco road, Stagolee was as impulsive, as
vulgar, as daring, and as adventurous as they wanted him (and

themselves) to be. My uncles, who were my male role models, and their friends recited their rhymed, obscene praise of Stagolee's badness. At the end of the day the same men gathered in J. C. Himes's jook joint to dance with the girls, drink whiskey, and fight. Their nocturnal activities, I thought, were an extension of Stagolee's.

As I grew up, I realized that many other young black men also knew Stagolee. In fact interest in Stagolee is widespread among black men throughout America, not just on southern farms and in industrialized northern ghettos but also in Oklahoma, Montana, and California.

The origins of the Stagolee legend coincide with the origins of the blues in the 1890s. The legend had its first expression as a field holler of former plantation slaves as they migrated to the levee camps along the Mississippi. From there the legend moved to southern prisons, where it was honed and shaped into a work song. Stagolee also expressed the worldview and feelings of poor white hillbillies, who adopted the legend as one of their own.

Carl Sandburg loved singing "Stagolee,"[1] and writers such as Gwendolyn Brooks, Howard Odum, Richard Wright, and James Baldwin have used the song as a model for short stories, poems, and plays. Duke Ellington and Sidney Bechet arranged and performed versions of it, and more recently Stagolee has been the subject of a musical comedy.

Stagolee is a metaphor that structures the life of black males from childhood through maturity. I have heard versions of it, spoken and sung, many times during and since childhood, and the core image continues to have meaning for me in middle age. Not long ago I recited a few stanzas of the ballad to my eight-year-old nephew Lionel, and soon afterward he asked me to tell him all about Stagolee. The legend survives because black men pass it on. As culture critic Greil Marcus observes, Stagolee "is a story that black America has never tired of hearing and never stopped living out, like whites with their Westerns."[2]

Black people hold Stagolee before them like a charter whose meaning is implicit. The comment "He's just another Stagolee" in reference to the actions of a well-known black figure evokes the black male ethos. The other person might reply, "There's no shame in Stagolee's game." Stagolee is an in-group catchword conveying knowledge of what it means to be a black man. A well-known black painter told me that it is impossible to understand what Stagolee is about until one understands that Stagolee "wouldn't allow anybody to 'touch' his hat." He emphasized "touch" with a great deal of body language, imitating Stagolee's own taboo against anyone's putting a hand on his apparel.

Enslaved Africans might have recognized Stagolee as a variant of Shango, the Yoruba deity of thunder. But the ballad of Stagolee didn't come into existence until 1895, after one Lee Shelton, a thirty-one-year-old resident of St. Louis, shot one William Lyons. The field hollers and field blues predated the ballad. Like other slave verbalizations, the field hollers and slave ballads contained elements of protest. Some were about escaped slaves, like the one about "St. Malo," a rebellious slave who was hanged.[3] Thus, before the murder of Billy Lyons in 1895, there were probably already several ballads with what folklorist David Evans calls "floating stanzas" that expressed themes similar to those found in the Stagolee ballad. Charles Haffer, of Coahama County, Mississippi, recalled having first heard of a Stagolee ballad in 1895.[4] As a ballad, Stagolee evolved from then to the 1970s, when it was appropriated by black revolutionaries like Bobby Seale, who used it as a symbol of the enduring black male struggle against white oppression and racism. We see its vestiges today as gangster rap.

In short, Stagolee is authentic African-American folklore. What accounts for its profound influence upon the worldview of African-American men? What is Stagolee? Is it simply a ballad? A toast? An epic? A subtype form of oral literature? Is Stagolee a political hero? A cultural hero?

Stagolee has taken musical shape as ballad, as blues, as jazz, as epic, as folk song, and as rap. There are at least twenty jazz recordings, by musicians ranging from Cab Calloway, Jimmy Dorsey, and Peggy Lee to Duke Ellington. More than a hundred bluesmen, from Champion Jack Dupree and Sonny Terry to Mississippi John Hurt, have recorded it. During the 1930s and 1940s John Lomax and his son Alan collected it from prisoners across the South, in the form of a strictly folk protest music; at least a dozen recordings survive in the Library of Congress. And it has thrived as a soul tune rendered by James Brown, Neil Diamond, Fats Domino, and Wilson Pickett. Performers of Stagolee have ranged from levee workers to white female "coon-shouters," from whorehouse pianists to black female blues shouters, from hundreds of "unidentified Negro convicts" to famous contemporary musicians such as Huey Lewis and the News, Bob Dylan, and the Grateful Dead, and from 1920s Hawaiian guitarists to 1970s English groups like the Clash.

The earliest recordings, in 1923, were made by two white dance bands, Fred Waring's Pennsylvanians and Frank Westphal and His Orchestra. The next recording was made in 1926 by Ma Rainey, one of the first blacks to popularize vocal music. Australian rocker Nick Cave last recorded it in 1996. What accounts for the longevity of this tune? And how is it that the same song can mean so many different things in so many different forms of music?

While I was learning the Stagolee toast from my Uncle Lindsey, Hogman Maxey, a black prisoner, was singing the following version to collector Harry Oster at the Angola State Penitentiary in Louisiana. By then the Stagolee tradition was already six decades old. Yet Maxey's version remains close to the original in substance.

> I was standin' on the corner
> When I heard my bulldog bark;
> He was barkin' at the two men
> Who gamblin' in the dark.
> It was Stagolee and Billy,
> Two men who gamble' late,
> Stagolee throw seven,
> Billy swore that he throwed eight.
> Stagolee told Billy,
> "I can't let you go with that;
> You have won my money
> And my brand new Stutson [Stetson] hat."
> Stagolee went home,
> And got his forty-four,
> Says, "I'm goin' to the bar room,
> To pay the debt I owe."
> Stagolee went to the bar room,
> Stood four feet from the door
> Didn't nobody know when he
> Pulled his forty-four.
> Stagolee found Billy,

"Oh please don't take my life!
I got three little children,
And a very sick little wife."
Stagolee shot Billy,
Oh he shot that boy so fas'
That the bullet came through him,
And broke my window glass.
Some folks don't believe,
Oh Lord that Billy dead
You don't believe he gone,
Jus' look what a hole in his head.[5]

In the version I heard forty years ago, Billy Lyons also asked for mercy. Invariably his plea is based on his wife's sickly condition and his three children:

"Have mercy!" Billy groaned. "Oh please spare my life.
I've got two little babies and an innocent wife!
Don't! Don't shoot me anymore!"[6]

How is it that I can still remember the image and the rhythms of this song so many years later? How is it that people from as far west as Oregon and as far south as Florida remember exactly the same imagery? The image of Billy Lyons begging for his life, for example, made a deep impression on my young mind. I can still remember the emotions that it evoked. Billy Lyons has been begging for his life for many decades now. He has made his plea on the lips of thousands of tellers, singers, liars, actors, and ordinary folk. From David C. Rubin's study *Memory in Oral Traditions,* we know that ballads can transmit imagery orally for hundreds of years. The ballad

6

"Lord Thomas and Fair Annet," for example, which dates to before 1690, is still sung in North Carolina.[7]

As an oral narrative, Stagolee has what folklorist Albert Lord called "multiformity," which allows "the existence of alternative forms of a particular component of a theme."[8] My Uncle Lindsey chanted the saga of "bad man" Stagolee; Hogman Maxey sang it to guitar accompaniment. But whether it takes the form of a "bad man" ballad, a talking blues (combining singing and talking), a folktale, a drama, or a musical, the story is essentially the same. This book is about Stagolee as a black oral narrative and the rich relationship it reveals between oral literature and social life.[9]

As an oral narrative, Stagolee is keyed not only to the events recounted in the narrative but also to liminal, unofficial black social organizations such as the black four hundred clubs, black-and-tan clubs, and the bordello milieu. One reason Stagolee has survived so long is that any performance of it grants the participants—performers and audience alike—"time out" from the pressures of life in a racist American society. This time-out is ritualistic in Turner's sense of that word.[10]

What keeps Stagolee alive, then, is its ritualistic performance. The performance is set off from the ordinary, the mundane. Whether it takes place in a tobacco field or in the poolroom of a juke joint, it constitutes a privileged space and time.

The performance is a central feature in a three-phase rite of passage characterized by the ethnologist Arnold Van Gennep as separation, transition, and incorporation in a series of "rites of passage." In the first phase, novices, candidates, and neophytes are detached from a previous society. For young black boys, who are being separated from female society, hearing and reciting the legend of Stagolee is part of a symbolic separation. During the next phase, the neophyte is in transition, on a threshold, poised between childhood and maturity. In the third phase, the subject returns to a "new, relatively stable, well-defined position in the total society."[11] In adulthood the black male assumes the role of a keeper of tradition by passing the legend on to youngsters.

Some folk songs seem to have been helped to survive by the medium of print. But Stagolee survived primarily through oral traditions. It was so dirty that many would not print it. When it was printed, it was heavily censored for "obscene" words. The fact of censorship itself (chiefly through white Americans' control of blacks' access to the print media) has ensured Stagolee's survival as an example of oral memory.[12] The fact that Stagolee was a pimp ensured that white Americans would not see him as a subject of serious interest.

Was there a real model for the Stagolee myth? Did Stagolee exist at all? If he did, was he born in St. Louis, New Orleans, or Memphis? The first Stagolee ballad ever collected consisted of eight stanzas sent to John Lomax in February 1910 by Miss Ella Scott Fisher of San Angelo, Texas, with the following note: "This is all the verses I remember. The origin of this ballad, I have been told, was the shooting of Billy Lyons in a barroom on the Memphis levee by Stack Lee. The song is sung by the Negroes on the levee while they are loading and unloading the river freighters, the words being composed by the singers. The characters were prominently known in Memphis, I was told, the unfortunate Stagalee belonging to the family of the owners of the Lee line of steamers, which are known on the Mississippi River from Cairo to the Gulf. I give all this to you as it was given to me."[13]

8

Miss Fisher must have thought that Stagolee was a white man, if she believed that he was the son of the Lee family. She went on to describe the song's effect on the listener: "The effect of the song with its minor refrain is weird, and the spoken interpolations add to the realism. It becomes immensely personal as you hear it like a recital of something known or experienced by the singer."

> 'Twas a Christmas morning,
> The hour was about ten
> When Stagalee shot Billy Lyons
> And landed in the Jefferson pen.
> O lordy, po' Stagalee!

Everything but the hour is true to the historical record. The next stanza introduces Billy Lyons' wife:

> Billy Lyons' old woman,
> She was a terrible sinner,
> She was home that Christmas mornin'
> A-preparin' Billy's dinner.

Next comes the news:

> Messenger boy came to the winder,
> Then he knocked on the door,
> An' he said, "Yer old man's lyin' there
> Dead on the Barroom floor."
> O Lord, po' Stagalee!

Then Billy's wife addresses Stagolee:

> "Stagalee, O Stagalee,
> What have you gone and done?

You've gone and shot my husband
With a forty-four gatlin' gun."

In the next stanza Stagolee's friend asks him why he didn't run. Then the policeman, "a little scared of Stagalee," addresses him. In the next stanza Stagolee addresses his jailer:

"Jailer, O Jailer,
  I jest can't sleep;
  For the ghost of Billy Lyons
  Round my bed does mourn and weep."

After this scene, the "Counsel for the Defense" addresses the court. Finally, the judge sentences Stagolee, and he is hanged.

When he published the ballad "Stagolee" in 1912, University of North Carolina professor Howard Odum had no information about the hero's true identity.[14] More than seven decades later, British folklorist and music scholar Paul Oliver called Stagolee "a shadowy and uncertain figure" and questioned whether there was an actual man behind the legend.[15] The distinguished American folklorist Richard Dorson also doubted his existence.[16] In his doctoral dissertation on African-American "badmen," Frederick William Turner noted that "despite the best efforts of scholars to track him down, History has been silent about the identity of Stagolee."[17] Even when John W. Roberts discovered Stagolee's true identity and wrote the only book on the influence of Stagolee on black culture, he ignored the facts behind the story.[18] Roberts identified Lee Shelton as the man behind the myth, but he didn't go further. Perhaps his greater interest in the myth's impact on the black community overrode his interest in the actual person behind it.

Did Stagolee actually live? Most black men with whom I have

discussed this question believe that someone like him did exist, but they usually have in mind a particular gangster who lived in their own neighborhood. A typical response is the one by the poet and professor of black literature Eugene Redmond: "I grew up in East St. Louis, and I know the place where Stagolee shot Billy Lyons. Stagolee's real name was Luther Heyward, and he lived right here in the projects and used to drive a red Corvette." Another black man will claim that Stagolee lived in Cleveland, and yet another that he was from New Orleans. Wherever there was a murderer, there seems to have been a Stagolee. Sometimes a murder wasn't necessary. Walter Hood, a professor of architecture at the University of California, Berkeley, told me that his mother always called the "hot man" (the local man who sold stolen goods from the back of his car) "Stagolee."

But there was indeed a real Stagolee, a well-known figure in St. Louis's red-light district during the 1890s, a pimp who, when he shot and killed William Lyons, was the president of a "Colored Four Hundred Club," a political and social organization. In December 9, 1937, Tyrrell Williams, a law professor at Washington University, wrote an article in the *St. Louis Post Dispatch,* claiming that the Stagolee ballad was based on "the killing by a Negro bully named Stacker Lee (or Stack O' Lee) of another Negro named Lyon, because Lyon accidentally spit in the Stetson owned by Lee." He claimed that his information had come from William Marion Reedy, a journalist and critic who was active during the 1890s (and about whom we shall learn more later). Reedy had told Williams "that Lee was an actual character and that the lawyer who defended him was Nathaniel Dryden." A sketchy narrative of Lee Shelton's life is also available from newspaper articles and other public records.[19] A look at the man himself and the social setting of 1890s St.

Louis affords valuable insight into why this act of violence, rather than five other murders reported in the "Bloody Third" ward on the same night, made it ballad material.

We must also consider why many scholars are ignorant of Stagolee's true identity. One reason has to do with who the actual person was and what he did to earn his place in the folk culture. We Americans love our folk heroes and the ballads made about their lives. Yet we are reluctant to admit that many of those heroes come from the lowest levels of society. Like the "Frankie and Albert" ballad, "Stagolee" may have originated with a pianist in a bordello. The "hero" of the ballad was a pimp, and the "heroic deed" was the murder of a defenseless black man. How much of this can we really applaud?

Kevin Mumford's book *Interzones: Black/White Sex Districts in Chicago and New York in the Early Twentieth Century* casts some light on why Stagolee was associated with the subcultures of bordellos and prostitution. As Mumford suggests, these subcultures are closely linked with sex and class. They are also coded with criminality.[20] After studying the counterculture in America for many years, jazz critic Albert Goldman came up with an intriguing insight:

> One idea I summed up in the formula of the counterculture is the criminal culture. This meant two things, first, that the roots of the counterculture as a defiant revolutionary way of life lay not so much in the sources that the kids were proud to show—the political treatises of Marcuse, the racial theories of Fanon, the Eastern religious doctrines of Zen . . .—but rather in that culture that had always been the most antagonistic to conventional values and codes of behavior, the culture that had

always acted out the most basic fantasies of the American psyche and created the whole underground world of drugs, violence, street argot and antisocial defiance: the criminal culture.[21]

As one of the earliest examples of the antihero, Stagolee is a figure who embodies and perpetuates a counterculture. Many scholars do not want to know who the real Stagolee was, because he was not a hero. This is as much as admitting that although we enjoy the folk hero, we have no idea how he came to be.

It is true that the American public has been interested in other black folk heroes such as John Henry and Joe Louis. But rarely does one hear their names associated with popular figures today. Stagolee's name, however, is frequently linked to sports figures like O. J. Simpson and Jack Johnson and rap stars like Tupac Shakur.[22] For example, after Tupac's arrest, Randee Dawn reported in the *New Musical Express* that the "fans of Tupac accuse the white community of missing the point . . . They say Shakur is a black hero in the tradition of the blues archetype Stagger Lee [Stagolee], who created a system for himself based on his own perceptions."[23]

John Henry, Jack Johnson, and Joe Louis are folk figures who worked within the white system, but O. J. Simpson and Tupac are perceived as working outside and against it. A Christian who worked from nine to five on a railroad, John Henry sacrificed his life for that system. In contrast, one cannot imagine Stagolee giving his life for a system that oppresses the black man.

Instead of using written texts to develop their heroes, blacks use social dramas. Stagolee's shooting of Billy Lyons is a social drama, complete with beginning, middle, and end. The social drama produces narratives and cultural performances such as the singing of ballads.

The Stagolee paradigm not only provides explanations for the behavior of members of black communities; it also accounts for why so many musicians have Stagolee in their blood. As Greil Marcus observed,

> In the blues, Stack changed names, but little else. He was the Crawling Kingsnake; Tommy Johnson pouring Sterno down his throat, singing "Canned heat, canned heat is killing me"; Muddy Waters's cool and elemental Rollin' Stone; Chuck Berry's Brown-Eyed Handsome Man; Bo Diddley with a tombstone hand and a graveyard mind; Wilson Pickett's Midnight Mover; Mick Jagger's Midnight Rambler . . . When the civil rights movement got tough, [Staggerlee] took over. And Staggerlee would come roaring back to the screen in the '70s, as Slaughter, Sweet Sweetback, Superfly.[24]

The Stagolee paradigm has produced political figures such as Adam Clayton Powell, Malcolm X, Muhammad Ali, H. "Rap" Brown, Robert Williams, and Bobby Seale. Seale not only named his son Stagolee but used the narrative toast version as a recruiting device to get young black men into the Black Panther party. It is also the paradigm for such literary figures as Bigger Thomas, the protagonist in Richard Wright's *Native Son*.

In contemporary African-American critical thought, scholars and writers make frequent references to "Stagolee, the bad nigger." Usually the reference is to a violent act by some black man. Robin

D. G. Kelley provides such an instance in his book *Race Rebels*. In recounting the behavior of black servicemen in uniform who voiced their objections to taking their assigned "place" on the bus and were put off the bus by white bus operators carrying guns, Kelley characterized them as "'modern-day 'Stagolees,' 'baaad niggers' who put on public displays of resistance that left witnesses in awe."[25]

Kelley correctly terms Stagolee a "folk hero," although, he writes, "the Stagolee-type is not always regarded as a hero to other working-class black passengers." Likewise, in his biography of Jackie Robinson, Arnold Rampersad asserted that Robinson joined the pantheon of "folk heroes like Stagolee."[26]

Part I of this book focuses on the city of St. Louis and the events central to the Stagolee narrative. Today St. Louis is the eighteenth-largest city in America, but in the 1890s it was the fourth largest.[27] As a cultural center in the Midwest, it was second only to Chicago. European stars performed to a well-educated upper class, and some of the nation's richest industrialists lived in the West End. Like New York, San Francisco, and New Orleans during this period, St. Louis had a large red-light district along Market, Chestnut, and Targee Streets, an area known as "Chestnut Valley." As the only place in the city where blacks and whites could commingle, this district was what Kevin Mumford calls an "interzone": "Simultaneously marginal and central, interzones were located in African-American neighborhoods, unique because the (often transient) inhabitants were black and white, heterosexual and homosexual, prostitute and customer . . . [They] were . . . areas of cultural, sexual, and social interchange."[28] About ten blocks south was another red-light district, called "Deep Morgan." It was in this area that Lee

Shelton, called "Stago Lee," shot William "Billy" Lyons. "This area," according to William Barlow, "was a magnet for the St. Louis sporting crowd even before the turn of the century."[29]

In the 1890s blacks in St. Louis sought political protection through their right to vote. During this period, known as the Progressive era, politicians across the country tried to close the red-light districts. Other Progressive reform efforts resulted in prohibition, commercialized leisure, and populist politics.[30]

Seeking to escape the constraints of the Victorian era, Mumford notes, "American urbanites turned from their homes into the dance halls, speakeasies and amusement parks."[31] As a ballad, Stagolee both reflected and enabled these changes. Part II traces its evolution and transmission, in the course of which the bordellos and black saloons where Stagolee was sung became dance halls and amusement parks where the ballad was sometimes banned.

From 1895—the birth year of the ballad of Stagolee—to 1930, when the song attained its widest circulation, America was confronted with two major events: the Great Migration of thousands of African Americans from the rural South to the industrial North, and the sexual revolution. Both Republican and Democratic politicians sought the black vote. Most blacks in St. Louis voted Republican, but when the Republican convention in the summer of 1896 ignored their interest, many broke with the party. This break owed much to the black pimps in St. Louis, who, operating with saloon-keepers and gamblers through "sporting" clubs, frequently called "four hundred clubs," solicited Democratic votes.

But the Stagolee tradition also fits into a larger, nonpolitical context, one associated with music and class and with Walter Benjamin's ideas about the city and its marginal inhabitants and his concepts of the flaneur, commodities, and modernity. As a disfranchised group, many blacks in St. Louis during the late 1890s were unemployed and marginal figures. Recently transplanted from the southern plantations, these men sometimes became pimps. This was St. Louis's "rag" (Marx's "lumpen") proletariat. Like the French flaneur with his aesthetic of boredom, the members of this "rag" proletariat rebelled against the work ethic; they rebelled not because they were bored with the bourgeoisie, as perhaps the flaneur was, but because whites kept them out of white-collar jobs. It is not coincidental that the music that first celebrated the Stagolee ballad was called ragtime. Born in St. Louis and nursed in ragtime's arms, Stagolee grew up in the Progressive era and has been translated anew in each decade.

Since the publication in English of Vladimir Propp's *Morphology of the Folktale* in 1958, structuralism has had a profound impact on folklore analysis. But very little structural analysis has been applied to African-American narrative folklore; as we have seen, most socio-psychological scholars have limited themselves to the psychology of Stagolee and its relationship to the theory of deculturalization. Given the number of important insights produced in other areas, the investigation of a relationship between structuralism and African-American oral narrative becomes all the more intriguing and urgent.

For Stagolee to become a ballad, meter, music, and meaning had to come together. But more than purely musical elements were involved in its persistence over a century. What internal and external factors enabled Stagolee to exert such a lasting influence on American culture? Part III explores the "bad nigger" influence of Stagolee on literature, black politics, rap music, and, by extension, the American cultural identity.

One word of caution. In the following chapters there is a lot of repetition. In literate tradition, one is asked not to repeat, but in the oral tradition repetition is the essence of communication. It creates the meaning of the message in Stagolee. Performers of the ballad depend on this clichéd quality of the core images, out of which they create their own intended meaning. Like them, in many cases I have had to repeat stanzas and motifs.

There will be many apparent repetitions, but in fact each represents only a variation on a stable theme. According to my method, the reader should not be bothered by generic differences among Stagolee as a ballad, a legend, or a field holler. Just as Vladimir Propp showed that the functions of a fairy tale are invariable, and as such provide it with an abiding structure, so I have attempted to show that the structure of Stagolee remains stable. Although each performance of Stagolee produces a different version even when several performers use the same motifs, the sequence of events and the kind of figure created through the narrative remain essentially the same.

I

Stagolee and St. Louis

1

Stagolee Shot Billy

"Stagolee" was one of the verses that went into numbers that was wrote and rewrote in St. Louis. Stagolee and Billy Lyons about the milk white Stetson hat.

—JELLY ROLL MORTON, 1938

It was in the year of eighteen hundred sixty-one,
In St. Louis on Market Street where Stackalee was born
Everybody's talkin' 'bout Stackalee.

—"STACKALEE," 1941

A cold wind blew through the streets of downtown St. Louis that Christmas night in 1895. In the Third Ward, better known as "Chestnut Valley," well-dressed Negroes strolled up and down Market Street, which was lined with high-class whorehouses. A large crowd had gathered in Tom Turpin's Rose Bud Saloon, at 2222 Market, where Turpin sat beside a Christmas tree that was "beautifully illuminated by scores of electric lights in all colors."[1]

About ten blocks away, two men came out of the Bridgewater Saloon at the corner of Eleventh Street and Lucas Avenue and watched the crowd: women gaily dressed as though going to a church parade, men sporting spats and high-roller derbies. One of the watchers was William Lyons, a stout man in a derby. The other was his friend Henry Crump. Joining the moving crowd, the two men ended up a few blocks down the street at the Bridgewater's rival establishment, the Bill Curtis Saloon, at 1101 Morgan Street, at the corner of Thirteenth in the Bloody Third District.

Between Morgan and Christy Streets, as one newspaper put it, the heart of black society "throbbed" with vaudeville theaters, bordellos, shoe-repair shops, and billiard parlors.[2] In fact the Bill Curtis Saloon was the epicenter of the vice district.

When they arrived at the Bill Curtis Saloon, Lyons stopped at the door and asked Crump to lend him a weapon. Everybody knew the saloon's reputation for crime. Murders had taken place in the rowdy atmosphere. Billy Lyons didn't have to read the newspapers to know that the saloon was the "envy of all of its competitors and the terror of the police," or that newspaper owner and moralist Joseph Pulitzer regarded it as one of the "worst dens in the city . . . patronized by the lower-class of river men and other darkies of the same social status."[3] Billy knew from firsthand experience what the saloon was like; one night he had had to pull his knife on a fellow.[4] Every time he went into the saloon, Billy told Crump, he got into trouble with "those bad niggers."[5] Crump had a knife and agreed to lend it to Billy. After Crump handed him the knife, the two men entered the saloon.

They walked deep into the bar, near the stove. A ragtime band was playing happy, delightful music. There were good-looking belles sitting at the tables. In the back, on a platform, a craps game was in session.

After ordering beer, Billy Lyons noticed that people were looking toward the door. Turning to see what they were looking at, he saw that Lee Shelton, known as "Stack Lee," had entered.

Shelton was dressed in a pair of tailored shoes known as "St. Louis flats," with almost no heels and long toes pointing upward. On the top of the toes were tiny mirrors that caught the electric light hanging overhead and sent sparkles upward. A pair of dove-colored spats covered Shelton's shoe tops. Gray-striped pants hung over his spats. The flaps of his black box-back coat fell open to reveal an elaborately patterned red velvet vest and a yellow embroidered shirt with a celluloid standing collar that kept his chin high in the air. Knuckle-length sleeves almost covered the gold rings on his manicured fingers; his left hand clutched the gold head of an ebony walking cane. The other hand took a long cigar out of his mouth. On his head was a high-roller, milk-white Stetson. Along the hatband was an embroidered picture of his favorite girl, Lillie Shelton.[6]

Lee Shelton belonged to a group of exotic pimps known in St. Louis as the "macks." The macks were not just "urban strollers"; they presented themselves as objects to be observed.

According to eyewitness George McFaro, Shelton asked, "Who's treating?" In reply, someone pointed out Lyons. Shelton approached him. Apparently, he and Lyons drank and laughed together for some time until the conversation turned to politics. Soon they began to exchange blows by striking each other's hats. Shelton grabbed Lyons' derby and broke the form. Lyons said he wanted "six bits" from Shelton for damaging his derby.

Then Lyons grabbed Shelton's Stetson. When Shelton demanded it back, Lyons said no. Shelton said he would blow Lyons' brains out if he didn't return it. Next Shelton pulled his .44 Smith & Wesson revolver from his coat and hit Lyons on the head with it.

Billy Lyons' death certificate. Courtesy of Judith Ann David.

Still Lyons would not relinquish the hat. Shelton demanded the Stetson again, saying that if Lyons didn't give him his hat immediately, he was going to kill him.

Then Lyons reached into his pocket for the knife his friend Crump had given him and approached Shelton, saying, "You cockeyed son of a bitch, I'm going to *make* you kill me." Shelton backed off and took aim. The twenty-five people in the saloon flew for the door. Only the bartenders Thomas Scott and Frank Boyd and a few others—Henry Crump, George McFaro, and Leslie Stevenson—were left drinking at the bar. Both bartenders later testified to the coroner that they saw Lee Shelton shoot Billy Lyons.

After shooting Lyons, Shelton walked over to the dying man, who was still holding on to the bar, and said, "Nigger, I told you to give me my hat!" He snatched his hat from Lyons' hand, put it on his head, and walked out. Shelton walked to his house, a few blocks away, checked his gun in with his landlady, went upstairs, and presumably went to sleep. Meanwhile, Billy Lyons was taken to an infirmary; later he was moved to a hospital, where he died about four o'clock in the morning.

At three o'clock that morning, police officers John Flanigan and A. Falvey went to arrest Lee Shelton. Not knowing where he lived, they went to "a lady at No. 307 [Sixth Street]." There they found a woman "carrying a note to this man's [Stack Lee's] girl. We suspected that Stack Lee wrote it and sent it out there. We went down there and got Stack Lee, in bed."

Shelton's Sixth Street address was a tenement building near Spruce Avenue in "Tamale Town." Sixth Street was the district's main artery of vice. Blacks, lower-class whites, and Chinese were the principal inhabitants. With available living space reduced by the growing number of factories, public buildings, hotels, and business establishments in St. Louis, six hundred of Tamale Town's fourteen hundred black residents lived in this one block.

After arresting Lee Shelton, Officer Flanigan went back and asked "the woman of the house" if she had "Stack Lee's revolver." The landlady said yes, she had put it in a drawer. "I went to the bureau drawer and took out the .44 Smith & Wesson, fully loaded, every chamber was full," Flanigan said. Perhaps Shelton had put another bullet in the chamber to eliminate evidence that he had fired his gun.

They took Lee Shelton to the Chestnut Street police station. Like the railroad's busy Union Station, the Chestnut Street station was in the center of the high-class prostitution area. Once in the station, Shelton was taken into the Four Courts.

The Four Courts was notorious. For many, like the young Theodore Dreiser, who was there frequently as a crime reporter, it was a symbol of injustice. "A more dismal atmosphere than that which prevailed in this building," he wrote, "would be hard to find." The complex consisted of "the city detention wards, the office of the district attorney, the chief of police, chief of detectives, the city attorney, and a 'reporters' room' where all the local reporters were permitted to gather and were furnished paper, ink, tables." Dreiser saw the Four Courts as an embodiment of corrupted institutions. "Harlots, criminals, murderers, buzzard lawyers, political judges, detectives, police agents, and court officials generally—what a company!" he exclaimed. "The petty tyrannies that are practiced by underlings and minor officials! The 'grafting' of low, swinish brains! The cruelty and cunning of agents of justice!"[7]

By Friday, December 27, Lee Shelton had hired a lawyer, Nat Dryden. Dryden was a brilliant if eccentric advocate from a well-known Missouri family. He had been the first lawyer in the state of Missouri to gain a conviction of a white man for murdering a black. Since no black lawyer was admitted to the bar in St. Louis until 1894, Lee Shelton was unlikely to have been able to hire a black lawyer.

What was unusual was that Shelton had Dryden, who seems to have been one of the best lawyers, if not the best, in town. Dryden was an alcoholic and opium addict, but in the courtroom he was flamboyant and dramatic, a brilliant cross-examiner and gifted orator, with a good record of beating murder convictions. The fact that he could afford Dryden suggests that Lee Shelton was a man of means. In addition, Shelton could afford to post a bond as high as $4,000.

Dryden's decision to take on the defense of a man like Stack Lee Shelton raised some speculation. There may have been a combination of reasons. Perhaps Dryden found Stack Lee's status in the St.

Nat Dryden. Tintype. Courtesy of Missouri Historical Society, St. Louis.

Louis underworld appealing in some way. A lawyer of Dryden's caliber would have been attracted to high-profile cases. He was currently defending a prominent doctor accused of murdering his wife.

An inquest in the Lee Shelton case was set for December 27 at 1:00 P.M. Shelton was brought to the Eleventh Street entrance of the coroner's office in the Four Courts. As Shelton, Dryden, and the police escort turned the corner to the coroner's office, a crowd of about three hundred angry black people, described by a journalist as the "Henry Bridgewater faction," greeted Shelton with "hisses, curses, and other indignities."[8]

Henry Bridgewater, reputedly one of the richest blacks in St. Louis, was Billy Lyons' brother-in-law. He was also a black Republican, as doubtless were many members of the crowd. The police called for reinforcements. As the growing mob "surged towards the door," the police had to draw their weapons.

Once the prisoner was inside, Coroner W. J. Wait, M.D., began the inquest. Shelton was brought before the dead man's body and several eyewitnesses. While the crowd raged outside in the courtyard, the witnesses gave their accounts to Coroner Wait. One of them was Frank Boyd, the bartender at the Bill Curtis Saloon that night.

"What do you know about this affair?" Wait asked Boyd.

> "Well, at the time it started, there was a crowd of men at the bar, drinking . . . I suppose there was 25 men in the room when this trouble first started."
>
> "At least 25 men?"
>
> "Yes, sir."
>
> "Well, how many were there about, when the shooting was done?"

"Now, I could not tell you."

"Was the room full?

"No, sir."

"Well, was there 6 or 8?"

"Oh, I suppose there was that many."

"6 or 8?"

"Yes, sir, I suppose there was, I could not say for sure, because right there it was an exciting time, I don't know just how many there was, I didn't pay any attention as to how many there were."

According to Boyd, Lee Shelton shot Billy Lyons at close range with a .44 Smith & Wesson. Lyons fell back and staggered momentarily, still clutching Shelton's hat. George G. McFaro heard Shelton say, "Give me my hat, Nigger," and then, "You have got my hat." Then Shelton went over and snatched his hat from Lyons' hand and walked "coolly" out of the saloon.[9]

Frank Boyd had known both Stack Lee and Billy Lyons for ten years. Thomas Scott had known Lee for twenty years, since "he was a little boy." Both bartenders testified that Lee Shelton and Billy Lyons were "good friends" and had never quarreled. Coroner Wait asked them if Stack Lee was "behind the bar" and "if he was working that night," questions that imply that Shelton might have been a waiter—he was listed as a waiter in a newspaper article—and might have recently worked at the Curtis saloon.

Another witness, Leslie Stevenson, a farmer, "just happened to be in there when the row occurred." He described Lee Shelton with respect, calling him "the gentleman" and "Mister Lee." But although he lived at 1008 Morgan Street, close to where Shelton and Lyons lived, Stevenson did not know Shelton personally.

The other witness, George G. McFaro, who "had heard of" Stack

Lee, was the only witness to see Shelton enter the saloon. According to McFaro, "Stack came in and says, 'Who is treating?'" So somebody told him that Billy Lyons was treating, and Stagolee walked to where Lyons was standing. McFaro said,

> "I thought he [Stack Lee] was playing and he hauled off and broke his [Billy Lyons'] hat, his derby."
>
> "Was that in play, or quarreling?"
>
> "No, sir, they wasn't quarreling, just playing, and so he says to him when he grabs Stack's hat, Stack goes to him and he says, 'give me my hat,' and he says, 'I ain't going to give it to you, I want pay for this.' Stack says, 'how much do you want?' He [Billy] says, 'I want six bits,' and he [Stack] says, 'six bits will buy a box of those hats.' He [Billy] says, 'I want six bits,' and he [Billy] said, 'Well, what made you break my hat, my derby,' and Stack done that way (indicating) and then they stood and talked awhile, and Stack snatched out his pistol, and he said, 'if you don't give me my hat, I will blow your brains out.' He [Billy] said, 'I am not going to give you the hat, you can kill me.' So when he pulled the pistol out, I walked out, I didn't stay any longer."

McFaro was outside the saloon a few minutes later when two men brought Billy Lyons out after he had been shot.

Coroner Wait asked the next witness, Leslie Stevenson, "What did you see after the shooting?"

> Well, then he just walked there, and stands there, it looked like about 2 or 3 seconds, he staggered against the side of the bar, leaned against the railing, holding the hat in his fingers like that, and it seemed he was getting

weak, and he let the hat drop out of his hands. About that time, Shelton says, "Give me my hat, Nigger," and he says, "You got my hat," and he takes and picks it up and walks out into the brisk air.

Another person, identified only as an "informant," told Wait that Lee Shelton shot Billy Lyons because of a vendetta against the Bridgewater establishment. Billy Lyons' stepbrother Charles Brown had killed Lee Shelton's friend Harry Wilson, and Shelton had sworn to avenge the murder.[10] The coroner said he would take that for what it was worth and would look into it.

When the inquest came to an end, Dryden's task was to get Lee Shelton safely out of reach of the mob that had gathered outside the morgue. The crowd, however, would not disperse until Coroner Wait told them that Shelton would be held in custody pending an indictment for first-degree murder. Nevertheless, in the interests of Shelton's safety, late on the afternoon of December 28 Dryden requested a warrant to get him out of the holding cell and into a jail. Judge David Murphy signed the warrant against Shelton for first-degree murder.[11]

On January 3, 1896—the beginning of an election year—Lee Shelton, "alias 'Stack Lee,'" was bound over to a grand jury by Judge Murphy but was released on a $4,000 bond, equivalent to about $100,000 today, and released on January 5, 1896.[12] Six months later, on June 26, 1896, the *St. Louis Globe-Democrat* reported that Lee Shelton, "also known to the police as 'Stack' Lee, was released from jail yesterday on bonds of $3000 dollars."[13] Although the article mentioned that "he was the slayer of William Lyons, who was killed last Christmas night," it did not say why Lee Shelton was in jail this time. Was he in jail for another crime? We may never know.

What we do know is that on July 15, 1896, nearly seven months after he killed Billy Lyons, Lee Shelton went on trial for Lyons' murder. The presiding judge was a Judge Harvey. On Tuesday morning, July 14, 1896, the *St. Louis Globe-Democrat* reported:

> In the second division of the criminal court Judge Harvey
> spent yesterday impaneling a jury to try a case of the
> State against Lee Shelton, alias Stack Lee, colored, ac-
> cused of murder in the first degree. Shelton has been out
> of jail on bond since shortly after the murder, which oc-
> curred last Christmas night. The man who is now on
> trial for his life was shooting craps with William Lyon,
> also colored, in a saloon at Morgan and 11th Streets. The
> men quarreled, and Shelton whipped out a revolver and
> shot Lyons. The victim died almost instantly. This was
> one of five similar crimes committed in St. Louis Christ-
> mas day. Col. Nat C. Dryden will defend the murderer,
> and Marshall F. McDonald has been engaged as a special
> counsel for the State to assist attorney Orrick C. Bishop,
> assistant circuit attorney. The trial promises to develop a
> very pretty and interesting legal fight.

Two errors stand out in this article. First, according to the witnesses, the men were not shooting craps. Second, Lyons didn't die instantly. Whether these errors were due to a confusion among the witnesses or to bad reporting, such discrepancies fostered many different episodes in ensuing versions of the ballad. For example, some ballads concentrated on the actual murder, while others concentrated on the trial, like the following version, from New York City, dated 1927:

> They took him to the court house
> Judge Murphy sat on the bench

An' the first one to put her can in a chair
Was Stack-o-lee's loving wench
Oh poor, ole Stack-o-lee.[14]

The other person mentioned in the *Globe-Democrat* article, Orrick
C. Bishop, was to play an important role in city politics in 1903, as
part of a team created by Mayor Joe Folk to close down "policy
shops" (illegal gambling sites) and other gambling operations.[15]

In a St. Louis version dated 1903, the judge (now called MacDonald) claims that no amount of money will help Stagolee's "loving
wench" to plead his case, because he is going to make an example
out of "this here pimp."

At last she went to Judge MacDonald,
Says Judge what his fine!
I got a hundred cold iron men saved up
In nickels, quarters and dimes,
And I can't live without my papa Stackerlee.[16]

Nat Dryden argued that Lee Shelton shot Billy Lyons in self-defense. At noon on July 18, after deliberating for twenty-two hours,
the jury returned, unable to agree on a verdict. The last ballot stood
seven for murder in the second degree, two for manslaughter, and
three for acquittal. The jury was discharged; the case would be tried
again. Shelton was taken from jail by a deputy sheriff and arranged
for a bond from friends that would be given on Monday for his release. Apparently, Shelton returned to his job running the Modern
Horseshoe Club.

On August 26, 1897, before he could defend Lee Shelton at his
second trial, Dryden died. His young wife had been kept in the dark
about his drinking problem, and she offered him a glass of sherry.

This glass of sherry caused Dryden to go on a drinking binge, which killed him.

The *St. Louis Post-Dispatch* ran a long obituary, including an interview with his widow. It was a combination of biography and hagiography, a character study of a nineteenth-century "brilliant man." Dryden's death was "felt throughout the state."[17] Although he was an addict to the end, it was Dryden's brilliance and expertise at Shelton's first trial that had resulted in a hung jury. The Stagolee oral tradition celebrates their relationship:

> On one cold and stormy winter night
> Stack'lee and Billy Lyons had an awful fight.
> Do-do-de-do-o-o, de-do-de-do-o-o
> P'liceman, p'liceman, what you think of that?
> Stack'lee, Stack'lee, don't take my life
> I got three chillun and a dear, lovin' wife.
> Next Monday morning preliminary was tried
> Don't be afraid, Stack, Nat Dryden is by your side.[18]

Although we have no records of the second trial, Shelton must have been tried soon afterward, because on October 7 he entered the Missouri State Penitentiary at Jefferson City to begin serving a twenty-five-year sentence.[19]

In the penitentiary in March 1899, Shelton was given five lashes for "loafing" in the yard. On June 14 of that year, he was reprimanded for "shooting craps." But because he helped the authorities to detect a "systematic thief" in the prison (and perhaps also because of petitions from many powerful and influential Democrats), he was recommended for parole.[20]

Lee Shelton was paroled on Thanksgiving 1909. He arrived at the Benevolent Order of Peerless Knights, Othello Lodge No. 1, to be-

Lee Shelton's prison death certificate. Courtesy of Judith Ann David.

gin work in the yard. But two years later he was in trouble again. In February 1911, Assistant Circuit Attorney Charles B. Davis declared in a statement that Lee Shelton—alias Stack Lee—had on January 26 assaulted William Akins and taken sixty dollars from him.[21] In an account of this episode in the March 17, 1911, *St. Louis Post-Dispatch,* Shelton "is accused of robbing the home of William Akins, another Negro, last January, beating Akins on the head with a revolver and breaking his skull." We must remember that three witnesses claimed Shelton had pistol whipped Billy Lyons. Shelton was sentenced to five years and returned to prison on May 7, 1911. A. H. Myerdick, the prison doctor, reported that Shelton "is getting pretty low and I fear he cannot live much longer."

When Shelton reentered prison, he was sick with tuberculosis. Governor Herbert S. Hadley was impressed by Shelton's weakened condition; his weight had dropped to 102, down over 20 pounds in less than six months. Under pressure from other Democrats, the governor granted him another parole, effective February 8, 1912. But Elliot Major, Missouri's attorney general, objected to the parole, and Shelton died in the prison hospital on March 11.[22]

The Shelton/Lyons murder case is a classic example of Victor Turner's concept of social drama, which has four phases: "breach, crisis, redress, and either reintegration or recognition of schism." Social dramas are cultural markers that express the "drama of living."[23] They occur on both small and large scales, ranging from the Boston Tea Party to the power struggle between Henry II of England and Archbishop Thomas Becket, and in our own time from trials of black superstars such as O. J. Simpson and Puff Daddy to the events immediately surrounding September 11, 2002.

The essential structure of Stagolee follows Turner's four stages of social drama. First Billy Lyons "wins," cheating Stagolee out of his hat. This is a breach in the norm—an interdiction that has disastrous consequences for the breacher. The crisis is when Stagolee kills him. The trial is the redress phase: Stagolee is sentenced and either goes to jail or is hanged. In some versions there is a fourth phase, in which he goes to hell and there takes over from the devil.

It is during the redress phase that artists create their works. The social drama provided the context for the Stagolee ballad, and stanzas were probably added to it as that drama evolved.

As we shall see, the other context that sheds light on how this social drama was crystallized into a memorable ballad is the world of St. Louis during the fading of the steamboat era and the rise of the modern one. In the final years of the nineteenth century and the first years of the twentieth, St. Louis epitomized the riverboat culture. "Until the World's Fair of 1904," writes Nathan B. Young, "St. Louis was known as a 'sporting town.' The golden era of the steamboat on the Mississippi reached its peak between 1870 and 1880. Packet lines centered a growing commerce on St. Louis, then a city of 250,000 population. The levee was an apron of the industry, and Negro stewards, cabin boys, porters, deck hands and roustabouts were a part of this colorful busy scene. This era is symbolized by the Negro roustabouts and the octoroon ladies."

The search for the truth cannot be a "prudish" one, Young contends. "Out of the 'Chestnut Valley' came the most beautiful music. Out of the green scum and muck grow the fairest lilies and valuable hardwood trees; out of old Chestnut valley sprang the stock of popular American music, nurtured and flavored by Negro musicians.

"American ragtime, out of which the blues and swing music evolved, should have a St. Louis label on it."[24]

Who was Lee Shelton, the man behind the Stagolee legend? How did he fit into this transitional setting?

2

Lee Shelton: The Man behind the Myth

According to his prison records, Lee Shelton was born on March 16, 1865, in Texas, the son of a Negro named Nat Shelton. He was thirty at the time of the killing and the trial. When he entered the Jefferson City penitentiary on October 17, 1897, he was thirty-two. When Uncle Lindsey told me about Stagolee, he was always big, black, and bad. But although Shelton had big feet—his shoe size was eleven—he was only five feet seven and a half inches tall. The prison records describe his hair and eyes as black, his "complexion" as "mulatto." Under the column "marks and scars," the authorities noted: "L[eft] eye crossed. 2 scars [on] R[ight] cheek. 2 scars [on] back head. 1 scar on L[eft] shoulder blade."[1]

As we have seen, one witness said that just before Lee Shelton shot him, Lyons taunted Shelton: "I'm going to make you kill me, you cockeyed son of a bitch." This may have been a reference to Lee Shelton's crossed left eye.

The *St. Louis Post-Dispatch* (March 17, 1911) described Lee Shelton as "formerly a Negro politician" and the "proprietor of a lid club for his race." What was a lid club? One suggestion is that "lid" referred to a guidebook on prostitution. A "lid book" existed in New Orleans as a "supplement to the Blue Book," the famous whorehouse guidebook. Because it was smaller than the Blue Book, "it could readily be given away free without serious loss to the distributor, and issues were usually handed out in the railway station to single men."[2] But in fact a lid club was an underground establishment that kept a "lid" on such criminal activities as gambling while serving as a front for other activities.

According to *Gould's St. Louis Directory* for 1894, "Stack L. Shelton" was a waiter living at 1314 Morgan Street. Three years later he was listed as "a driver" living on North Twelfth Street.[3] The newspaper reporting the murder of Billy Lyons said that Shelton was a "carriage driver."[4] As the driver of a hackney cab, Shelton would have been in a position to direct white male visitors to St. Louis bordellos. As one writer describes the situation in Storyville, New Orleans, "the visitor came out of the Southern Railroad Station on Canal Street, looking for a hack . . . a hotel room and then for a night on the town. White or black poontang. And many tried the colored joints first."⁵ Henry Townsend, a St. Louis musician whom I interviewed in 1998, and who arrived in St. Louis as a boy in the early 1920s, had also heard that Lee Shelton was a carriage driver who made connections with well-heeled men looking for prostitutes. "He was instrumental in delivering them to, or getting in touch with, the ladies or whatever," Townsend said. Shelton's job would thus have put him in the role of a "go-between" for prostitutes and their customers. Kevin J. Mumford has identified "the go-between[s] of vice" as "taxi drivers, doormen, and porters who earned money on the side for connecting prospective customers with prostitutes."⁶

At the time of the murder Lee Shelton owned a lid club called the Modern Horseshoe Club, a name that related nicely to his profession as a carriage driver. According to blues scholar William Barlow, the Modern Horseshoe Club was in the "center of the tenderloin's night life" on Morgan Street, ranking among the most prestigious underworld nightclubs along with the Chauffeurs Club, the Deluxe Club, the Jazzland Club, and the Cardinal's Nest in the 1920s.⁷

In *Interzones* Mumford describes the vice districts of New York and Chicago in the early 1910s. Here gambling, prostitution, and interracial mixing, which had been pushed out of the white areas, took hold the African-American neighborhoods. "The internal migration of vice into growing black neighborhoods was covert, quiet—its purpose to elude police. The changing sexual terrain . . . was not obvious but was hardly invisible." In St. Louis this migration of nightlife into the "interzones" seems to have occurred as early as 1895.

There is no reason to doubt that Shelton's club catered to gambling and prostitution. Given that ragtime and blues music would have flourished in such a place, it is not surprising that Stagolee first emerged as a blues song.

Deep Morgan, where Lee Shelton killed Billy Lyons, was the home of the sporting fraternity of the Third Ward. Henry Townsend, who learned to play blues shortly after arriving in St. Louis, recalled that Deep Morgan then was still much as it had been in the 1890s. "It was mostly black people," he said. "Some of them were considered wealthy; they lived above the poverty line." Even so, white journalists writing about "Lower Morgan Street" commonly stereotyped the blacks living there as colorfully dressed but lazy. According to an article titled "Snap Shots of Daily Life on Lower Morgan Street," published the very day Stack Lee Shelton shot Billy Lyons,

> On Morgan Street, by day or night
> You'll find the festive coon,
> As thick as dogs that bark and fight
> And bay the summer noon.
> They labor not a single jot
> To earn their bread and cheese;
> Yet Solomon in all his pride was not
> Arrayed like one of these.[8]

The article reflects a growing trend in urban slumming, where one could encounter the black world. Such articles repressed overt references to sex and race, but language like "festive coon" was laden with an implicit sexual energy. According to Mumford, "By the opening of the twentieth century, these narratives of urban exploration described the ways in which race 'colored' the contours of the city, emphasized the sexualized and hence immoral characteristics of the slum, and consistently linked the most vicious of vice to the incidence of black/white sexual relations."[9] One notorious whorehouse called "The Bucket of Blood," a few blocks from where Lee Shelton lived, shows up in many versions of Stagolee.

Jim Crow ruled in St. Louis during the late 1890s. Between 1860 and 1870 the black population of St. Louis increased almost sixfold, and from 1880 to 1890 it grew by 21 percent. Black migration from the South created slums, where landlords exploited the crowded conditions by charging blacks a higher rent than they did whites. Although the city was burgeoning with possibilities for whites, 85 percent of black St. Louisans lived in only 2 percent of the area. Lee Shelton inevitably interacted with whites as neighbors, landlords, tenants, and ward bosses, but in very limited ways. He might have ridden with whites on one of the city's streetcars, but he would have had to sit up front; the whites sat in the back, where they would not be exposed to the rain and smoke. Hotels remained strictly segregated, as did churches, theaters, and most other public amusements. Blacks competed with whites in "athletic events such as baseball," and Washington University had admitted a few blacks to some departments in the 1880s, but it ended that practice in the 1890s. The two black graduates of the law school left the city in 1891, and the the next year the alumni association rewrote its constitution in order to bar the two graduates of the Manual Training School from the annual alumni banquet. Although blacks received the vote in 1870, they "failed to achieve . . . equal citizenship rights . . . through the power of the ballot." Civil rights became the main goal of black voters, who judged candidates and parties by their racial politics.[10] Efforts by Democrats to stop racial segregation proved unsuccessful. A 1901 referendum prohibited blacks from establishing residences on blocks that were at least 75 percent white.[11]

Although the ballad of Stagolee is about one black man killing another, it also evokes the world of segregation and rejection. The singers of Stagolee used the ballad to depict white brutality, and fantasized how Stagolee would escape their injustice:

> De hangman put de mask on, tied his [Stagolee's] han's behind his back,
> Spring de trap on Stagolee, but his neck refused to crack.
> Hangman, he got frightened, he said: "Chief, you see how it be,
> I can't hang this man, you better let him go free."
> Chief Maloney said to de hangman, "Befo' I'd let him go alive—"
> He up wid his police special an' shot him six times in de side."[12]

According to an article in the *St. Louis Star-Sayings* on December 29, 1895, "the killing of William Lyons by Lee Shelton was the result of a vendetta. The informant told Coroner Wait that Shelton was the president of a negro club which has headquarters at Curtis' place . . . [that] Lyons, who was a relative of Henry Bridgewater, the negro saloonist, belonged to a faction which held forth in Bridgewater's saloon, [and] that the feud which resulted in Shelton killing Lyons commenced five years ago when Harry Wilson, a noted negro character and friend of Shelton's, was shot and killed in Bridgewater's place, on Eleventh Street by Charley Brown, a step-brother of Lyons, Shelton's victim. Brown escaped conviction, and it is said that Shelton then swore he would avenge Wilson's death. It is said he had trouble with several of the Bridgewater crowd."

A short time after this was published, J. C. Covington, the financial secretary of the Four Hundred Club, wrote a letter to the editor disputing the fact that the club was located in the Bill Curtis Saloon. "In justice to the '400' allow me to make a correction of the false statement concerning a social vendetta," Covington wrote.

"There is no part of the statement that is true, and it only goes to show that some enemy . . . of the Four Hundred is striving to place our club in a false light before the public, or perhaps, some festive reporter has drawn greatly upon his imagination and made a startling discovery of a mythical vendetta." The Four Hundred Club had not been organized, Covington went on to say, until December 6, 1895, which meant that it could not "have influenced the life of Charley Brown," who had been killed in 1892.[13]

The Four Hundred Club was a "social club," but such clubs always had a moral front. Apparently black social clubs like the Four Hundred were always in trouble with the police. The Four Hundred Club may have been a type of black-and-tan club, catering to an interracial clientele, and as such would have been under pressure from reform policies.

The Sunday *St. Louis Star-Sayings* included this letter to the editor in its follow-up article on the Lyons murder. The article focused on Lee Shelton and his relationship to the Four Hundred Club. "The Four Hundred was organized," the article said, "for the moral and physical culture of young colored men. We contemplate no acts of violence, and as law-abiding citizens and voters we stand ready and willing to protect the laws of our city, State, and United States." Covington went on to laud Lee Shelton: "Mr. [Stack] Lee was our captain. We deeply regret the situation into which our unfortunate member and brother has fallen, and he has our heartfelt sympathies, both individually and collectively, and our hope for him is the best."

The ballads convey the impression that Stagolee was a loner, a man who went "stag," that is, without friends. But according to Covington's letter, Lee Shelton was not a loner. This group of men supported him. Moreover, as their "captain" it seems he was also a leader. Shelton appears to have been a man with responsibilities to others.

Where did Stack Lee get his name? One scholar claims that the real Stagolee was a black man with "a bad eye" who worked as a cabin boy on the Anchor Line, a Mississippi steamboat company. Another tradition has him working as a stoker.[14] John and Alan Lomax claimed alternately that "Stack Lee . . . was the son of the Lee family of Memphis who owned a large line of steamers that ran up and down the Mississippi" and that the name Stack Lee came from the riverboat of that name.[15]

In 1967 one Stagolee scholar, Richard E. Buehler, published evidence that Lee Shelton took his nickname from a white riverboat captain called Stack Lee. Buehler speculated that the real man behind the ballad worked for the Lee shipping line, that he had worked on one of the ships as a waiter, and that if we could find the records of the Lee Line, we would discover his real identity.[16]

Shields McIlwayne claimed that because of the popularity of the river captain Stack Lee, there were "more colored kids named Stack Lee than there were sinners in hell." Unlike the white riverboat captain Stack Lee, according to McIlwayne, this black one was a killer. When people referred to the killer, some thought they were referring to the river captain, and this "queer turn of folklore" gave the name of Jim Lee's son a mistaken immortality. Stack Lee, the Negro, was a killer, and the rousters sang about his deeds. In these songs, the reference to "Stack-o-Lee" is not to a man but to a riverboat of that name:

> Stack-o-Lee's in de Bend
> He ain't doin' nothin'
> but killing up good men.[17]

There is some evidence that Lee Shelton took the name from the riverboat *Stack Lee*. Many of the riverboats were the subjects of "coonjining" (conjoining) songs. These songs, according to Garnett Laidlaw Eskew, "eulogized the boats themselves." "There was something intensely personal about a steamboat. To the men who manned and owned and operated them, steamboats had personality. Hence the qualities of certain boats live today in Coonjine songs."[18]

The *Stack Lee* belonged to the Lee Line of riverboats. Blacks were particularly fond of this line and of the Anchor Line. Anchor Line boats (running from 1869 to 1911) were noted for speed, sumptuous cabins, elaborate cuisine—and prostitution. In the following song, quoted by Eskew, there is some indication that the man in the song gives his money to the chambermaid and gets sexual favors in return. As Eskew claims, "The boats of the Lee Line, in the Memphis–New Orleans trade until a few years ago, fed the passengers and crews well, but paid notoriously low wages. Still the Negroes liked to work for the Lee Line. The reason is to be found in this song:

> Reason I likes de Lee Line trade:
> Sleep all night wid de chambermaid.
> She gimme some pie and she gimme some cake,
> An' I give' her all de money dat I ever make."[19]

If there was prostitution on the *Stack Lee* or other riverboats (as the song suggests), and if Lee Shelton was a pimp even before arriving in St. Louis, the epithet "Stack Lee" would have fitted him admirably. Using epithet in this way is one of African Americans' signifying practices, much like what contemporary rappers do when they adopt stage names instead of using their own. In any case, this use of epithet is a feature of the oral tradition from Homer down to the latest rap artist.

According to the newspaper account of the murder, Shelton "lived at 911 North Twelfth Street," yet the police told the coroner that they had arrested him on Sixth Street in the Tamale district. Why was he arrested in one place if he lived in another? One would assume that he was hiding out. Since Sixth Street was in the slum and North Twelfth Street was in a better neighborhood, one can assume that Lee Shelton was moving up in the world. Or perhaps he was living in several places at once. If he was a successful pimp, we may assume that he maintained several places, one of them his official residence.

Despite two major attempts to eradicate the red-light district, city officials unwittingly left the brick house at 911 North Twelfth Street, the home of Stack Lee. Today the rear of this dwelling retains vestiges of crib houses constructed for Stag's working girls. Each crib was equipped with a bed, a washbasin, and a towel. Stag Lee allowed the girls to keep their tips and gifts; in contrast, madams were strict about allowing the whores to keep expensive gifts. Perhaps this is why so many whores sing his praise. He seems to have provided them a place to work, and perhaps, because these streetwalkers were not tied down to a madam and her house, they felt freer.

But not all the prostitutes sang Stack Lee's praise. In the 1903 St. Louis version of the ballad, Stack's street gals say:

> It's too cold out there,
> The sidewalk's full of ice and sleet,
> Damned if we'll hustle to get him out
> Up and down this damn cold street,
> Cause he's a good-for-nothing p.i. [pimp] Stackerlee.[20]

Lee Shelton's house at 911 North Twelfth Street in St. Louis, with the cribs at the rear. Photograph by Kate Partridge.

The person speaking here is a streetwalker and probably black. As we known from Mumford's research, black streetwalkers appeared in urban areas in disproportionately large numbers at the turn of the century and continued to do so "throughout the era of migration." In the 1920s, for example, although black women represented roughly 2 percent of the population, they accounted for 20 percent of convicted prostitutes.[21]

Streetwalking was the least desirable form of prostitution. "Excluded from the brothels," Mumford asserts, "black women were viewed as 'natural' streetwalkers, deserving of harsh punishment." Although reformers in the 1910s argued that streetwalking had been eradicated, investigators reported that black streetwalking still occurred in black neighborhoods. The White Slavery discourse implied that white women had been forced into prostitution by some "sinister, dark men" and were not to be blamed for their behavior. But whereas white women could be reformed, black women were stigmatized as biologically degenerate.[22]

In such circumstances, black streetwalkers may have looked upon Stagolee as a kind of savior. Who else would take a real interest in them if not someone who shared their worldview and their situation in an oppressive urban setting? If we are to believe the oral literature of Stagolee, he was a liberator.

3

That Bad Pimp of Old St. Louis: The Oral Poetry of the Late 1890s

We have learned what we can about Lee Shelton from public documents such as prison records and trial transcripts and from newspaper articles. Although these sources provide no definitive proof that the Stagolee of the oral literature is the same as the Stack Lee of the St. Louis newspapers and other documents, neither do they disprove it.

We may learn something more by casting backward from the oral literature, the ballads and the blues. "Living means leaving traces," Walter Benjamin wrote.[1] These traces of the living are left behind by the modern city dweller and must be carefully preserved. We are looking for "traces" of a life that has been been hidden or destroyed by the city. Although the ballads are not themselves historical documents, they are based on historical incidents and on real names.

There are two variants of the basic type of Stagolee ballad. One of them is called the 1903 variant because it was collected then.[2] The other one, called 1927, was privately printed in that year.[3] Its first lines run:

> Stack-o-lee was a good man
> Everybody did love
> Everybody swore by Stack
> Just like the lovin' stars above.
> O, Stack, O, Stack-o-lee
> Stack-o-lee was a good man.

Here Stack-o-lee is "a good man" who loves and is loved by everybody. How could a pimp, or mack, be a good man, except perhaps from the point of view of those whom he helped? The next lines reveal that Stack-o-lee is the local hero of a specific group of people—other pimps and whores:[4]

> The pimps and whores all swore by Stack—
> By the everlasting stars above
> They all loved Stack-o-lee!
>
> Now what you know 'bout this!
> An' what you all know 'bout that?
> They say he killed old Billy Lyons
> 'Bout a damned old Stetson hat
> Oh! poor, poor, Stack-o-lee.

The Folklore Archives at the University of Oregon yield a single handwritten couplet transcribed either from an oral performance or from a memory of such a performance:

> Go tell little Lilly Sheldon to get out on these icy blocks
> And rustle for to get her Stackerlee some rocks.

Lilly Sheldon appears not only in the ballads but also in Stagolee's prison records and in newspaper articles. The references to a Lilly or Nellie Sheldon as Stackerlee's "girlfriend," "wife," or "old lady" indicate the presence of a hidden history.[5]

The name Sheldon provides an essential link with the identity of Stagolee. It seems plausible that through frequent retellings and re-hearings the letter *t* in "Shelton" was changed to *d*, producing "Sheldon," which was easier to pronounce (or to hear). If this is correct, then this name connects the ballad to the historical person Lee Shelton, a pimp who became a legend.

The earliest version of the ballad that I have been able to locate, dating from 1903 in Memphis, offers a portrait of an old pimp called Stackerlee and his whore, called Nellie Sheldon. The details are so realistic that it is hard not to conclude that the song was about actual people. There are explcit references to the world of prostitution:

> Poor old Nellie Sheldon.
> When she heard the news,
> She's sittin' on the bed side,
> Lacing up her high-heel shoes,
> Bulls got my sweet-fuckin' papa Stackerlee.

The image of a woman sitting on a bed lacing up her shoes as news of her lover's death arrives harks back to the era of bordellos, ragtime music, honky-tonks, blues, the cakewalk, and murder ballads. By 1903, fashions had changed from high-topped to high-heeled shoes, but the vestiges of the earlier style remain in the act of lacing. Dozens of variants carry this image, including this one, reportedly first heard in the gold-mining town of Cripple Creek, Colorado, in 1899 or 1900:

Little Lillie Sheldon when she first heard the news,
She was sittin' on her bedside a lacing up her shoes.[6]

Lee Shelton's real-life girlfriend, or "bottom woman," worked for him as a prostitute. Although her first name may differ from version to version, in every case she has the same function, that of the hero's helper.[7] At the inquest on Billy Lyons' death, Police Officer Falvey testified that he went to "No. 307 on Sixth Street," where he "requested the woman of the house, asked her if she had Stack Lee's revolver. She said, yes, she had put it in a drawer. I went to the bureau drawer and took out a .44 Smith & Wesson, fully loaded, every chamber was full."[8] This detail has resurfaced in many versions, as in this one by Tom Rush from 1963:

Now Staggerlee come running
In the red, hot, boiling sun,
Said, "Reach down in the drawer, Roberta,
Get me my forty-one."[9]

In the 1903 version the narrative shifts from "poor old Nellie Sheldon" to the confrontation between Stackerlee and Billy Lyons:

When Stackerlee and Billy Lyons
Sat down to that game of cards
If Billy'd known like old bad Stack
He'd have made it up with his God,
Cause he laid poor Billy's body down, bad Stackerlee.

The third and fourth lines imply that Stackerlee already knew what was going to happen, endowing him with an evil premeditation. Billy is innocent and doesn't have time to pray, to "make it up with his God."

The background characters mentioned in the next stanza, "the Rounders and gamblers," provide another clue to the time when the ballad crystallized:

> The Rounders and the gamblers
> Won't forget that night.
> A bottle of booze and a Stetson hat
> Caused that fatal fight,
> And he laid poor Billy's body down bad Stackerlee.

According to the *Oxford English Dictionary*, *rounder* is an American term, first used in 1891, meaning "a habitual criminal, loafer, or drunkard"—clearly a figure that would have been familiar in the red-light district of St. Louis.[10] The causes of the fight and murder are "a bottle of booze and a Stetson hat"—the one fairly general but the other strikingly specific. The order of mention is the same as the order of events recounted in the inquest testimony.

There follows an account of the fight itself:

> Billy Lyons made just one move,
> He couldn't make no more.
> They had to put his body on a shutter
> Before it hit the floor.
> Yes he laid poor Billy's body down bad Stackerlee.

The next stanzas develop the escape episode in which Stack eludes the police, who are afraid of him. In other versions he is running through the forest, where the wind is "howling" and "moaning."

> Round the corner of Fourth and Main.
> Stackerlee did run,

And in his hand he held
A blue Colt smokin' gun,
Cause he'd laid poor Billy's body down bad Stackerlee.

The news spread quickly round the town,
and all the gang came to see
what cop would have the nerve to pinch bad Stackerlee.
That quick-shootin' two-gun-totin' Stackerlee.

Policeman and Sergeant Frisbie seen Stack behind a tree.
Frisbie was the toughest copper on the Force,
Says, You better come along with me,
Count of how you laid poor Billy down bad Stackerlee.

After Stackerlee's arrest the ballad switches to the street "thirty long days, thirty long nights" later. Stackerlee is still in jail, and somebody is trying to get his "street gals" to cough up enough money to get that "hip-shakin', heart-breakin' papa Stackerlee" out of jail. But Stack's street gals say no; they're not going to hustle to get him out; it's too hard to come by the money. The women who are willing to prostitute can't be depended on when the pimp goes to jail.

The mack is usually not the person who goes to jail. In the world of prostitution, the pimp functions as a combination of bail bondsman and lawyer, advising the girls on their rights if they get arrested and providing ready cash to bail them out. In this ballad, however, it is the mack who is in jail, and the girls are supposed to come to his aid; but they "blow," or leave him in the lurch.

Not even Stack's "chippy gal in the parlor house" will help him:

Stack's chippy gal in the parlor house
Says I've got a lot of ready dough,

But I've turned over a new leaf, boys and girls,
I keep no goddam pimps no more,
No, no, not even papa Stackerlee, that p.i.

The chippy gal was probably a white prostitute who earned more money than a black prostitute who walked the streets. White prostitutes often preferred working in a house. Other prostitutes preferred walking the streets because they had more freedom to refuse customers, an important consideration for white women who wished to avoid contact with black men.[11] The chippy gal's assertion that she's not going to "keep no goddam pimps no more" implies that she did keep Stagolee at some point. Like most prostitutes, she would give her money to her pimp not only for protection but also for sex. Presumably she was keeping Stagolee not because he was an obligation but because he was an indulgence. This suggests that Stack was her lover whom she paid. But as we learn in the next stanza, he also took money from Nellie—one of his "bottom women"—and gave it to the insincere, parlor house whore.

The police testified that they found Stack Lee through his woman: "We knowed where she lived and went down there and found Stack Lee." The police looked at the note she was carrying and suspected that Stagolee had written it. Like the mack he was, Stack Lee had used one woman to communicate to another woman. The following version comes from Lodi, California, and was printed in 1927, but it is similar to the one found in the oral tradition around St. Louis in 1903.

Says the Captain to the Police
Just keep still as any mouse,
And we will sure catch old Stackalee
At his woman's house.
That bad man Stackalee.[12]

The woman of the "house" is probably the madam of the bordello. We know that Sixth Street was lined with bordellos and that the most famous of them all, Madam Babe's Castle Club, was located at 236 Sixth Street. Elsewhere in the police testimonies, the officers refer to the "landlady" and the "boarding house," all code words for "madam" and "bordello." We can gather from the implicit text that this "boarding house" was a house of prostitution and that the "landlady" was a madam.

Just as in the real event, the police go looking for Stagolee's bottom woman:

> At last they found Stack's old girl,
> The one who'd been with him twenty years or more.
> The same poor old bitch he'd taken the money from
> And give to the chippy parlor house whore,
> She was crazy about her Papa Stackerlee.
>
> Nellie she was Stack's old girl,
> Poor old gal was about sixty,
> Not a tooth or a strand of hair,
> She says Since all of his whores have gone back on him,
> Watch his sweet mamma go from here,
> Watch me get it for my sweet man Stackerlee.

Nellie turns tricks all night and all day to help her man:

> All night long and all day long
> She hustled up and down the street.
> Wouldn't even spend a dime
> To buy herself a bite to eat.
> She was gettin' it for her sweet papa Stackerlee.
> She says John if you ain't got a dollar,
> I'll take you on for a dime,

I've got to feed this hungry pimp of mine.
I'm out here hustlin' for my sweet papa Stackerlee.

She takes her money and offers it to the judge. But the judge, a typical reform figure of the era, refuses:

Judge says even if you sold your horse and buggy
And every stick of wood,
We're goin' to make an example out of this here pimp,
And money's goin' to do him no good,
Cause he laid poor Billy's body down bad Staggerlee.

When the trial comes up, Stack's old girl pleads with the judge once more:

At last when the day of trial came up
She had a hundred dollars in her hand
(All in nickels dimes and quarters).
She says, Judge take all of this money
But give me back my sweet fuckin' man
Cause I can't live without my papa Stackerlee.

But the jury comes back with the news that Stack is to hang:

The jury went out on poor old Stack,
Came back and began to speak,
Stackerlee we condemn you to hang
On Friday of next week,
Cause you laid poor Billy's body down bad Stackerlee.

On the gallows, Stack makes a speech to "young pimps":

When old Stack got up on the gallows,
He said, I want to say a word or two,

I want to tell young pimps what shootin' high craps
And sportin' women will do
See what they've done to Stackerlee.

Next comes the funeral procession:

The horses and the carriages
Stretched out for about a mile.
Everybody whore and pimp had gone in hock
To put Old Stackerlee away in style.
Cause he was crap-shootin' coke-sniffin' hop-smokin'
Bad pimp Stackerlee.

In the St. Louis basic type, or archetype, there is a graveside scene. Structuralist Alan Dundes has called such a scene a "motifeme," a slot that marks a typical trait, to be filled in by the performer with a detail, called an "allomotif."[13] This detail may vary. In the 1927 variant, for example, a pimp takes out his bamboo and smokes his opium. During the 1890s there were opium dens all over downtown St. Louis. In the 1903 version, a pimp pulls out a needle and takes a jab. In this version, the drug of choice is cocaine:

When the funeral got out to the graveyard
Coke Jimmy had a word to say,
I want to tell you somethin' nice about old Stack
Before you lay my pal away
He was always a damn good friend of mine Stackerlee.
Many times I had a yen so bad I was about to croak,
All I had to do was to find old Stack
And get a sniff or two of coke,
Cause he never refused a pal poor Stackerlee.

The funeral procession and the graveside scene signal another step in the apotheosis of the real Lee Shelton to the mythic Stagolee.

There were many famous funerals given by the friends of famous pimps by 1895. Blacks lavished large amounts of money on underworld funerals. The occasion was the perfect site to elevate actual incidents to the status of legend, and thence to myth. Accounts of the fabulous wealth spent on the casket, of how many horses carried the possessions, of how the whores cried and wanted to jump into the grave with the pimp, and of speeches delivered at the graveside would spread far and wide by word of mouth.

Appropriately, the last person to speak at the gravesite is Nellie:

> Stack's old gal Nellie said I've had men
> From Maine to Tennessee,
> But I never had a man to grind me and make me like it
> Like old Stackerlee, that hip-shakin' back-breakin'
> Sweet-fuckin' papa
> Stackerlee.

We can assume that the ballad was well known among the "sporting" people of St. Louis and even that Lee Shelton heard it when he came out of prison in 1909. He would probably have been amused to hear a song that narrated his death while he was still living.

The 1903 version of the ballad ends with an account of Billy's and Stackerlee's ascent to heaven:

> Billy Lyons and Stackerlee
> Went to heaven looking mighty curious
> Michael and his angels announced

Two dudes from East St. Louis
Poor Billy Lyons and that bad pimp Stackerlee.

The angels' announcement of "two dudes from East St. Louis" ties the origins of the ballad still more closely to the world of prostitution in St. Louis during the late 1890s.

Both the 1903 and 1927 narratives are variants of the basic type. The basic type itself is hypothetical; no written version of it exists. But it is nonetheless real, surviving in all the available narratives of Stagolee that I have examined that retain similar traits, most of which refer to the historical events.

How do we relate this image of Stagolee as a pimp with the images of him as a carriage driver, a waiter, and a saloonkeeper? Are they contradictory images? Is there another meaning beneath them? Perhaps the key to the puzzle lies in the identity of other players, such as Billy Lyons.

4

"Poor Billy Lyons"

When the trail of the historical Stagolee dried up, scholars turned to other figures in the legend for clues. Richard E. Buehler suggested that Billy Lyons might be a useful starting point.[1]

William Lyons died of bullet wounds at four o'clock on Thursday morning, December 26, 1895. The next day his body was taken to the medical examiner, where an inquest was held with the suspect Lee Shelton present. A few days later, Lyons was interred in the Henry Bridgewater lot at St. Peter Cemetery, where he now rests. He is the coactor in the Stagolee ballad drama. Of the hundred versions I have examined, there is only one in which Billy Lyons is not the victim. Who was he?

Billy Lyons was born in 1864 in Missouri, but the exact place of his birth is lost to history. Although Lyons apparently came from a respectable, well-to-do family, the names of his father and mother were not on his death certificate. The *St. Louis Globe-Democrat* described him as a "colored levee hand." *Gould's St. Louis Directory* for 1894 listed him as "a watchman."[2] Both occupations were considered unskilled labor, which was how most African Americans in urban areas were employed.[3]

At the time of Billy's death his father was married to Marie Brown. It was this stepmother's son, Charles Brown, who in 1892 killed Harry Wilson—Lee Shelton's friend—in the Bridgewater Saloon. According to John David, Billy Lyons' sister, Eliza, was married to Henry Bridgewater, who owned the saloon. The newspaper account of Charles's murder has Charles at the same address that was given as Billy's; they were brothers-in-law who lived together on Gay Street. Billy Lyons may also have worked at the Bridgewater Saloon.[4]

Although he was not married—his death certificate listed him as single—Billy Lyons had three children. In the version of the ballad collected by Harold Courlander, Billy pleads for his life for their sake:

> Billy O'Lyons told Stagolee
> Please don't take my life
> I got three little children
> And a dear little lovin' wife.[5]

60

Billy Lyons' children, Florence, Marie, and Buddy.
Courtesy of Judith Ann David.

In another version, recorded in Kentucky in 1937 for the Works Progress Administration's American Folksong Collection project, Billy Martin sings Billy Lyons' plea for his "three children" and "weeping wife."[6] Most of the ballads, however, mention only two children, probably because this number made it easier to create a poetic opposition (male/female), which in turn aids the memory in recalling the line.[7] An example is this version, in which Billy pleads:

> Stackerlee, Stacker don't take my life.
> Think of my two children and my loving wife.

Stagolee's answer is:

> I know your two children
> I know your loving wife
> One is a boy, other is a girl
> But if they ever see their Dad again
> It will be in some other world.[8]

Why didn't Liz Bridgewater, their aunt, or Marie, their grand-mother, adopt them? Poverty was one of the reasons most black families gave children up for adoption—but this family was not poor.

We do not know the answers to this question, but we do know that the Bridgewater family exerted a great deal of effort to ensure that Shelton was convicted and that he stayed behind bars. When Shelton's parole came up in 1909, Lyons' sister and stepmother wrote the parole board:

> And in conjunction with my mother I hope and pray that
> you will never agree to let a man who never worked a day
> or earned an honest dollar be turned out to meet us face

to face. As far as his character is concerned ask any officer
on the police force from Captain down to patrolman.
Again as a sister I beg you not to turn a man like him on
the community at large. If justice had been done he
would have hung. Just think he has not served half his
term.

Yours respectfully,

Mrs. Henry Bridgewater, sister

Marie Brown, mother[9]

John David discovered a letter from a sheriff to Judge James
Withrow stating that Bridgewater was active "in the prosecution of
Lee for the crime." Billy's sister Eliza, his stepmother Marie, and his
brother-in-law Henry Bridgewater hired C. Orrick Bishop—one of
the best lawyers in St. Louis—to convict Lee Shelton of the murder.
Henry Bridgewater may also have hired or influenced the appointment of Marshall F. MacDonald as a special counsel for the state to
assist Bishop.[10]

The facts are that in the 1890s there was a woman named Marie
Brown who owned the Bridgewater Saloon, that her son Charles
Wilson killed a man in that saloon, that her stepson Billy Lyons
was killed by Stack Lee Sheldon (Stagolee), and that both Marie
and Billy's sister sought full punishment for Shelton's murder of
Billy. References to these incidents persisted into the 1950s and
1960s, in toasts such as this:

Mrs. Billy she went runnin' an' screamin': "Stack, I do b'lieve
    it's so.
You an' my lil Billy been frien's since many long years ago."
Stagolee tol' Mrs. Billy, "Ef you don't b'lieve yo man is dead,
Come to de barroom, see de hole I shot in his head."

Mrs. Lyon fell to her knee, an' she said to her oldes' son,
"When you get lil bit bigger, gonna buy you a 41."
Then the bartender's mother comes running out. She says:
"Your name may be Stack, but you'd better not be here
When my son Billy Lyons get back."[11]

The toast is a narrative that is chanted, usually to a beat. Usually its themes center on incidents—sometimes violent, often comical—involving a fictional folk figure or a legendary hero. This toast, which I call the Billy Lyons version, presents a subtype of the prototype Stagolee in the 1903 ballad. This Stagolee is a bully, who replies that he

will be there when time comes to pass—
And you can tell your son Billy Lyons to kiss my ass!

When Billy Lyons does come in, Stagolee kills him too. This version recounts the two historical murders, one in the Bridgewater (involving Charles Brown and Wilson) and the other in the Bill Curtis Saloon (involving Billy Lyons and Lee Shelton).

Another toast version sustains the bully image of Stagolee:

Stag went to Mrs. Lyons, say, "Miz Lyons, Miz Lyons, you know
   what I've done.
I went out there and killed your last and only son."
Mrs. Lyons looked at Stag, say, "Stag, Stag, you know that can't be
   true!
You an' Billy been good friends for the last year or two."
He say, "Look bitch if you don't believe what I said,
Go down there and count them holes in his motherfuckin'
   head."[12]

We have fewer facts about Billy than about his brother-in-law, Henry Bridgewater. His saloon, at 814 Christy Avenue, was only a few blocks away from the Bill Curtis Saloon. Bridgewater's patrons were wealthier and more popular. For example, Peter Jackson, a famous pugilist as well as a noted actor in a theatrical production of *Uncle Tom's Cabin*, visited there when he was in St. Louis. In addition to being a celebrity hangout, the saloon was known throughout the city for its "expert billiardists" and as the "principal exponent of the western sporting fraternity." Bridgewater was himself one of the wealthiest black men in St. Louis, owning a house worth $4,500 and other real estate worth over $11,000.[13]

In 1933 St. Louis officials widened Morgan Street from thirty feet to eighty feet, and many historic structures had to be torn down. One of them was Bridgewater's Saloon. "And who remembers when Eleventh and Morgan was the stomping ground of Henry Bridgewater?" one newspaper columnist asked. "Bridgewater always entertained the visiting sporting celebrities of his color: Peter Jackson; Isaac Murphy, the 'Colored Archer,' who rode more Derby winners than any jockey in history."[14]

Bridgewater used the two-story building housing his saloon for Republican politics: the Republican Central Committee of St. Louis often held small gatherings on the second floor. The Republican party was the favored party of blacks with a stake in the system. But the saloon itself was described as "a den of vice" in the account given by a St. Louis newspaper of a murder that took place there.[15]

Yet most saloonkeepers in this era were both politically involved and community minded. Bridgewater's prominence in the black community was enhanced by his attempt to purchase land to start a manual trade school for blacks. In this move he may have been in-

fluenced by the ideas of Booker T. Washington, who had argued
that blacks should concentrate on manual schools to improve their
political and financial condition.

In several toast versions, Stagolee comes into a saloon or restau-
rant for something to eat and is served badly. For example:

> I waded through water and waded through mud,
> I went to the bar and ordered something to eat,
> The bartender give me a muddy-assed glass of water and a tough-
> assed piece of meat.[16]

The oral tradition crystallizes Henry Bridgewater as "the bartender," who treats Stagolee badly. First he threatens to call the
police on him. The ensuing dialogue in the toast unfolds from
Stagolee's point of view:

> I said, "Bartender, you don't know who I am."
> He said, "Frankly motherfucker, I don't give a damn."
> I said, "Well, you'd better look up and see,
> 'Cause I'm that bad motherfucker, my name's Stacka Lee."
> He said, "Well Stack, I heard you was down this way,
> But I meet bad motherfuckers like you each and every day."
> Well, two seconds later, that motherfucker lay dead,
> 'Cause I done put a hole in his motherfuckin' head![17]

Perhaps Buehler was right, and Billy Lyons is a key to the
Stagolee mystery. Billy Lyons appears to have his own narrative,
which tells a different version of the murder. This narrative provided the content of the toast version of Stagolee. In the toast version, there is no fight over a hat. The hat is symbolically displaced
by the bartender's insulting treatment of Stagolee. The Billy Lyons
version of the event always narrates two murders. In that version,

66

Stagolee first kills the bartender for serving him "a muddy-assed glass of water and a tough-assed piece of meat"; then he kills Lyons.

One more fact remains to be told: it seems that it was William Lyons—not Lee Shelton—was known to the police as "Billy the bully." Lyons was a "rowdy bully" from a "respectable family" background with "means to prosecute Stack Lee," a man who at the time "bore a pretty hard name." James L. Dawson, the city jailer of St. Louis, writing to the governor, "recalled an earlier experience in Curtis' saloon [where Lyons was killed by Lee Shelton] in which Lyons terrorized the patrons with a 'long knife very sharp on both edges.'"[18]

In an early version of the ballad published by Howard Odum in 1911, it is clear that the black community did not regard Stagolee's "victim" with favor—he is simply a nameless "bully":

Stagolee shot bully; fell down on de flo'.
Bully cry out: "Dat fohty-fo' it hurts me so."
Stagolee done kill dat bully now.

Sent for de wagon, didn't come.
Loaded down wit pistols an' all dat gatlin gun.
Stagolee did kill dat bully now.

There follows a vivid scene at the funeral where a collection is taken up for the dead "bully." The first-person narrator expresses his own disapproval, and his sense of alliance with Stagolee, in these lines:

Some give a nickel; some give a dime;
I didn't give a red copper cent, 'cause he's no friend o' mine.[19]

Billy's helpers are usually his son, his wife, or both. Despite the black community's low regard for Billy, several members of his family responded to his death and even sought revenge for his murder. In some versions Billy's wife tells her son that he must grow up to kill Stagolee. In 1934 in Goul, Arkansas, a black convict sang this version to John Lomax:[20]

> When I was a little boy sitting on my mother's knee
> She often told me of that bad man Stagolee.
> "Son, O Son, when you get to the age of twenty-three,
> I want you to kill that bad man Stagolee."

But the boy is afraid:

> "O Mother, O Mother, I don't see how it can be.
> Stagolee killed my daddy and he might kill me."

At the end of this version, the son fails to kill Stagolee, leaving the job to the "Sargent," who shot Stagolee "dead on the barroom flo'."

In other versions, Billy Lyons' wife dismisses the son and shoots Stagolee herself. Robert Hunter wrote such a version, which the Grateful Dead made popular. Hunter claims that he wrote this as an anthem for a band called The Dinosaurs back in the mid-1980s.

> 1940 Xmas evening with a full moon over town
> Staggerlee met Bill DeLyon
> And he blew that poor boy down.
> Do you know what he shot him for?
> What do you make of that?
> 'Cause Billy DeLyon threw lucky dice,
> Won Staggerlee's hat . . .

In Hunter's version Billy's wife, Delia DeLyon, tries to get the policeman to arrest Stagolee, and when he refuses, she takes a gun and goes after Stagolee herself.

Big Delia said just give me a gun
He shot my Billy dead now I'm gonna see him hung
She waded to DeLyons's Club through Billy DeLyon's blood
Stepped up to Staggerlee at the bar
Said Buy me a gin fizz, love
As Staggerlee lit a cigarette she shot him in the balls
Blew the smoke off her revolver, had him dragged to city hall
Bail, Bail, see you hang him high
He shot my Billy dead and now he's got to die.[21]

Billy Lyons may have been a big, burly "bully" in real life, but in the ballad, toast, and blues, he is a small, pathetic figure, a man lacking dignity, begging for his life. Stagolee has assumed at least seven "subtype" forms throughout his evolution, but Billy is always on his knees, begging. As teenagers, my friends and I would reenact this request for mercy when we wanted to ridicule our own behavior or that of others. The image remains with me today as a paradigm of pathos.

In the preceding account I have attempted to separate the facts from the Stagolee legend, but in the performance of oral literature, the performer tries to do the opposite: to fuse the facts with the fiction, to make his story live dramatically. In the process, as we shall see, he often creates oppositions and inversions that in reality never existed.

5

Narrative Events and Narrated Events

In looking over the Stagolee and William Lyons material, we notice that the oral tradition changes the facts. Why did Stagolee get cast as the bully when in reality it was the man he killed who was the bully? This is what is meant by "inversion." The social drama, with its breach, crisis, and resolution, influences the way the events are remembered later. As Victor Turner makes clear, the values of the social drama are inverted to permit the assignment of values and meaning in the third, redress, phase of a dramatic (or, in our case, an informal oral) performance.[1]

Just as in dreams, the process of inversion is at work in the social drama of ordinary people without a print literature. This process transforms actual historical incidents (narrative events) into oral literature (narrated events) by recounting them from the viewpoint of the desires of the people hearing the story. Despite the historical references found in the hundreds of existing versions of the Stagolee song, the legend is not based on facts. Rather, the legend exploits the facts according to the emotional and psychological needs of the teller and his or her audience.

There were many "unofficial" social dramas unfolding in St. Louis in the 1890s, including those involving the black social clubs and their affiliations with crime, politics, and music. Many of the narrated events in the Stagolee texts make sense when placed in the context of the actual (narrative) events that these social dramas spun. These contributed to the oral literature of Stagolee.

Stagolee is an oral narrative that is based in both the social events and oral literature. It is a tale, but it is more of a myth than a folktale. Folktales—such as the "Signifying Monkey"—do not use historical figures, whereas the ballad, as we will see, is full of names that refer to historical people, places, and rituals. Stagolee, however, is not a historical document, a saga, or a legend. Like other traditional tales, its main ingredient is poiesis.

Stagolee is a myth in the sense that it is a traditional tale that can be retold and reapplied to different situations. It is a myth in the sense that the classicist Walter Burkert meant: "a traditional tale with secondary, partial reference to something of collective importance."[2] This leads us to a conception of an oral literature in which Stagolee is an archetype.

As a form of oral literature, the original Stagolee is based on facts. But like much of oral literature, it is a combination of facts and fictions. As oral literature, it is a verbal performance—a mode of verbal communication. As Richard Bauman has observed, "Oral narrative provides an especially rich focus for the investigation of the relationship between oral literature and social life because part of the special nature of narrative is to be doubly anchored in human events. That is, narratives are keyed both to the events in which they are told and to the events that they recount, toward narrative events and narrated events."[3] Walter Benjamin also described the interdependence of narrated events and the narrative events: the storyteller takes what he tells from his own experience or that reported by others, and in turn makes it the experience of those who are listening.[4]

Richard Bauman's ethnographic perspective of oral performance requires that we look at folklore as a "verbal art, as a way of speaking, a mode of verbal communication."[5] By looking at the narrative events—political, cultural, and musical—that occurred in St. Louis around the time of Lee Shelton's killing of William Lyons, we can see why the storytellers narrated certain events but not others. This interdependence will in turn give us an insight into the larger picture of how Americans—African Americans in particular and society in general—make sense of the American experience. We can begin to understand how a bordello ballad like Stagolee can become a classic American ballad.

The "eyewitness" accounts are the narrative events. These accounts show that elements of the legend are derived from the actual killing of Billy Lyons: the importance of the hat, the "cool" character of Stagolee, the coroner's inquest, Lilly or Nellie Sheldon, Nat Dryden, Judge Murphy, and the bartender Ben Scott—these are references to real facts and real people.

Crystallization occurs when the folk organize the narrative events itself into oppositions. Contrast and symmetry are agents of crystallization. Walter Burkert explains it this way: "the combat tale, the ending of which is victory, will not introduce two medium-sized, medium-minded, average people to fight—they would rather shake hands"; the "prospective victor and the antagonist are made opposites in every respect: the victor will be bright, handsome, nice, young, perhaps slim and small . . . while the adversary will be dark, ugly, repulsive, big and powerful, but dissolute and lecherous."[6]

The prevailing contrast in the Stagolee oral literature is that between Billy's plea for mercy and Stagolee's refusal to be merciful—a refusal that exemplifies Stagolee's "hardness," his "badness." Thus the Stagolee folklore structures the narratives in order to maximize Stagolee and Billy Lyons as opposites. Billy Lyons violates the interdiction on stealing, or in any way damaging a "bad man's" hat. By stealing or damaging Stagolee's Stetson Lyons sets in motion a series of events that constitute the narrative, including Stagolee's response to this violation.[7]

Both the anthropologist Claude Lévi-Strauss and the folklorist Alan Dundes also see opposition as a basic structure of myth and folktales.[8] Lévi-Strauss claims that there are always two opposite terms with an intermediary, which always tend to be replaced by two equivalent terms, which allows a third one as a medium (such as a mermaid—a conlfation of woman and fish—or a flying horse—a conflation of horse and bird). Dundes believes that the oppositions can be found in male and female, hero and villain, trickster and dupe, or in a single character, half human and half animal (e.g., mermaids). These oppositions are also found in themes such as life and death, good and evil, truth and falsehood, love and hate, large and small, child and adult. The device of contrast is not new; Danish folklorist Axel Olrick has identified it as one of the three principles of the epic.[9]

The oral tradition crystallizes—and inverts—Billy Lyons and Stagolee as opposites in every way possible. Not only is Stagolee made to be the hero and Billy the villain, but Stagolee becomes the single guy and Billy the family man; in reality, Billy was single, and Stagolee was a married man. Whereas the legend presents Stagolee as a rootless character, in reality John David found him to be "a man who felt a sense of responsibility to both his mother and his father."[10] We have seen that he was a leader of a social club and owned a saloon that may have been a site of political meetings. If not a pillar of the community, he was probably somebody who aimed for that position. Morover, we know that after the murder, Lee Shelton wrote at least one letter to one of his girls to be given to his woman. If he is the man on whom the Stagolee ballad tradition is based, he was not the illiterate thug portrayed in the oral tradition. But the principle of contrast required that one of these two men become the "bad guy" and the other the "good guy."

The oral literature exploits the historical events in several ways. One of them relates to Billy Lyons' behavior after Lee Shelton shot him. Frank Boyd testified that Lyons stood at the bar after he was shot, and that the hat fell from his hand. When it did, Stack Lee picked it up: "Well, after he got shot, he staggered or stepped, partly staggered across the room, and taken hold of the top rail that is in the room, and stood there for a moment, and some of the boys, I forgot who they were, says, 'Don't let him stand there, let's take him to a Doctor,' and they taken him to the Doctor."[11] William Marion Reedy published a strikingly similar version of these movements in 1919:

> Billy Lyons, Billy Lyons, staggered
> Through the door,
> Cause Stackerlee had got him with his
> Great big forty-four—
> Everybody talk about Stackerlee.[12]

Another example is the survival of the real Judge David Murphy, St. Louis' chief of criminal corrections, in the ballads, as in this version from 1927:

> Judge Murphy pronounced the sentence
> His eyes were filled with tears.
> "I'm goin' give you 'bout ninety-seven years
> O poor-poor Stack-o-lee."[13]

According to historian Lawrence Oland Christensen, "Blacks looked upon Murphy as a special friend."[14] The white majority at the 1896 Republican city convention shouted down black delegates who tried to renominate Murphy as judge of the Court of Criminal Corrections. This is the same Murphy whose name appears on Lee Shelton's murder indictment.

One of the reasons for blacks' support of Murphy was his stand against police brutality. Beginning with his appointment in 1894, Murphy had fought against excessive use of the billy club. The *St. Louis Star* noted in his obituary in 1916 that he had begun his one term on the bench "with a denunciation of the police for using their clubs too freely on prisoners." Next he forbade policemen to wear guns in his courtroom, and when they complained, he fined them and sent them all to jail for contempt.[15]

One story about Judge Murphy that all the Negroes living in the Third Ward must have heard was the case of Thomas Wright, a Negro, who shot a policeman who had come to arrest him. The policeman also shot Wright. Both recovered from their wounds. When the case came before Murphy, Wright argued that he had shot in self-defense, because the patrolman was beating him with his club. After hearing testimony, Murphy let Wright go. Outside the Four Courts, a mob of policemen attacked the man. In response Murphy had the policemen put in jail.[16]

In the summer of 1896, several events took place that influenced the Stagolee legend. First, a black delegation arrived at the national Republican convention in St. Louis to complain about their failure to benefit at all from patronage. Not long afterward, at the Republican city convention blacks sought to renominate David Murphy as judge of the criminal courts, and white Republicans rejected their effort. A few days later, James Milton Turner, the best-known black Republican leader in the state, denounced the party for not defending blacks against racism. The white Republicans' rejection of Murphy prompted blacks in St. Louis "to form an independent

David M. Murphy. Engraving, ca. 1898.
Courtesy of Missouri Historical Society, St. Louis.

political organization and also to move toward the Democratic party." Murphy became the black independents' choice for the old office. Governor Lon V. Stephens, a Democrat, persuaded Turner and other black leaders to come over to the Democrats, offering among other things to appoint a black policeman to the city force.[17] Ninety percent of black voters supported the Democratic ticket in Missouri's 1896 elections.

Given this political context, it is understandable that Judge Murphy's name would surface in the Stagolee narratives about police brutality, white justice, and murder. Sometimes the judge is sympathetic to Stack Lee; in others he is cruel, telling Nellie Sheldon that "he's going to make an example of this here pimp."[18]

In the ballad tradition, Stagolee stands in front of Judge Murphy and gets his sentence, from twenty-five years in some versions to life or hanging in others. Yet in reality it was not Murphy who sentenced him. He did sign Lee Shelton's indictment, but by the time of the trial, in June 1896, he was seeking renomination. Since he was not reappointed, the case went to a Judge Harvey, but as we know, after that trial Lee Shelton was released because of a hung jury. The actual sentencing occurred after the retrial in March 1897, under Judge James Withrow. Withrow's name never appears in the ballad tradition.

Why did the collective memory pick Judge Murphy and not Judge Withrow? One reason may have been that blacks saw Murphy as sympathetic to them, whereas Withrow clearly was not. When Withrow died in May 1931, the *St. Louis Globe-Democrat* wrote that "when the Police Department was waging war in the late '90s, he ordered the police to make a bonfire of several thousand dollars' worth of gambling equipment." He was also hard on delinquent taxpayers: on March 4, 1895, the *Globe-Democrat* noted, he "disposed of the largest number of delinquent tax cases, having cleared his docket of 2665 cases [in a single day]."[19]

Compared with Murphy, Withrow was dull. He stayed on the job, went along with the police department, made a lot of successful investments, and left his wealth to his only son, Edgar. Although Murphy served only one term, his defense of blacks against police brutality clearly made a lasting impression. The ballad tradition rewards him for his effort.

The actual Thomas Scott appears to be a model for the bartender. At the inquest Scott described the event to Coroner Wait. The following version of the ballad gives Scott a different first name, but it describes essentially the same events:

> He [Stackalee] run into Ben Scott's Saloon
> And before the bar did stand
> Take my pistol Bar boy
> I dun killed another man;
> That bad, that bad man Stackalee.[20]

The similarity in names indicates that the ballad singer, consciously or otherwise, retained the name of one of the bartenders on duty that night.

Yet another example is the description of Shelton's journey to and presence during the inquest:

> He laid down at home that night, took a good night's rest
> Arrived in court at nine o'clock to hear the Coroner's inquest.
> Crowds jammed the sidewalk, far as you could see,
> Tryin' to get a good look at tough Stackalee.
> Over the cold, dead body Stackalee did bend,
> Then he turned and faced those twelve jurymen.[21]

This is a graphic description of a terrifying event from the viewpoint of the narrator/victim. It owes its power to crystallization.

As in a dream, Stackalee stands in a morgue facing a jury. Dorothy Todd, director of the Office of the Medical Examiner in St. Louis, told me that in the 1890s it was normal procedure to hold inquests with both the dead body and the suspect present while the coroner took testimony from witnesses.[22] Thus much of this passage from the ballad is a speaking picture of what actually happened.

The political connection between Stagolee the Democrat and Henry Bridgewater the Republican may provide more links between the reality and the legend of Stagolee.

6

Stagolee and Politics

As a prosperous Negro in St. Louis, Henry Bridgewater could count himself among the city's important blacks in his affiliation with the Republican party. For example, Walter Farmer, a black graduate of the Washington University Law School and the first to defend a black client before the Missouri Supreme Court, was a Republican. The first black lawyer admitted to the St. Louis bar and the first black to prosecute in a St. Louis court, Albert Burgess, was appointed by Republican mayor Cyrus Walbridge.

Just a few months after they received their freedom, on January 11, 1865, St. Louis blacks founded a black organization to fight for voting rights. On March 30, 1870, when the Fifteenth Amendment went into effect, they got that right.

When St. Louis blacks went to the polls for the first time in the fall of 1870, the Republican party had already "won their allegiance as the party of Abraham Lincoln, emancipation, and black rights."[1] Although they were only 6 percent of the population, blacks made their presence felt, because, according to the Democratic *St. Louis Republic*, they "had the balance of political power in the city."[2] Because Republicans had passed national legislation and three amendments that helped secure black citizenship rights, black St. Louisans were loyal to the party of Lincoln.

But by the mid-1880s blacks were unhappy with the Republican party. The leading black newspapers complained about the lack of Republican patronage benefits for the black community.[3] During the 1896 Republican national convention in St. Louis, things came to a head. Restaurants had pledged to allow black customers if the Republican party would hold its convention in St. Louis. The Republicans committed to the pledge, but the restaurants reneged. When the Republican party didn't hold the restaurants to their promise, blacks felt abandoned. To make matters worse, during one session of the national convention the white Republicans shouted down black St. Louisans when they tried to renominate Judge David Murphy.

Black St. Louisans also had encouragement from James Milton Turner, the most powerful black Republican politician in the state. Turner had been the U.S. ambassador to Liberia and was a significant defender of black rights. When he warned blacks that the Republican party had in effect abandoned them, they listened. He told a large group of black independent parties that "the Republican party had secured black voter allegiance by falsely depicting itself as the sole instrument of black emancipation, while in reality Democrats and blacks also had helped win the Civil War." The Republican party, he said, had enslaved blacks politically, because it had not given them representation in party decisions and patronage equal to their voting strength, and it had nominated none of them for office.[4]

Between 1892 and 1898 a significant number of black Republicans bolted from the party and formed an independent political movement. George B. Vashon, a respected newspaper editor, captured the feeling among young Democrats in St. Louis when he described the break as "slow self-emancipation from political slavery."[5] His decision to join the Democrats encouraged many blacks in St. Louis to do likewise.

Politically, St. Louis was, according to scholar William Barlow, "a ward system of government based on the ethnic composition of a large working class population."[6] Each ward was assigned an unofficial "mayor," such as the "mayor of Little Italy," the "mayor of Kerry Patch." Deep Morgan's, known as the "bully of the town," was usually a black who owned a saloon.[7] Because saloons also served as hotels, they were patronized by stevedores and roustabouts. In return for money he lent them, the lodgers would give their vote to the saloonkeeper.

The ballad of Stagolee celebrates the bully of the town, who in turn is rewarded by "the guv'ner of this State" :

> I ask ev'ybody did that bully come this way.
> I wus lookin' for that bully of this town
> Oh, the guv'ner of this state offered one hundred dollars reward.[8]

The most powerful bartenders in Deep Morgan were Bill Curtis, Henry Bridgewater, and "Bad Jim" Ray. As a saloon owner and the leader of a social club, Lee Shelton would also have been on that list. Like Shelton, Ray owned a saloon and was connected to the criminal underworld of St. Louis. Ray's Buffet was probably a lid club like Shelton's Modern Horseshoe Club. An impressive person physically, Jim Ray wore diamonds, drove fine horses, and married the most beautiful Negro woman in the West, who was so pale-skinned that one could hardly tell she was black. In 1895 he shot and killed a Negro, Sam Kelly, but escaped punishment with a plea of self-defense. While Ray was recuperating from a gunshot wound in the stomach from a white policeman, his wife eloped with his partner and friend Fatty Grimes. When he got well, Ray went after Grimes.[9]

Six weeks before his death, Ray came into a lot of money. According to John David, "All the newspapers agreed that his 'sudden' wealth was the result of political 'pull.'" Ray had been a bag man, or collector, for the Republican party since 1893. As the leader of a "political group," Ray "would ride about the Negro wards on election days in a wagon, shouting and doing other things in the interest of the Republicans." Around 1896 he suddenly underwent a political change of heart and began to support the Democratic party. In David's view, his sudden wealth came from "the Democrats in return for his assistance in swinging the Negro vote away from the Republicans."[10]

Some white politicians confessed to "giving [an alleged Negro Democrat] 600 dollars and a Smith & Wesson revolver to go to Eleventh and Morgan streets the night before an election 'to get the negro vote.'"[11] When he was gunned down in the streets, Bad Jim became the subject of a long ballad; like Lee Shelton, he was celebrated as a hero for a particular group of people.[12]

In 1885 a black group called the Stags—a "rather large group of colored sports"—voted for Edward Noonan, the Democratic nominee for mayor. Noonan won, and a year later the Stags supported another Democrat, Colonel Bob Claiborne, who also won.[13] There is no evidence that Lee Shelton belonged to this group, but he would have been twenty-one at the time and may well have acquired his nickname from membership in it. Like many young black males, he had little reason to vote for the Republicans. Moreover, we have evidence that Lee Shelton was a Democrat from someone who knew him. Addison "Booker T. Washington" Burnett, a black man, came to St. Louis in 1906. He knew Shelton and didn't like him. He was a "damned Democrat—a worthless Negro who never did anything for the Negro people," Burnett declared.[14]

In the spring of 1895 the Negroes of St. Louis held their first Democratic convention. Lee Shelton may have been there. The delegates were "armed," and a "jeering crowd of spectators [was] surrounded by a cordon of police." Black Democrats elected their first black official, Martron D. Lewis, to the office of recorder of deeds when Lee Shelton was still free. By the fall of 1896, "over 600 Negroes were in bona fide Democratic club organizations."[15]

Neither of the two major political parties was above corruption. Folklorist Nathan Young knew the history of St. Louis politics well. "These parties weren't what you would call politics," he told me in an interview in 1998. "Politics didn't mean what it means today. It wasn't so much about voting as about who was a boss. And you made the law and had your gun at your side to enforce that law. That's the kind of politics they had then." Political clubs consisted of a few rooms above a saloon or barbershop, where white political bosses came to give speeches to a group of blacks.

Like many blacks, Lee Shelton must have felt that the promises made to blacks by white Republicans were hollow. He had seen how southern whites had tried to regain power over blacks. During the 1890s, two hundred blacks per year were lynched in the

South. In 1898 St. Louis blacks had a mass rally against lynching, an event that brought black Republicans and Democrats together. Like most of his generation, Shelton would have had firsthand experience of discrimination, and perhaps also violence, by whites.

When Lee Shelton was in prison, Democrats mounted two petitions for his release. The first was signed by a St. Louis attorney, Charles P. Johnson, a former member of the Missouri legislature and a former Democratic lieutenant governor. The second was signed by a "mixture of blacks from middle-income professions," including George B. Vashon, editor of the *Negro World* and a prominent spokesman for African-American Democrats. This petition maintained that Shelton's suffering had outweighed his crime. The very fact of the two petitions indicates that Democratic officials in St. Louis respected Lee Shelton.

The Stags were probably the first party of pimps to become politicized, and Lee Shelton "Stagolee" was doing his part to help.

7

Under the Lid: The Underside of the Political Struggle

The hero of the novel *God Sends Sunday* is a black jockey and pimp named Augie. With his pockets full of money, dressed in the style of a mack, Augie arrives in St. Louis to see his relatives and find himself a girl. Within a few chapters we find Augie strolling down Market Street in Chestnut Valley on his way to a social party. At the party, Augie competes with the St. Louis mack Biglow Brown for the affections of a dazzlingly beautiful prostitute named Della.

Watching Biglow dance with Della, Augie overhears Biglow say to her, "You know right well whut kind o' mack I is. Any woman dat messes wid me gotta take de lumps. I'd slap yo' eyeteeth out, an I don't care when or where."

Augie steps up. "Lissen a minute Mistah Biglow Brown. Lil Augie can whup his own womens. An' there ain't no mack in St. Louis gonna do ma job. Lil Augie is loud as a six-gun."[1]

Black pimps were under pressure to make their women produce cash. The domestic relationships between the macks and their partners were reflected in the male's right occasionally to beat up the woman. This prerogative belonged only to him; hence "lumping," as it was called, became a symbol of his unique position.

Later in the novel, when Biglow gives Della her lumps, Augie feels more pain than he would have if Biglow had slept with her: "If he had been intimate with her in some other way, it would not have been as bad. But this invaded the one province that Augie believed to be his own."[2] For this insult to his manhood, Augie gets a gun, shoots Biglow dead, and willingly goes to prison to pay for the crime.

This episode is a fiction, but it depicts the reality for most black people living in Deep Morgan. Arna Bontemps's *God Sends Sunday* is the only novel written about life in the black bordello culture of St. Louis, and it is set in the period of the Lee Shelton / Billy Lyons murder.

Some variants of the Stagolee ballad suggest that Stagolee's beef with Billy Lyons was over a woman, a woman perhaps like Della:

> It was no Stetson hat
> He didn't have a good excuse

They say he killed old Billy
'Cause he gave his gal abuse.[3]

The abuse may refer to "lumping," which in the world of St. Louis macks would have had sexual connotations.

Chestnut Valley was known for its beautiful women. W. C. Handy, the father of the blues, visited St. Louis at this time. Handy was so poor that he had to sleep on cobblestones, but he was so impressed by the beautiful women that he wrote the classic ballad "St. Louis Blues." He was probably talking about some well-dressed streetwalkers.

Saint Louis woman wid her diamon' rings
Pulls dat man roun' by her apron strings.
'Twant for powder an' for store-bought hair
De man I love would not gone nowhere.[4]

Every major American city had a Stroll, a street where blacks dressed up in the most expensive and stylish clothes they could afford and walked about leisurely, looking and being looked at, showing off their status. In St. Louis the main streets for strolling were Market and Targee Streets, in Chestnut Valley. Jelly Roll Morton recalled that every sport "strove to acquire at least one Sunday suit, because without that Sunday suit, you didn't have anything."[5] As the title of Arna Bontemps's novel reminds us, it was on Sundays that the Stroll was most crowded.

Strolling involved more than just walking; *how* one strolled was also important. Jelly Roll Morton describes the preferred form of strolling: a real sport "moved down the street with his shirt busted wide open, revealing a red flannel undershirt, shooting the agate." Shooting the agate, he explains, involved "putting your hands at your sides with your index finger stuck out and you kind of struts with it."[6]

This kind of behavior would have been inconceivable in a white-controlled public space. In Chestnut Valley blacks took over the street and imbued it with their own kind of competitive display and freedom to improvise.

Prostitution was so prevalent in Chestnut Valley and Deep Morgan that blues singers made it one of their themes. In his song "Deep Morgan Blues," "Hi" Henry Brown explains why women were prostitutes.

> Well, it's down on Deep Morgan just about Sixteenth Street, [repeat]
> Well, it's a selling a business, where the women do meet.
> Well, it's down in a basement, where they work so hard, [repeat]
> Well, it's all on account of their husbands ain't got no job.[7]

Henry Townsend grew up in St. Louis during the 1920s and learned to play the blues from the older generation of bluesmen from the South. When he visited Oakland in 1998, I had the pleasure of speaking with him after his concert. I asked Townsend why there was so much prostitution in St. Louis during the 1890s. "I don't know why it was widespread," he laughed, "but it was." There were many black women selling their bodies to white men, he said, but there were also some white women selling to black men. "But you had to be very careful about that," he said, because the white men would force the women to say that they had been raped, and for this black men would be lynched.

In his analysis of black popular culture, Robin D. G. Kelley asks why the pimp enjoyed such exalted status in the late 1960s and early 1970s. Searching for an answer, he recalls the influence of black comics like Redd Foxx and Richard Pryor, and the popularization of the pimp as hero in the writings of black nationalist militants like H. Rap Brown, Eldridge Cleaver, Bobby Seale, and Huey P. Newton. "The Pimp, not just any 'baaad-man,' became . . . elevated to the status of hero."[8]

Adrienne M. Seward offered a psychological explanation for why the black pimp was considered a hero, an explanation based on the history of the slave South and its culture of white sexual supremacy. During slavery, the black man sat back and watched the white man sexually abuse black women without being able to do anything about it. After emancipation, and especially beginning late in the nineteenth century, the situation was reversed: the black man had control of the women, and the white man came to the pimp for his satisfaction. Both the pimp and the prostitute looked on the white man, the "trick," as their "client," an inferior position in a business transaction.[9]

But it is difficult to understand the reason for recent glamorizations of the pimp's image without also looking at the origin of the pimp in the 1890s in cities like St. Louis. The rise of the black pimp was tied to a more general changing American attitude toward men, reflected in the burgeoning concept of "sportsmen."

Timothy J. Gilfoyle has labeled this new model of sexuality a "promiscuous paradigm." It rested on an ethic of sensual pleasure that distanced men from women and at the same time bonded them with other males of all ages, classes, and colors. According to Gilfoyle, "sporting-male ideas and activity served to promote a certain gender solidarity among nineteenth-century urban males. Through the milieu of commercial sex, urban heterosexual males demarcated part of their subculture. The glorification of male heterosexual freedom and bachelorhood permeated not only New York but much of America."[10]

88

During this time, blacks living in Chestnut Valley were sympathetic to the pimps, who were, after all, embodiments of the "sporting spirit" for which St. Louis's downtown was well known. Blacks' sympathy for the mack had a specific historical basis that could not possibly obtain for white pimps. Black men like Lee Shelton—the first generation out of slavery—were part of this new male sporting culture, which continued to grow well into the twentieth century. Combined with the rise of ward politics, the culture of the sportsman produced the pimp.

Out of ward politics emerged the career politicians who used gangs to keep opponents from the polls, guard ballot boxes, and manipulate political elections. But although the career politicians controlled the votes, they lacked ready cash to oil the political machinery. In order to get cash, ward politicians resorted to bribery and extortion of saloons, gambling dens, and houses of prostitution. Prostitution became one of the sources of revenue for politicians.

Gangs of black men were hired by politicians to control and police the brothels. In addition to pressures from gangs and ward politicians, the prostitutes were directly threatened by a general burgeoning of violent attacks against working women by white males from all walks of life who unleashed pent-up frustration by attacking a visibly independent, autonomous, and sometimes materially successful woman. The "brothel bullies" were middle- and lower-class males who were seldom arrested for their crimes. In St. Louis, white males talked openly about "storming the Castle," a practice of breaking into the whorehouses, usually during a drunken spree. Whereas the "vigilante attack" on a brothel was a "public protest," a spree was "a source of fun."[11]

Because most women were unable to defend themselves against strong men, and because the courts refused to view prostitutes as legitimate victims, their main defense against brothel bullies was the pimp. Black men were hired to live in the brothels, providing physical protection and performing services such as buying groceries, repairing the house, and serving the guests.[12] Thus while white men allowed themselves a new freedom in the red-light districts, the black man came to represent a sexual threat. The pimp became a negative figure for white men, but for most black people in areas like Deep Morgan and Chestnut Valley a hero.

In St. Louis, pimps were known by the French word *maquereaux*, which became shortened to "macks," a term that is still used by African Americans. The mack of St. Louis was a well-dressed sportsman who wore the finest clothes and lived in Chestnut Valley. Black and white women gave the mack money and gifts in exchange for sexual favors. In *Nigger Heaven,* his novel about slumming in Harlem, Carl Van Vechten describes "authentic" black men "so virile and sexually attractive that they are 'kept' by women." Similarly, in *White Women / Coloured Men,* French writer Henry Champly, in a chapter titled "Black Bullies," claims that it was "quite common" both in Chicago and elsewhere to find black men who were "supported by several women, some White, others Black."[13]

Prostitution, or the "social disease," was widespread in St. Louis. Dreiser complained about the hypocrisy of newspapers that cried out about immorality but did not dare bring up the subject of prostitution even when prostitutes were plying their trade right outside the doors of the leading newspapers. "In the heart of St. Louis, in Chestnut Street," he wrote, "was a large district devoted to just such orgies [prostitution]. But these streets were somehow never in the public eye and [you] could not for your life, put them there . . . You couldn't write newspaper articles about them . . . or arouse any particular interest . . . The police were supposed to extract regular payments from one and all in this area."[14]

As we have seen, ward politics had created political parties that demanded money—cash money. One source of that money was prostitution. And prostitution came from black people. But now there was a new element, the newly emerging "sporting" atmosphere. And with the rise of the sportsman culture and the political wards came the creation of the pimp.

In the city, anything and anybody becomes a commodity. In order to survive, even the marginal figures must sell themselves. Such figures include the gambler, the prostitute, the idler, the journalist, and the ragpicker. All were aspects of Lee Shelton's life in 1890s St. Louis. Karl Marx had his own list of such marginal types. He called them the lumpenproletariat:

> Alongside decayed roués with doubtful means of subsistence and of doubtful origin, alongside ruined and adventurous offshoots of the bourgeoisie, were vagabonds, discharged soldiers, discharged jail-birds, escaped galley slaves, swindlers, mountebanks, lazzaroni, pickpockets, tricksters, gamblers, *maquereaux,* brothel-keepers, porters, literati, organ-grinders, rag-pickers, knife-grinders, tinkers, beggars, in short the whole indefinite, disintegrated mass thrown hither and thither, which the French term La Bohème.[15]

The maquereau, or pimp, and the prostitute surely qualify as the most marginalized figures, for they are the ultimate expression of putting one's body in the marketplace. The pimp, according to Graeme Gilloch's study of Walter Benjamin's writings on the city's marginalized figures, combined aspects of the sauntering flâneur and the self-conscious dandy. Like Lee Shelton, he seemed to make an art of idleness. The pimp, like many of the new type of black sportsman who inhabited American cities in the 1890s, was "an incipient version of the bourgeois consumer": he could dress in nice clothes as though he were prosperous, but he might not have had a dime in his pockets. Like the flâneur, the mack didn't generate commodities as middle-class manufacturers did, nor did he consume enough commodities to make a difference. Instead, he was a facilitator, an in-between, someone who made his living "on the luck of what the city could provide."[16]

The ragpicker, another figure left out of society, was a symbol not only for Marx but also for Scott Joplin, who put a picture of a ragpicker on the first cover of his new music, which was called "ragtime." During the Jim Crow era, many blacks were in this marginalized class.

In the first rap, "The Message" (1982), Grand Master Flash also has a list of lumpenproletariat. Addressing a youth in the ghetto who is "living second rate," Grand Master Flash admonishes him:

> You wanna grow up to be just like them, huh
> Smugglers, scramblers, burglars, gamblers
> Pickpockets, peddlers, even panhandlers.[17]

As we shall see, when Stagolee became a symbol for Bobby Seale, founder of the Black Panther party, it was because Stagolee represented the lumpenproletariat for young black men in the 1960s.

8

The Black Social Clubs

Two influences in St. Louis combined to create a tense, brutal atmosphere in Deep Morgan and Chestnut Valley. One was ward politics; the other was the black social clubs. Henry Bridgewater's saloon and Shelton's Four Hundred Club were merely metonymies for the Republican and Democratic parties, respectively. The black neighborhoods were divided into a fiefdom of saloons, each one hosting political meetings, gambling, prostitution, and general gatherings.

Two years after Lee Shelton started his Four Hundred Club, Tony Williams started a Black Four Hundred Club in Sedalia, Missouri, an hour away by train. But whereas Shelton's club supported Democrats, Williams on at least one occasion in 1898 rented his to "Republican party politicians who were invited to speak to black voters."[1] Since we have more information on the Black Four Hundred Club in Sedalia, it may provide a fuller picture of the patterns of political affiliation, music appreciation, and violence in Lee Shelton's and other such unofficial organizations.

Just as Shelton's Four Hundred Club had its rival in the Bridgewater Saloon a block away, the Williams Four Hundred Club in Sedalia had a rivalry with the Maple Leaf Club. One prominent member of the latter was a young musician named Scott Joplin. His

93

"Maple Leaf Rag," one of the first published rags, was dedicated to the club.

"An important part of Joplin's social and musical life in the 1890s," Edward A. Berlin notes in *King of Ragtime*, "was connected with Sedalia's black men's clubs: the Black 400 Club, and the town's brightest and most enterprising young black men, some of whom were among Joplin's closest associates." Like Shelton's Four Hundred Club, the black clubs in Sedalia purported to exist for the betterment of young men: the purpose of the Black Four Hundred Club, according to its charter papers, was "to form and maintain a club, and to maintain a club house for the purpose of advancing, by social intercourse." But the black social clubs were always in trouble with the city, and when Sedalia's Democratic mayor threatened to close the Black Four Hundred Club, Williams accused him "of closing the clubs for political reasons, of trying to prevent blacks from unifying under the Republican banner in the coming election."[2] Political organizing seems to have been one of the main functions of the black social clubs, but the organizing was only unofficially connected to the Democratic and Republican parties.

These clubs also had a liminal social function: they were sites where blacks and whites could meet on an equal basis. Whites were often invited to sit and watch blacks as they played music, put on musical shows, and made speeches. As such, these social clubs resembled the black-and-tan clubs described by Kevin J. Mumford in *Interzones*: from the outside, "the Black and Tans were immoral, even frightening, in part because they represented a world in which the rules and conventions of the mainstream were literally inverted. In the Black and Tan, black men were in the lead—black men were on 'top.'"[3]

The black churches in Sedalia, the main opponents of the clubs, offered votes to the mayor if he would close the clubs on the grounds that they were immoral. But "the city authorities refused to grant the pastors' request, and the clubs continued operating. Within the week, [the] clubs had dancing events, and a report noted that at the Black 400 'a large crowd of white people were given seats of honor on the platform on the south end of the hall.'" When the clubs applied for incorporation, the court denied their application, chiefly on the basis of the pastors' claims that the Maple Leaf and Black Four Hundred were "worse than any of the town's many saloons."[4]

The most crucial parallel between the rival clubs in Sedalia and St. Louis is that they were the sites of many bloody fights. One such fight took place in Sedalia in October 1899, less than four years after the Billy Lyons murder. It started in the Maple Leaf Club, but it soon became a "street brawl with the use of knives and beer bottles, with women participating as enthusiastically as men." The highlight was a fight involving Arthur Marshall, a ragtime musician and a close friend of Scott Joplin. Earnest Edward had brought his favorite girl to the dance at the Maple Leaf, but Arthur took a liking to her and tried to escort her home. The two young men quarreled and went out to the street to continue their fight. There Arthur pummeled Edward with his cane, which was weighted. Edward, in the words of one newspaper, "who comes of fighting stock, pulled his gun and commenced to shoot, while Marshall commenced to run." Another newspaper reported that "from what authorities can learn, he is still running yet."[5]

Lee Shelton's shooting of Billy Lyons must be placed in the same context of rivalry and violent revenge.

These social clubs probably had much to do with bootlegging and prostitution. A little later that October, the entire night shift of the police department raided the Maple Leaf Club and arrested the proprietor, Walker Williams, for "selling liquor without a license." Two months later the club was in the news again: two women had been engaged in a vicious brawl in the clubroom. The black social clubs in Sedalia were closed on January 25, 1900.[6]

Many members of the Maple Leaf Club were arrested for consorting with white women, even though most of the women were prostitutes. Ada Carol, "a white woman and a frail wreck," was "in the company of Tom Ireland . . . and Ed Gravitt—two members of the black Queen City Cornet Band [Scott Joplin's band and friends]—when apprehended." The Queen City Cornet Band was the first band to play ragtime, and its members belonged to the Maple Leaf Club. When the police came, Carol ran to the front window, raised it, and leaped out into the darkness onto the icy pavement. According to contemporary accounts, "She fell straight down from the window ledge and her body broke on the stone steps below." Carol recovered and continued her profession. The men were fined thirty dollars each, but the fines were later reduced to ten dollars each.[7]

White women were severely punished for being caught in intimate situations with black men. When a white prostitute, Lottie Wright, was caught with her regular beau, Emmett Cook, the Cornet Band's drummer and a singer with Joplin's Texas Medley Quartette, each was fined a hundred dollars. The fines were stayed provided the two left the city. Apparently they did leave for some time, but they returned: Lottie opened her own brothel, and both Arthur Marshall and Scott Joplin worked for her as pianists.[8]

White violence against sex between black men and white women was so prevalent that white madams didn't allow their prostitutes to have black customers. "White whores who had black boyfriends were looked down upon," recalled Nell Kimball, a madam who worked in St. Louis at that time:

I had one whore named Gladdy, who got herself a high
yalla fancy man, a nigrah lawyer who had gone to college
up north. I told Gladdy . . . she couldn't have him talked
about with her and some guest would hear and object to
getting into bed with her when she had just been screw-
ing her nigrah the day before. Gladdy got lippy and said
the black stud was a great fighter for rights, human
rights. Most likely he was, but not in my house. I had her
pack and get out. I didn't want any Klan trash to burn
down my house. Or lynch the high yalla on the lamp post
before my doorsteps.[9]

Compounding the violent image associated with the social clubs
was the "bad man" reputation of the saloonkeeper himself. Sometimes the "bad man" reputation took on a supernatural aura. There
were many legends of the "bad man" similar to that of Stagolee.
One involved Aaron Harris, one of the most notorious killers in
New Orleans around 1910–1912. Jelly Roll Morton, who knew him,
sang the "bad man" song about him until "certain people" told
him he should stop because singing it would not be "healthy."
Like Stagolee, who in some versions of the ballad possesses access to magical power, Harris was supposed to have a voodoo
woman, which explained why he was able to escape paying for his
crimes:

Aaron Harris was a bad, bad man
. . .
He killed his sweet little sister, and his brother-in-law
About a cup of coffee, he killed his sister, and his brother-in-law
He got out of jail every time, he would make his ill
He had a hoodoo woman, all he had to do is pay the bill.[10]

Harris killed several people, including gamblers like himself. He twice escaped hanging or a penitentiary term for his slayings, and finally was shot to death by George Robertson, better known as "Bear Dog." The journalist William Turner discovered that it wasn't supernatural aids that kept Harris out of jail, but his secret association with the corrupt police of the ward. In an article in the *New Orleans Times-Picayune* on July 15, 1915, Turner revealed that Aaron Harris was a "police 'stool pigeon.'" Further investigation of the police record revealed that the claim was true.

As we have seen, Lee Shelton had connections with important ward politicians in St. Louis's "Bloody Third." It is probable that he, too, had supernatural motifs that were a cover for his real relationship with the judges and policemen who helped him get away with his crimes. Black social clubs like the four hundred clubs were the birthplace of Stagolee as a song. Like Joplin's "Maple Leaf Rag," perhaps "Stagolee" was initially a song dedicated to Lee Shelton's club.

9

Hats and Nicknames: Symbolic Values

"Les Bricks," the red light district is called, after the barges moored a hundred paces away at the jetty of the old harbor . . . Has anyone yet probed deeply enough into this refuse heap of houses to reach the innermost place in the gynaeceum, the chamber where the trophies of manhood—boaters, bowlers, hunting hats, trilbies, jockey caps—hang in rows on consoles or in layers on racks?

—WALTER BENJAMIN, "MARSEILLES," 1929

What does the Stagolee epic really say? It says a man's hat is his crown.

—BOB DYLAN, 1993

STAGOLEE'S STETSON

The Stagolee song was born in the whorehouses and saloons of St. Louis, in the 1890s world of ward politics, racism, prostitution, and pimping. It was published as sheet music at least as early as 1924, but by 1911, six months before Lee Shelton's death, Negroes were already singing it in Georgia and the Carolinas.[1] The following lines come from Georgia in 1911:

> I got up one mornin' jes' bout four clock;
> Stagolee an' big bully done have one finish fight:
> What 'bout? All 'bout dat raw-hide Stetson hat.[2]

This version, told from the point of view of an eyewitness, casts Stagolee against a "big bully" and identifies the crux of the fight as a Stetson hat.

In his analysis of Malcolm X's early life, Robin D. G. Kelley demonstrates that "fashionable ghetto adornments"—the zoot suits and conk hairdos—were an essential element in Malcolm X's journey to political consciousness. Articles of clothing—along with the lindy hop and the language of "the hep cat"—were loaded with oppositional meanings for young black men in the postwar era.

The zoot suiters and hipsters sought "alternatives to wage work and found pleasure in the new music, clothes, and dance styles of the period." Such announcements of difference made them conspicuously identifiable as "race rebels."[3]

Likewise, articles of clothing held symbolic meaning for Lee Shelton and other St. Louis macks in the 1890s. "When it came to dress and fraternal deco St. Louis Colored sports were unique," according to Nathan Young. The macks "wore special full-cut suits out of import fabrics. Their styles were copies of the West Bank in Paris, plus their own western ingenuity such as hats." Their choice of hat undoubtedly made their membership in a particular subculture as readily apparent as a Raiders cap on a Los Angeles gang member today. The hats had "a special high felt crown" but "were not as tall as the regular toppers. They came in colors, seldom black. The brims were slightly rolled with a silk binding. They had to be 'Stetsons' and no other brand!"[4]

Although there is no mention in the eyewitness reports of the kind of hat being fought over, the first singer of the ballad may well have assumed that it was a Stetson, since it was typical of Chestnut Valley. The Stetson was the archetypal western hat; in the 1890s its inventor had christened it "Boss of the Plains."[5] In that era it was a mark of highest status for blacks, coming to represent black St. Louis itself.

Black folklore has a dream form, and it should be deciphered by the same means used to decipher dreams, that is, by symbols. Symbols in dreams are displacement, condensation, and distortion. Indeed, black narrative folklore is a "dream plot."[6] To find the true meaning of Stagolee, we must search for the symbolic meaning behind constantly recurring motifs such as the Stetson hat.

Lee Shelton knocked William Lyons' hat off his head, and Lyons grabbed Shelton's.

The hat in Stagolee is a symbol of masculinity. The legend portrays Billy Lyons as wearing a derby, a round hat with a small brim, and Lee Shelton as wearing a wide-brimmed Stetson. Clearly, in this context, the Stetson symbolizes greater masculinity.

Freud claimed that in dreams the hat is a symbol of "the genital organ, most frequently the male." He goes on to say that this symbolism may derive from the fact that since the hat is an extension of the head, taking off one's hat is a sign of castration.[7] Thus knocking off someone's hat also symbolizes his castration. Black male culture adds a fatal measure of determinism to such symbolism, such that a black man must kill anyone who challenges his masculinity. This is why in most versions the refrain says that Stagolee was *bound* to take Billy's life," conveying a sense of inevitability.

As late as 1917, the Stetson was a symbol of power and status among black males. "In those days," Louis Armstrong said, "when a fellow wore a John B. Stetson, he was really a big shot, as big shots went at that time."[8] Black musicians like Armstrong and black sportsmen like Lee Shelton mapped their ideas about masculinity, pride, and "sharpness" (in dress) on the Stetson hat. To hurt a man symbolically, one could do no worse than cut his Stetson.

Whereas the hat is a metonymy of the black man's masculinity, the razor represents the castrating device that threatens the black man. During the early formation of the Stagolee ballad, such symbols abounded in folk songs. Like most coon songs, the 1903 prototype of the Stagolee song contains the razor-toting black:

I'm a-lookin for dat bully, and he must be found
I'll take 'long my razor, I's gwine to carve him deep.
And when I see dat bully, I'll lay him down to sleep.[9]

The stereotype of blacks carrying razors was based on whites' fear of blacks. On a visit he made in 1920 with the chief of police to a black saloon in the levee, Lafcadio Hearn asked his companion how many blacks he supposed were carrying razors. The policeman answered, "All of them. Including the women."[10] This stereotype was popular with whites at a time when many whites castrated black men. It was black men who had to fear the white man's razor, not the other way around.

THE "STAG" AND "STACK"

The *St. Louis Star-Sayings* of December 29, 1895, refers to Lee Shelton as "Stag" Lee; the coroner's report calls him "Stack" Lee. The nicknames cover two different contextual streams, but they converged in Lee Shelton's way of life.

"Stag" certainly has some associations with "Stagg Town," which, along with "Buck Town" (designating not only a young male deer but also a young black male), was widely used in the nineteenth and early twentieth centuries to refer to a "negro" settlement.[11] A "Stagg Town," as Charles Dickens noted when he visited America in the late 1800s, was "a place where 'dogs would howl to lie.'" Such districts were known for their black-and-tan "saloons," where "all kinds of underworld and salacious activities could supposedly be bought for the right price."[12] Such communities were characterized by poverty, crime, and vice, including interracial sex and prostitution. Some of the burlesque theaters in Chicago at the turn of the century featured "peep shows" that "catered especially to boys, and provided entertainment for stag parties, which featured white women and black men."[13]

"Stag," as used in "stag parties" and "stag films," has long been closely tied to notions of male sexual potency. Pictures and heads of stags were found in most elegant bordellos in the late 1800s.[14] Like the stag's antlers, Lee Shelton's hat may have come to symbolize his potency and power. This association persisted at least into the early 1960s, when, according to Geneva Smitherman, "Stagger Lee" came to embody "a fearless, mean dude," and when "it became widely fashionable . . . to refer to oneself as 'Stag,' as in 'I ain't got to brag, uhm like Stag.' Or, 'Don't mess with me, cause I ain't no fag, uhm Stag.'"[15]

Nell Kimball, a young white woman of unusual intelligence, became a prostitute in St. Louis and kept a diary from the ages of fifteen to eighty. Coming from a farm in Missouri, where her family still spoke German, she remembered the lively parlor of the whorehouse where the piano played Strauss waltzes while a famous actor sat with two girls on his lap. "Guests in the hallway were hanging up their top hats on the stag horn coat hanger with the crest of the Kaiserschritzen on it."[16]

The horse was also associated with virility, and objects such as horseshoes and equestrian terms such as "stable" and "fillies" became linked with the world of prostitution. In Lee Shelton's time and place, it is surely significant that he owned a club called the Modern Horseshoe Club, drove a carriage, and was known to be a pimp.

"Stag" also has political associations. In St. Louis, white men of power and distinction met together at "stag" parties. William Marion Reedy, the first editor to publish a Stackolee ballad, was famous as a raconteur at such parties. As we have seen, there was also a political party called the "Stags," whose membership was "colored sports."[17]

"Stack," on the other hand, referred to the world of gambling, to "arranging the sequence of a pack of cards before the deal for the purposes of cheating." Stack Lee's girlfriend is called Stack-A-Dollars, referring to the stack of money won from gambling. The use of both epithets for Lee Shelton entails no contradiction, since he was both a pimp and a gambler. However fortuitously, the nickname "Stag" also converges with the world of gambling in the name of an "informal and illegal Craps game" called "stag craps."[18] And of course both worlds merge easily under the broad symbolic brim of the Stetson hat.

In 1941 Onah Spencer, a white writer working for the Chicago Works Progress Administration, collected folklore material from the South Side of Chicago about Stagolee. Among the narratives was one about Stagolee and his Stetson: "Stack was crazy about Stetson hats; specially them great big five gallon hats with dimples in the crown. And he had a whole row of em hanging on pegs and you could look at em along the wall of his rickety shanty on Market Street in St. Louis."[19]

In folklore Stack has a different color hat for each activity:

> Stack had a dimpled and lemon colored yaller hat, and a black Sunday one with two white eyes to wear to funerals with his new brogans, and lots of other ones, all kinds and colors. But his favorite one was an oxblood magic hat that folks claim he made from the hide of a man-eatin' panther that the devil had skinned alive. And like I told you, how come Stack to have it was because he had sold his soul to old Scratch.

Here Stack's hat is endowed with supernatural qualities, having been acquired through Stack's striking a deal with the devil in exchange for good luck at the gambling table. For his part, the devil promises Stack that "he could do all kinds of magic and devilish things long as he wore that oxblood Stetson and didn't let it get away from him." According to this myth, the devil tricked Stack out of his soul by "fix[ing] it so when Stack did lose [the hat] he would lose his head, and kill a good citizen, and run right smack into his doom."[20] And thus we return to the murder episode involving Lee Shelton and Billy Lyons.

10

Ragtime and Stagolee

Lee Shelton had many friends in Chestnut Valley. Among them was the ragtime pianist Tom Turpin (1873–1922). When Shelton was in the Jefferson City prison, Turpin signed a petition seeking commutation of his sentence.[1] Turpin had made his mark with ragtime music even before his friend Scott Joplin; in 1892 he had composed and published the first ragtime music and song, the "Harlem Rag." According to Nathan Young, "It was Tom Turpin down on Market Street here in St. Louis who first began to put this peculiar American form of music [ragtime] down on paper as a record so that it could be scattered and sold over five-and-ten counters eventually to a million buyers a year."[2] The Rose Bud Saloon, where Turpin played, was on Market Street, mentioned in many versions of the Stagolee ballad.

One indication that the Stagolee ballad was originally a ragtime tune comes from D'Arcy Fanning, who lived in St. Louis at the same time as Stagolee and Turpin, and who recalled that the

Stagolee ballad was supposed to "be played in a 'slow ragtime.'" In John David's opinion, Turpin himself created the ballad, adding the Lee Shelton events to the popular song "Looking for the Bully," also called the "The Bully of the Town" and the "Bully Song":[3]

> I ask ev'ybody did that bully come this way.
> I wus lookin' for that bully of this town
> Oh, the guv'ner of this state offered one hundred dollars reward
> To anybody's arrested that bully boy
> I sho lookin' fo that bully of this town.
> I pull out my gun 'n' begin to fire,
> I shot that bully right through the eye:
> An I kill that bully of this town
> Now all the wimmins come to town all dressed in red
> When they hear that bully was dead;
> And it was the last of that bully of this town.[4]

Turpin may have heard this song in Madam "Babe" Connors' bordello, where he often played piano. Madam Babe was the daughter of a white man, P. T. Connors, who may also have been her owner. Born Sarah Connors in Nashville, Tennessee, she changed her name when she moved to St. Louis and opened a bordello that catered exclusively to wealthy white men. Her newspaper obituary described her as a "mulatto, of a light brown hue, [who] was reared as a Catholic, though not baptized until just before her death."[5]

Well-heeled white men were acquainted with her bordello and its specialty of lighted-skinned black women. A famous writer described an evening at Madam Babe's with the European composer Paderewski, who was there as her guest. As they walked in, their eyes were blinded by the brilliance of the expensive chandeliers and of Madam Babe's sparkling diamonds. Babe, in full panoply, resembled a Tiffany's window. She enhanced the natural sparkle of her front teeth with diamond inlays. Diamond pendants dangled from her ears, and strands of diamonds encircled her neck, wrists, and ankles. So far as anyone knew, the jewels were real. Babe was a woman of substance, and she detested fakes.

Presenting a sharp contrast to this spectacle of a stylish southern belle, Mama Lou, "short, fat, black, often belligerent, and always herself," came out wearing "a calico dress, gingham apron, and head bandanna" and began singing. Young reports that nine-tenths of Mama Lou's songs were obscene.[6] Babe's bordello originated the "coon song" craze, which swept the nation. Mama Lou was the first black woman to sing blues commercially.

According to the gossip about Babe recounted by Young, she refused to have Oscar Wilde in her house because he was said to be a homosexual. On the other hand, she broke one of her cardinal rules that no women were allowed and invited the Canadian singer May Irwin into her salon. Irwin was from the town of Whitby, Canada, which had been a terminal for the Underground Railroad during the Civil War. She also became friends with some of the early pioneering black performers, including Bob Cole, Rosamond Johnson, Ernest Hogan, Will Marion Cook and Harry T. Burleigh.[7]

Apparently, Madame Babe allowed May to adapt the "Bully Song" for her stage show *The Widow Jones*. W. C. Handy said that when he arrived in St. Louis as a young musician, he stood on the levee and "heard Looking for the Bully sung by the roustabouts, which later was adopted and nationally popularized by May Irwin."[8] May Irwin may have stolen the "Bully Song" from Madame Babe's bordello. According to William Barlow, black songs were so popular during the 1890s that white composers went to black bars and clubhouses with the purpose "of stealing songs, then publishing them under their own names."

The "Bully Song," a form of the coon song, is about a bully who beats up the "bully of the town" and is rewarded by the authorities. The plot of the Bully Song and of some variants of "Stagolee Shot That Bully" are the same. In both, one bully kills another and becomes the "boss bully." This plot mirrors St. Louis ward politics, where bullies were hired to go out and get votes and do "dirty" work. If one bully got into trouble for killing another, he would get support from the whites he worked for. One of May Irwin's favorite performing stunts, as described by Nathan Young, "was to sing three or four verses with the audience participating in the round-round-round chorus . . . for an encore she led a little Negro boy seven or eight years old onto the stage, going through the 'bully scene' with him." The mock fight between the white star and her pickaninny "brought the house down." The following lines come from May Irwin's version of the song:

> Have you heard about dat bully dat's come to town?
> He's round among de jiggers a-layin' their bodies down
> I'm a-lookin' for dat bully an' he mus' be found
> I'm lookin' for dat bully an' I'll make him bow
> When I walk dat levee round, round, round round!
> When I walk dat levee round, round, round round!
> When I walk dat levee round, round, round round![9]

William Marion Reedy, editor of the *Sunday Sayings* (a scandal sheet, according to Nathan Young), praised May as a favorite with the sportsmen. "Every time May Irwin comes to town," he wrote, "there is a grand review of the old fellows who were sports in the days gone by." According to Reedy, "Her slang is as expressive as Emerson's prose." She was to America what Yvette Gilbert was to France, he thought. "Her fun is not elusive," he went on. "It knocks you in a heap. It smacks of the saloon, of the stale, of the craps game, of all the commonest life—and yet it is fun of the finest kind." She was, for Reedy, the first woman to catch the "sporty spirit." "She can't sing, musically," he confessed. "But she can sing a 'nigger' song inimitably, and she can gag the part unceasingly . . . Twenty years ago this woman was worth seeing. Today she is the perfect profundity of her vulgarity."

According to Isaac Goldberg, the singing—or ragging—of ragtime involved the use of an interpolated vowel, as in "I'm a hust-a-ling-acoon-a, and-a that's-a I-a am."[10] The most famous example of rag singing comes from black composer Rosamond Johnson's "Under the Bamboo Tree":

> If you lak-a me, lak I lak-a you
> And we lak-a both the same,
>
> . . .
>
> I lak-a change your name.[11]

T. S. Eliot, another St. Louisan, used a stanza from this song in *The Waste Land*, reflecting the influence of ragtime on the modern world.

The mystery of the origin of "Stagolee" is solved when we consider "Stagolee" as a ragged version of Stag and Lee. In the ragged version, Stag and Lee become "Stagolee," with the *o* interpolated. In the same way, Stack and Lee become "Stackalee," "Stackolee," "Stag-ger-Lee," or "Stack-A-Lee."

While this was going on with ragtime, the blues was lending its mood to the song, too.

11

The Blues and Stagolee

By the late 1890s, blues had become a kind of folk or oral literature. St. Louis was a major center of blues activity; the ballads "Frankie and Johnny," "Brady and Duncan," and "Stagolee" began there.[1] The rise of the blues song in the interzones forged an aesthetic based on music, ideology, and identification.

The blues ethos developed as a form of resistance to the conditions prevailing in districts such as Deep Morgan and Chestnut Valley. According to W. C. Handy, black women often had to sell their bodies to feed their families, and blues music helped the prostitutes get through these difficult times.[2] In the 1890s blues musicians started playing in illegal honky-tonks—slum apartments from which the tenants were being evicted. To raise rent money, the tenants would have a party and sell corn whiskey for fifty cents a pint, and invited musicians like Henry Thomas would perform. Many of the early blues performers were subject to drug and alcohol abuse and homicide. One of Henry Townsend's first music teachers was shot down in the streets of St. Louis. John David interviewed several men in the 1970s who claimed that Lee Shelton was himself a blues musician.

The blues ballad was a direct descendant of the African-American ballad, or narrative song, which itself was the product of the syncretism of the Anglo-American ballad and African tradition. Before the emergence of such ballads, slave songs were the only form of expression for blacks.

Malcolm Laws was the first scholar to argue that there were distinctive differences between white ballads and black ones. Laws found the black ballads "at once realistic and imaginative," with "a poetic quality . . . suggest[ing] almost as much as they express." Another difference was that it was easy to trace the origins of the white ballad. The white balladmaker "frequently wrote a ballad out and had it printed and sold." In contrast, "The Southern Negro composer, who was certainly uneducated and probably illiterate, presumably sang his ballad among his people, who were then free to do with it as they would. They could and did add to it, alter it to fit new situations, and pass it along for further folk treatment."[3]

Laws, however, did not take into account the oral method of versemaking, in which the author deliberately weaves in old formulaic material. And in fact there were many professional songwriters like Gussie Davis and musicians like Tom Turpin who knew how to write down music; both Davis and Turpin sold music to Tin Pan Alley.[4] But most blacks who created songs probably sang them to friends without expecting a fee.

Laws also noted that all the black ballads dealt "with crime, usually with murder and its consequences." And unlike white ballads, which frequently expressed horror when recounting a crime, the black ballads usually described violent events "briefly and rather casually," dwelling instead on the ensuing "trials, hangings, and funerals" at "some length." The attitude expressed in the many "bad men" songs Laws discovered, like "The Bully of the Town," "Railroad Bill," and "Stackerlee," was one of "fear, admiration, disapproval, and pity."[5]

Stagolee clearly belongs to this genre which expresses sympathy for the murderer's plight. A black audience, Laws noted, would also sympathize, because "they can understand how, provoked beyond endurance, a man or woman may be driven to kill, and they know, sometimes from personal experience, the devastating effects of long years in prison."[6]

Laws described the singer of Negro ballads as a "dramatist first, moralist second": "In contrast to the white singer, who often lets his moralizing interfere with an otherwise vivid story, the Negro . . . is so keenly aware of the truth and realism of the story he tells that he holds his hearers by his own sincerity. Limited as they are in range and incident, these narrative folk songs of the Negro are moving and intense."[7]

White folklorists who have studied Stagolee and other black oral narratives have viewed these songs as examples of "crude realism."[8] This quality seems also to have been an important part of the slave song. According to Thomas L. Morgan and William Barlow, slaves sang secular songs that addressed moral issues but also incorporated "realism and parody." The following slave song provides an example of such realism:

> The big bee flies high,
> The little bee makes the honey.
> The black folks make the cotton,
> And the white folks gets the money.[9]

Such songs originated with the West African griots, known as the "living libraries" of Bantu-speaking tribes. Another source of the African song tradition was kaison, a song in which right- and wrongdoing are dramatized through humorous lyrics, as in the following:

O massa take that bran' new coat
and hang it on the wall
That darky take that same ole coat
and wear it to the ball.[10]

Another distinctive characteristic of the slave song was "double voicing," which Morgan and Barlow describe as a use of "lyrics to ensure that black and white listeners came away with different understandings of the same song."[11] Whereas white audiences might view the song as innocuous, black audiences would laugh at the references to racist ideas.

"Story songs" or ballads were rare during slavery. According to music scholar Eileen Southern, the "unvarying routines of slave life" were incompatible with a narrative form. Because the slave had no control over his own body, there was no scope for adventures; the slave "knew in advance the consequences of any action he might take, and he knew that there was nothing he could do to avert the consequences."[12]

Nevertheless, there were in fact narrative slave songs, with rebels against slavery as their heroes.

The Anglo-American ballad consisted of a long series of stanzas that told a story about either a tragic love relationship or an "ill-fated folk hero." One of the changes that the African slaves made to this form was to interject more refrains between the stanzas. "This variation on the West African call and response song pattern," notes William Barlow, "allowed for more breaks in the music, more rhythmic input, and more audience participation."[13]

A more significant change was the substitution of a rebellious figure, usually black, usually a slave, as the hero of the narrative. One such ballad was about Gabriel Prosser, the Virginia slave insurrectionist who was executed in 1800 after his plan to attack white slave owners in Richmond was divulged by house servants. In this ballad, another slave, "Billy," breaks through fourteen guards to rescue Gabriel from his cell. They escape on a horse to a spot ten miles away from "dat hangin' tree."

An' den dey called fo' a vic'rry dance,
An' de crowd dey all danced merrily;
An' de bes' dancer 'mongst dem all
Wuz Gabr'l Prosser who wuz jes' sot free![14]

After the Civil War, the heroes of African-American ballads were "bad niggers" instead of rebel slaves. Often these ballads immortalized famous black desperadoes such as John Hardy, Railroad Bill, Roscoe Bill, Eddy Jones, Lazarus, and Aaron Harris. Saloonkeepers also featured as subjects, and so did figures like "Peetie Wheatstraw," a figure from black folklore who was the "High Sheriff from hell, the devil's son-in-law."[15]

A blues musician named William Bunch took the name "Peetie Wheatstraw," encouraged the notion that he, too, was an agent of the devil, and preached a blues message of hedonism, an anti-Christian, antiwork ethic. "Work has two fools," he declared, "a fool and a mule." I asked Henry Townsend, who had known Peetie Wheatstraw, if Peetie himself had believed he was the devil's agent. "That was just a rhyme he had made about himself," he told me; "he was a kind of 'jive' person."

"The blues was the music of the poor and the down-and-out, an embarrassment to the aspirations of the black middle class," writes Giles Oakley. "It had low-life connotations going back long in St. Louis' history, from the days when the wide open red-light district with gambling and bawdy houses had first become part of the world of civic corruption and racketeering." A black librarian told Paul Garon, Peetie Wheatstraw's biographer, that she'd heard of Wheatstraw "when I was a little girl . . . but of course we had nothing to do with people like that . . . no, you won't find any pictures of [him], even in the colored newspapers, not unless he got into trouble."[16]

Oakley claims that "Wheatstraw came across as the man who has seen it all, knows what it's all about, has got it made; he has seen hard times . . . likes his whiskey, has plenty of girl friends, knows their double-crossing, deceiving ways, knows how to handle them. That is the image, the rounder who isn't going to marry and won't settle down, who drinks, fights and believes women are no-good, false-hearted, and exploit hard-working men."[17] This is also the image of Stagolee in the blues ballad.

When Lee Shelton died, on March 11, 1912, in the prison hospital in Jefferson City, Missouri, he died alone. There was no gathering of macks and girls, no widow, nobody giving speeches. No notice appeared in any newspaper.[18] Yet somewhere in Deep Morgan, perhaps in the Modern Horseshoe Club, some anonymous poet cried out the name "Stagolee," then sang the song as people who lived in the district knew it. When he got to the graveyard scene, he described all the pimps and whores:

The horses and the carriages
Stretched out for about a mile.
Everybody whore and pimp had gone in hock
To put Old Stackerlee away in style.[19]

In reality, it wasn't like that at all. Nobody drove a horse, and no carriages stretched down the block. Nobody spent any money to put Lee Shelton away. He died with only a hundred and fifty-four dollars to his name. Lee Shelton had been a pimp, a political figure, a saloonkeeper, the proprietor of a "lid club," the president of a four hundred club, and the hero of a ballad. Now he was to become a legend. The graveyard scene establishes his burial place as a holy site, a shrine to a god who redeemed the lowest of the low—the black prostitute and her pimp. This scene effects the crystallization of the Lee Shelton tale into legend.[20]

As the body of Lee Shelton, waiter and carriage driver, sportsman and pimp, was dropped into an unmarked grave, the prototype Stagolee song rose from it. As the actual Lee Shelton passed into oblivion, his legend dispersed throughout the country, thanks, in part, to the music.

II

The Thousand Faces of Stagolee

12

Jim Crow and Oral Narrative

After the murder in St. Louis, the ballad of Stagolee began appearing in various places in the American South and West. A circus performer heard it in the Indian Territory in 1913. At about the same time a white youngster hunting with his father heard Negroes singing it in the Dismal Swamps of Virginia, and in 1911 hoboes were singing it in Georgia. By 1927 it had made its way to New York City.[1] As hoboes, roustabouts, and bluesmen traveled from St. Louis to other parts of the country, they took the ballad with them and created their own versions of Stagolee.

As the Stagolee ballad traveled across the landscape, it also traveled through history. But until the civil rights movements of the early 1960s, its historical context was dominated by Jim Crow.

As a way of characterizing black people, the term *Jim Crow* had its origins in minstrelsy in the early nineteenth century. Thomas "Daddy" Rice, a white minstrel who used burnt cork to blacken his face, popularized the term to characterize a dance routine he had appropriated from a slave stableman who belonged to a Mr. Crow. By the 1830s Jim Crow minstrelsy had become one of the most popular forms of mass entertainment and reinforced the distorted images that many whites, northern and southern, had of black life.[2]

By the 1840s abolitionist newspapers employed the term to describe separate railroad cars for blacks and whites in the North. By the 1890s, after the demise of Reconstruction, "Jim Crow," according to Leon Litwack, had come to mean "the subordination and separation of black people in the South, much of it codified, much of it still enforced by custom and habit."[3]

Aiding Jim Crow in the oppression of blacks was the doctrine of manifest destiny. In the 1840s a Jacksonian Democrat, John O'Sullivan, coined the term to describe "a providentially assigned role of the United States to lead the world to new and better things."[4] The doctrine came to mean that whites had the right to conquer and control all other, darker races.

While Jim Crow theater flourished as an official form of American popular culture, there were no "legitimate" venues for performances of Stagolee. Like rap music a century later, Stagolee became a trope for the resentment felt by people marginalized by the dominant white society. For almost seven decades, Stagolee remained a symbol of rebellion, oppositional, subversive, "underground," and largely invisible as part of the unofficial subculture of prostitutes, gamblers, criminals, and other "undesirables."

In a lecture in 1983 Nathan B. Young asked why this was so, then answered himself: "The very apparent reason to begin with is that he [Stagolee] was a BAD BLACK Man."[5] For blacks, such rebellious figures were essential to survival in an era when white southerners were exploiting, threatening, and murdering African Americans with little fear of punishment.

As the son and grandson of sharecroppers in North Carolina, I saw how hard, bitter, and miserable the lives of blacks were under Jim Crow. I also saw what kept these black men and women alive and hopeful.

What kept them going from day to day was their rich oral tradition. Through folk songs, ballads, folktales, sermons, hollers, and work songs, blacks were able to dispel some of the pressure and express some of the frustrations of living under such a system. My father and grandfathers, my uncles and aunts used the humor and double voicing of the oral traditions to lighten their oppression, exclusion, and drudgery.

Occasionally Stagolee was lifted into visibility (if not respectability) by white performers who cast him as a white outlaw or by recordings by black musicians such as Duke Ellington and Sidney Bechet. For the most part, however, Stagolee was not the kind of song that decent people heard. With a few exceptions (as we shall see), its venues were limited to barbershops, black social clubs, hunting and drinking parties, and bordellos.

Oral literature—in our case the Stagolee song—is dependent on the context in which it is created and subsequently shaped. In the case of the Stagolee legend and the Stagolee song, the setting—whether a saloon, a riverboat, a levee work camp, or a race recording studio—was almost always informal, and the performers—whether ragtime or blues singers, riverboat roustabouts or leaders of the work gangs—were, at least in the early days, almost certainly illiterate. In such settings, whatever the occasion of the performance, the audience—whether black sportsmen and whores, a black work gang, or a white folklorist—inevitably influences the performer's material. As the African scholar Isidore Okpewho notes, "an audience is the only context within which an oral performance makes any sense," and "the oral piece that was performed for one particular audience is likely to reveal some of the effort

made by the performer to please that audience or some of the ways
in which the audience tried to influence the performance."[6]

The following chapters explore some of the ways in which
Stagolee changed over space and time as its performers and audiences exerted their reciprocal influence.

13

Riverboat Rouster and Mean Mate

The Stagolee ballad began its odyssey on the riverboats. Nathan Young has observed that "the steamboat was the
southern economic world afloat." On the luxury craft the riverboat
culture was connected with the St. Louis vice district through the
availability of gambling and prostitution. But on all craft it was
connected through the presence of black laborers. After emancipation, the operation of a riverboat without a crew of black freight
hands, called roustabouts or rousters, was "inconceivable." Black
men and boys fed the voracious boiler, loaded the deck, served in
the cabins, tearoom, and saloon—and sang.[1]

Life on the river appealed to blacks because of its inherently
nomadic character, its constant changes of scenery, and hours of
pleasant idleness on deck between landings, when a black boy
could rest and sleep and roll the spotted ivories with his buddies.
The wages were relatively good, the food plentiful and substantial.
But for the small army of roustabouts aboard every riverboat plying
the Mississippi, Illinois, and Ohio Rivers, with frequent stops to

load and unload cargo, leisure was brief indeed. While it lasted, a roustabout's job—rolling cotton bales up and down the stage planks, carrying tierces of lard and sides of bacon, swinging a recalcitrant squealing pig or calf over the shoulder, working in all kinds of weather under the constant tonguelashings of a profane and two-fisted mate—was about as hard a job as could be found.

As they worked, the roustabouts sang narratives called coonjinings to lighten their labor. According to Garnett Laidlaw Eskew, who had spent many years of his youth watching the riverboats along the Mississippi, coonjinings "were composed sometimes on the spur of the moment, or garbled versions of songs previously heard." "Into these songs the rousters put the problems and the incidents of the day's labor, the characteristics of the people they met," such as "the peculiarities of a mate or captain or fellow rouster; the speed and qualities of a particular boat; the charms or meanness of a woman-friend."[2]

The mates and captain, far from objecting to coonjine, encouraged their roustabouts to sing. Eskew speculated that the motive was "purely economical": "A thousand tons of miscellaneous freight and a few hundred bales of cotton could be loaded, to the beat and time of Coonjine, in half the time that songless labor would demand. And there was another value to Coonjine," Eskew thought. "Moving in perfect time meant that the rousters' feet hit the stageplank with uniform precision. A wise thing, too! For if a rouster should step upon the vibrating boards out of time, and thus catch the rebound of the stage-plank, he was very likely to be catapulted [overboard] with his load."[3]

By 1939 the riverboat culture was passing. But while strolling down West Street in New York City one bright October afternoon in 1939, Garnett Laidlaw Eskew encountered a living vestige of that world.[4] Eskew liked walking along the Manhattan shoreline of the Hudson River, crowded with oceangoing and coastal vessels lying in at their berths or edging away from the wharves in the wake of straining tugboats. As always, on this day crowds of dock laborers were busily loading and unloading cargoes arriving from, or destined for, the ports of the world. They were Hungarians, Italians, Irishmen, Germans, and Swedes, with a fair scattering of Americans. But among them was an old, "powerful, gray-haired Negro," the only worker who seemed to be enjoying his labor, because he was singing.

Eskew stood transfixed by the old man's song. "Could it be! Coonjining! Was it possible," Eskew asked himself, "that here in New York there was a roustabout—a Coonjine Nigger from the Mississippi country?"

Eskew walked closer and looked at the old man. He could tell by the old battered hat with the brim turned up in front and the gunnysack fastened with nails across his chest and shoulders that this was the genuine article. But it was mostly the singing—"chanting, in a rhythmical barbaric sort of regularity"—that signaled his origins.

There came a lull in the unloading of the ship. The old man exhaled gustily, mopped his brow, chanced a glance in Eskew's direction, grinned, and shook his head. "Sho' is hot!" he announced, "and man is I tired!"

Eskew beckoned him over to one side. "Do you remember any more of those Coonjine songs?" he asked.

The old rouster at once became a trifle reticent and embarrassed. "Lawdy, hit wuz so long ago I mos' fergit 'em. I useter know a lot dem songs when I wuz a young buck. But sense I done got ole, I got me a wife and jined de chu'ch and fergit mos' all dem ole Coonjine

songs." But with a bit of encouragement from Eskew, he came up
with this:

> Sal Teller leave St. Looey
> Wid her lights tu'n down.
> And you'll know by dat
> She's Alabama bound. [repeat]
> Alabama bound!
> She's Alabama bound!
> Doan you leave me here! [repeat]
> Ef you's gwine away and ain't comin' back
> Leave a dime fer beer! [repeat]
> Brother, if you gwine away
> Leave a dime for beer!
> I ask de mate
> Ter sell me some gin;
> Says, I pay you, mister
> When de Stack comes in. [repeat]
> Says, I pay you mister,
> When de Stack comes in.

Eskew realized that the name "Stack" referred to one of the Lee
Line boats, the *Stack Lee*.

The blues scholar Paul Oliver believes that the early singers
of Stagolee were roustabouts, levee camp workers, muleskinners,
swampers, raftmen, and loggers, whose communities lined the bay-
ous and dotted the bottomlands of the Mississippi Basin.[5] And indeed, several of the ballads the old man sang for Eskew contained
stanzas that seem either to have come from or to have helped form
the Stagolee ballads. Thus,

De ole Lizzie Bay she comin' roun' de ben'
All she's a doin' is killin' up men

is similar to

Stack Lee she comin' roun' de ben'
All she's a doin' is killin' up men.

Yet another version from the Mississippi River, from about 1910, also seems at first glance to confirm the connection. Mary Wheeler collected this in 1944 from Negro riverboat roustabouts. One such worker sang the following praises:

Oh, Stack in the rivuh, turnin' all roun' an' roun'
An' I am prayin' fo' the long tall Stack to go down.
Oh, Stack in the rivuh turnin' all roun' an' roun'
An' I am prayin' fo' the long tall Stack to go down
When the women hollering, "Oh Mr. Stacker Lee
Have taken my husban', an' made a trip fo' me."
Oh, Stack has got ways jes' lak a natural man,
He'll steal yo' woman, an' in the woods he'll lan'."[6]

But here, as in the version above, the reference to "Stack" clearly is not to a man, but to a riverboat: the *Stack Lee*.

Another, less direct and more subtle, connection between Stack Lee Shelton and the roustabouts' coonjines seems likelier: The gangplank was the site of the drama between the white "mean mate," who ordered their movements, and the roustabouts. A black man who could survive a mean mate was a "bad nigger," or a "man in full"—in short, a hero. The Lee Shelton legend may have been modeled on these "bad niggers" and mapped onto the white "mean mate."

14

Work Camps, Hoboes, and Shack Bully Hollers

Gazing downriver from the passenger rail of the steamboat on which he was traveling, John L. Matthews could see a large group of black men driving mules on the riverbank. Although he had never seen one before, Matthews realized he was looking at a Mississippi levee work camp. A putrid stench from the sixty tents in the camp drove most of the passengers inside. "To these camps," Matthews later wrote, "commonly drift the ugliest and most criminal of their race, graduates from the convict camps being numerous in them. Gambling and drinking and quarreling pass away the idle hours, and murders are common occurrences."[1]

Under the inhuman conditions prevailing in these camps, blacks were worked as if slavery had not ended, victims of both the convict release system and the peonage system. In charge of each camp were the white levee contractor, armed with a shotgun or a Winchester rifle, and his muscular black assistant, the "shack bully," who kept the work gang in line.

Every morning about four o'clock, the white man with a shotgun and his big shack bully, who "always [went] armed with a pistol or club, always with the arrogance of an assumed prestige," would come around and rouse the work gang by beating on a tin pan, ringing a bell, or, sometimes, singing.[2] Throughout the day he operated as a merciless enforcer of the contractor's orders. Many people told of shack bullies beating workers to death. After studying this figure during his travels in the 1920s and early 1930s, the folklorist John Lomax reported that the shack bully was "one of the most thoroughly hated characters in the Negro construction camps in the South."[3] One levee contractor, Isum Lorentz, who was rumored to have "killed mo' men dan de influenza," and his shack bully, L. W. Simmons, became the stuff of legend and of several ballads.[4]

As they worked, the men sang and chanted a "shack bully holler," which in turn shaped the songs of the black hoboes who were common figures in the camps. Wandering around the southern countryside from the 1890s to the 1930s, they worked on the levees or on steamboats, often loafing when they couldn't find work. Before long the hoboes produced songs about the shack bully and Stagolee. In their versions, Stagolee becomes the hero.

> Stacker Lee is lookin' fo' the Bully,
> The Bully can't be found,
> Now we're goin' to walk the levee roun', roun',
> Goin' to walk the levee roun',
> I'm lookin' fo' the Bully uv yo' town.
> I'm lookin' fo' the Bully, the Bully mus' be found,
> I'm lookin' fo' the Bully boys, to lay the body down,
> I'm lookin' fo' the Bully uv yo' town.[5]

This "Stagolee" no longer refers to Lee Shelton. It refers to any hero who will defeat the enemy—in this case, the shack bully. Thus two different strains of the Stagolee legend—the rouster song about the riverboat *Stack Lee* and the "Bully Song" about the labor camp shack bully—merged into one.

During the era of levee construction, blacks were reluctant to express their resentment against white men in song; hence their displacement of the role of villain onto the white levee contractor's shack bully. Fortunately for us, in later decades they allowed a few white men in search of the country's underculture to record some of those songs. In doing so they allowed us to trace the otherwise invisible history of Stagolee.

15

William Marion Reedy's White Outlaw

By 1918 whites had appropriated Stagolee as an outlaw who spoke to the feelings of white men. William Marion Reedy, the well-known editor of a small St. Louis independent journal, *The Mirror,* played a key role in collecting and dispersing the Stagolee tradition among white audiences.

On December 22, 1918, Roy L. McCardell of the *New York Morning Telegraph*—journalist, poet, playwright, philosopher, humorist, and inventor of the comics section of daily newspapers—published an "exposé of William Marion Reedy," in which he quoted a verse from a "colored folk song, 'Everybody Talk about Stackerlee.'" Less than two weeks later, Reedy printed the entire ballad in *The Mirror,* claiming that his office had received "eleven requests for copies of the poem." Reedy asserted that the song had come to him from "Mr. D'Arcy Fanning, of Muskogee, Oklahoma."[1]

> On one cold and frosty Christmas night,
> Stackerlee and Billy Lyons had an awful fight.—
> Everybody talk about Stackerlee!
> Said Billy Lyons to Stackerlee, "Don't you take my life,—
> Remember my two children and my loving wife."

Fanning's version not only gets the date and place of the murder correct; it also names Shelton's girlfriend:

> Little Lillie Sheldon, when she first heard the news,
> She was sittin' on her bedside, just a-lacin' up her shoes.
> Everybody talk about Stackerlee!

The final stanza, though, recasts the identity of Stagolee. He is not an urbane mack, but a ruthless frontier outlaw.

> What a bold bad man he must be:
> With his forty-four and his Bowie knife,
> never hesitate for to take your life.—
> Oh, everybody talk about Stackerlee!

In 1927, when Charles J. Finger published *Frontier Ballads,* he included "Stackerlee" in the section "Outlaws and Hard-Cases." He wrote, "Lastly, I close this section with a very notable ballad, 'Stackerlee,' which my friend and associate, William Marion Reedy, rescued and printed in his *Mirror,* for I think it marked the beginning of all this fashion and taste for nastie . . . balladry."[2]

In his introductory remarks about the song, Finger claimed that Reedy had taken a few knocks for publishing "Stackerlee." Apparently readers had objected that the deeds of the songs were "anachronisms" and therefore "should be buried and numbered with [the] monstrosities of the past." Reedy (according to Finger) had responded: "There is a drop of rebel blood in the mildest of men which makes them give ear to songs about outlaws."[3] Reedy saw Stagolee as an embodiment of the "wild spirit" in man.

Perhaps the "monstrosities of the past" referred to the red-light district of downtown St. Louis, with which Reedy was well acquainted. Reedy was married three times, twice (briefly) to madams.

Born in December 1862 in the Irish section of northside St. Louis, William Marion Reedy, like Lee Shelton, was a child of Reconstruction. But unlike Shelton, Reedy was not held back or demonized by racial prejudices. The son of Patrick Reedy, an Irish-American policeman, he attended the best public and parochial schools and graduated from St. Louis University at age eighteen.[4]

Patrick Reedy had patrolled the Bloody Third Ward, where the ballads "Stagolee," "Frankie and Johnny," and "Duncan and Brady" originated as black protests against police brutality. The Irish policemen of St. Louis were well known for their brutal treatment of blacks, and Pat Reedy figured at least indirectly in the creation of the ballad "Duncan and Brady," based on an incident in which Duncan, a black bartender, killed Reedy's fellow Irish policeman Brady in Deep Morgan.[5] Jack Conroy claims that "The Bully of the Town," which also originated in St. Louis, was likewise a response to police brutality.[6]

In 1880, five months before Reedy's eighteenth birthday, his father got him a job as a reporter at one of St. Louis's oldest newspapers, the *Missouri Republican*. He apprenticed under the city editor, W. A. Kelsoe, who claimed that his young cub reporter was "brilliant."[7] In 1894 Joseph McCullagh, an editor at the *Globe-Democrat*, characterized Reedy as a successful feature writer "during the rare intervals when he was sober." By the time Reedy was thirty, he had become well known as "the hero of a cycle of alcoholic myths."[8] Soon afterward Reedy and a friend, D'Arcy Fanning, bought a little "scandal sheet" called *The Mirror*. After the journal went bankrupt, Reedy's influential multimillionaire friend James Campbell bought it, restoring it to him as a gift when Reedy sobered up.[9]

Although he lived at home until he was in his thirties, Reedy spent most of his days and evenings "downtown," the site of the municipal Four Courts, famous restaurants and hotels, the red-light district, and the burgeoning ragtime dance halls. Reedy was a "slummer" who crossed the "color line."[10]

According to his biographer Max Putzel, as a young man Reedy went looking for trouble. "He haunted the Four Courts and the jails." He would sit up all night with the warden and watch a man condemned to be hanged in the morning. They would chat interminably about immortality and atheism. In the morning, when the prisoner was marched out to face the crowd and the gallows, Reedy would note how the condemned man would glance up at the sky or at a bird perched on a tower, then look straight ahead with fluttering and swallowing in his throat. Later he would write of witnessing twenty hangings. "The sun came over the jail roof with a sudden glory, and made the crowd look inexpressibly mean as it poured out of the gate to meet the newsboys, crying, 'Extra: all about the execution!'"[11]

Caught between a Victorian sensibility and modern yearning, Reedy was a precursor to white slummers like Carl Van Vechten, who crossed the color line to Harlem in the 1920s. In many ways he embodied the moral ambivalence that ruled social life in St. Louis from the 1890s through the 1910s. It is also possible that Reedy knew Lee Shelton. His version of the ballad certainly indicates that he at least knew *of* him.

In his printing of the ballad in *The Mirror* in 1919, Reedy described it as a "rich example of the American Negro balladry . . . There are spots in it that remind one of polyphonic prose." It was performed in "a slow ragtime . . . The singer renders it, as in a dreamy reminiscence, in a low key. The refrain reminds one of those in Rosetti's poems 'Nineveh' and 'Tall Troy's on Fire.' It is a sort of swiftly foreshortened sketch of the story of a Negro murder that is said to have taken place in St. Louis."

This evaluation reflects Reedy's seasoned literary tastes. Certainly this was the first time anyone compared the Stagolee ballad with such literary masterpieces as Rosetti's poems. It was also the first time that the poem was associated with "a Negro murder that . . . has taken place in St. Louis."

If Reedy knew Lee Shelton and the circumstances that produced the poem, why didn't he say so? He claimed in his headnote to the ballad that it was based on real people. Reedy was probably afraid of what his readers would think if they knew he was acquainted with such underworld characters. He may have considered it sufficient to acknowledge that the facts were "said to have taken place." He was careful not to say by whom the facts were known. But Reedy's reference to the "slow ragtime" tempo of the ballad indicates that it was part of the black oral tradition of St. Louis of that time.

On December 29, 1895, a few days after the murder of Billy Lyons by Lee Shelton, Reedy published in the *St. Louis Star-Sayings* a long and detailed account asserting that the murder was a vendetta against another saloon down the street run by Billy Lyons' brother-in-law, Henry Bridgewater.

Reedy's *Mirror* became one of the most important literary journals in the country. It had a circulation of 50,000 a year, at a time when the *Atlantic Monthly*'s was about 5,000. Reedy established *The Mirror* as "a vigorous . . . organ of protest against the genteel tradition in Midwestern journalism," using it "boldly to shatter the complacency of church-going bride dispensers." Before long, however, Reedy also acquired an international reputation as a literary critic. He was an advocate for Theodore Dreiser and Stephen Crane at a time when nobody else even understood what they were doing. The young William Butler Yeats and Ezra Pound wanted to be published in his *Mirror*. According to his biographer, Reedy was the first critic to understand the American literary movement called Naturalism.[12]

As a man about town, Reedy was also a popular figure at dinner parties and "Stag dinners."[13] On one of these occasions, he may have recited the Stagolee song, and the term *toast* as applied to such recitations, whose significance we shall see later, may have come into being in this way.

16

Cowboy Stagolee and Hillbilly Blues

During the 1920s Stagolee surfaced in an array of places, musical forms, and character types, including the St. Louis mack, the black or white outlaw, and, by extension, the (outlaw) cowboy. In the early days of the Oklahoma Territory, blacks outnumbered whites by three to one.[1] They would have been likely transmitters of the song.

But there were other likely transmitters, too. By the 1920s, white men had discovered that figures in black folk songs such as John Henry and Stagolee appealed in many ways to their own circumstances and their feelings about those circumstances. In 1924 song-writers Ray Lopez and Lew Colwell published a sheet-music version called "Stack O' Lee Blues." This fact alone attests to the popularity of the song.[2]

During the 1920s Robert C. Gordon, a professor of English at the University of California, Berkeley, was so taken by the Stagolee song that he launched a campaign to collect it from sources throughout America. He did this by advertising in his magazine, *Adventure*, which was dedicated to cowboy folk songs. There he made a special plea to readers to send him any oral versions they had come by and stressed the need for authenticity.[3]

Between December 7, 1923, and February 18, 1927, Gordon corresponded with at least eight other white collectors across the country about Stagolee songs. The correspondence reveals that by then the unofficial culture of Stagolee had moved westward, into the plains of Oklahoma and the Indian Territory.

The best version that Gordon received came from S. J. Duffield of Lodi, California, in September 1925, who wrote:

> Dear Sir:
> I enclose you an old time song, which at one time was quite popular amongst the Sporting element in the early days of Oklahoma and the Indian Territory.
> At that time I was a Circus Musician and as we heard fragments of it everywhere we went in that part of the country, it aroused my curiosity and I finally got it in its entirety.
> It is founded on an actual happening in St. Louis in the early 80's.
> Trusting it will be new to you, I remain resp.
> Yours, S. J. Duffield[4]

In Duffield's version the singer or speaker summons his audience:

> Come all you sporty fellows,
> and listen unto me,
> I will tell you the awful tale
> of that bad man Stackalee.

Over twenty-four stanzas, the song is related to the basic type in that it contains an episode of a female helper, a "Mrs. Stackalee," who functions in the same way as Lillie Sheldon. Both go down to the court to bail Stagolee out. Here the helper

> rushed down to the jailhouse
> And fell upon her knees,
> "I'll give the thousand dollars
> Just to get the jailer's keys."
> That bad, that bad man Stackalee.

There are other elements that relate this version to the basic type, such as the name of the historical figure of the bartender. One of the real bartenders was named Thomas Scott. Here he retains part of that name as Stackalee briefly assumes the role of narrator:

> [Stackalee] run into Ben Scott's saloon
> And before the bar I'd stand,
> Saying, "Take my pistol, bar boy,
> I dun killed another man."

Although it is related to the basic type, some changes have been made to incorporate a Wild West ethos. Whereas in the basic type the confrontation between Stagolee and Billy Lyons takes place in a saloon, in Duffield's version the murder occurs in the street:

It was on this dark and
Cold stormy night
That Billy Lyons and Stackalee
They had that awful fight.
That bad, that bad man Stackalee.

Billy Lyons on the sidewalk
Dropped his razor from his hand;
In front of him a-shootin'
Old Stackalee did stand.
That bad, that bad man Stackalee.

After he shoots Lyons, Stagolee runs into the saloon. Ben Scott
sends for the police, who chase Stagolee into an alley. Stagolee is
hiding behind a tree, but policemen surround him, calling out:

"Your name is Henry Wells,
But they call you Stackalee;
You are my prisoner
Come and go with me."
That bad, that bad man Stackalee.

In this version, the name Henry Wells may have referred to a locally
known outlaw.

The judge sentences Stagolee to be hanged, despite his wife's
pleading. In the last stanza, the speaker delivers a blistering warn-
ing to his audience:

Now all you sporty fellows
That have listened to my tale,
Do not shoot another man

Or they'll hang you in jail
Like they did that bad man Stackalee.

Duffield, a white man who probably had no connections with St. Louis or the bordello culture, had nevertheless come across the song in a similar environment, "amongst the Sporting element" in the Indian Territory, which later became Oklahoma, in places where prostitution and gambling probably took place.

A few weeks later Gordon replied:

> My dear Mr. Duffield:
>
> I am delighted with the copy of "Stackalee" which you sent; it is the best and most complete that has yet come in . . . I should also like much to have the approximate date when the version of Stackalee was taken down—you refer in your letter simply to "early days"—and to have any other bits of information about its supposed origin or history.[5]

Duffield soon provided a further account of the song—and, along the way, of himself:

> Mr. R. W. Gordon, Dear Sir:
>
> In answer to your inquiry I will say that as near as I know now the song Stackalee was originated in the latter [18]80s, or early [18]90s. It undoubtedly was first started by some of the Sporting Fraternity around St. Louis, and then verses were added here and there by others of that class . . . It is a fact that sometime in the latter 80s two St. Louis gamblers one named Lyons the other Wells (alias Stackalee) had a fight one rainy night in which affair Lyons was killed.

What is of interest here is the persisting notion that the ballad was based on real people and events in St. Louis. But it wasn't the historical references that attracted Duffield to the song. What drew him "was the pecular [sic] melody. I never heard it sung completely (only fragments) until one night in a Resort in Anadarko Okla. shortly after the opening of that country it was sung by a Saloon Man and I played his accompaniment. And I remember He sang it bout twenty times."

Duffield assured Gordon that "if I should think of any others of interest I will certainly send them to you," although he also reminded the folklorist of his advanced age:

> But the Old Man is not quite as young as He used to be
> and his memory not being up to standard, I will do the
> best I can.
>   Yours S. J. Duffield, Lodi California
>   Permanent Address Imperial Hotel
> P.S. I am employed by one of the Fruit cos. here.[6]

On November 9, 1925, Gordon thanked Duffield for his information about the ballad and sent him the proof sheets of the version that would appear in the January 10, 1926, issue of *Adventure*. Gordon also promised Duffield credit for "authorship"; the song, he said, "will surely appear under your name" in the magazine. Thus, although Stagolee existed around the country in a multitude of versions, the moment it was published, the collector was given authorship, as if he had invented it. The folklorist John Lomax also followed this practice, taking not only credit for the songs he collected but also royalties for the books of folklore he published.

Gordon also carried on a correspondence about Stagolee with a Lieutenant F. Rorschach, serving on the U.S.S. *New York*. At the lieutenant's request, Gordon sent him a copy of "Staggerlee" and asked where and how Rorschach had first heard the song. Rorschach replied, "I heard them (i.e. 'Stackolee' and 'Frankie and Albert') originally sung by Negroes in the backwoods of southern Virginia, where I lived my boyhood—near the Dismal Swamp region, where my Father used to take me with him on his 'possum hunting expeditions in the fall and it is chiefly on account of that sentimental association that I was so anxious to obtain the words to them." In the fifteen years since, the lieutenant went on, "I have heard [Stagolee] only three times . . . once in a nigger barber shop in Seattle, once sung by a young Dane who makes his living playing for emotional effect at one of the big movie studios in Los Angeles, and once played by a dance orchestra in a cabaret."

Clearly, the ballad had traveled to diverse settings and moved across racial as well as national lines. Rorschach went on to speculate about the origins of Stagolee:

> My impression was that both these songs are of Negro origin . . . the Dane, who sings blues incidentally as if he were black as the ace of spades, and who is something of a fanatic on the subject, has told me that "Stackolee" is sort of an epic—that it originated in Kansas City, and was founded on fact—on an incident in the black colony there years ago—and that there were actually a Billy Lyons and a Stack o Lee and a [woman named] Lily Sheldon.[7]

In a letter to Gordon on February 14, 1927, another collector, a Mr. Nice from New York City, assured him that he was "glad to . . . be of some help in getting 'the low-down on Stack-o-lee.'"

> I don't know much about music, but I'll try to write it down, just as I heard it. It was during a trip I made one

season back in 1913-14 with the Buffalo Bill–Pawnee Bill Shows, as a performer and manager of a horse act. A hillbilly sort of person about twenty years old, drifted into the dressing room one afternoon and played it on a harmonica. Then he sang about thirty verses of it. As he was singing I wrote as many as possible and tried to remember the rest. The smutty lines may have been introduced to make it appeal to a rough crowd.

The tune is a sing song one so that may have been made up to fit also. However, I have an old square piano downstairs, and I'll try to pick it out on that. It should be very good on a ukulele. Well here's my first attempt at writing music.[8]

The reference to "thirty verses" indicates that this performer improvised considerably. The reference to "smutty lines" simply confirms what we have already guessed: that sung versions of Stagolee were more explicit than published versions such as Reedy's.

Thanks to Gordon's efforts, we have texts of Stagolee dating from the early part of the century. Although he collected very little of the music, only a few snatches of musical scribbling, his collections give us a hint of what the music must have sounded like. It was a typical ragtime tune of the times. Nice's letter provides the first explicit evidence that a "smutty" version of Stagolee was sung to music.

Apparently Nice sent Gordon a version that also contained "Frankie and Johnny"—"a marvelous mixture," Nice wrote, "part 'Stackolee' and part 'Frankie and Johnny.'" Gordon responded on February 18 that this was the "most interesting bit that has come in for some time. No I'm not criticizing you, or making fun," the professional folklorist reassured his amateur collector; "things like that happen sometimes, and they are most important to a student of folk song. What happens is that a new song is made out of the fragment of the two others. A rare but extremely interesting case. Hence my delight in capturing it."[9]

There is a close relationship, as it turns out, between "Frankie and Johnny" and the Stagolee song. Although different versions provide different narrative details, the melody and motifs are very similar. "Frankie and Johnny" and Stagolee may or may not have been created by the same person, but it is clear that both were shaped by the same aesthetic.

Born in 1897 in Raleigh County, West Virginia, Frank Hutchinson became a miner and played his banjo, guitar, and fiddle in mining camps and small-town schools and movie houses. According to Sherman Lawson, another fiddler who played with him, Hutchinson had acquired much of his knowledge of blues music from black musicians, especially Bill Hunt and Billy Vaughn. Hunt, who had been around Logan County since Hutchinson's boyhood, taught him "Worried Blues" and "Train That Carried the Girl from Town." It was Hunt who gave him the idea of playing slide guitar, "makin' it cry."[10]

When he recorded "Stackalee" on September 28, 1926, Hutchinson was already well known locally as a fine guitar player. "He could play ballads and songs like that," said banjoist Aunt Jennie Wilson, who also lived in Logan County and had known him around 1916. "And he played the blues by himself, and he really played them, too. He always specialized in the blues . . . He played the guitar laying on his lap," she recalled, describing the method of playing the slide.[11]

In his recording debut in 1926, Hutchinson started off with the two blues he had learned from Bill Hunt, "Worried Blues" and "Train That Carried the Girl from Town." Both sound as though he was merely imitating his black teacher's renditions. Then he performed "Stackalee," which he sang as a cowboy song, blending the elements of hillbilly music with the blues. Hutchinson's "Stackalee" is lyrically similar to other cowboy subgenres like Duffield's, omitting the motif of the female helper. Hutchinson's focus is not liquor, women, or police brutality, but the fetishized Stetson hat; a commodity had become a reason for murder.

When Bob Dylan recorded his version of the song in 1993, he took Frank Hutchinson as his model.

In 1928 the Fruit Jar Guzzlers, a group of white musicians, recorded a version called "Stack-O-Lee." The plot is a retelling of the St. Louis version, but without the references to pimping or macks. The urban motifs are replaced with motifs of the cowboy and white outlaw. Stagolee goes out of town with a forty-four in his hand, looking for Billy:

All about that broad-brimmed Stutson hat
He finds Billy, who begs for life;
Stack-O-Lee kills him; Sheriff comes looking for him.
A young boy tells the sheriff that he had a great big forty-four
in his right hand, for God's sake let him go.[12]

In the next stanza, Billy asks his mother not to pray for him. He is bound to die because of "that broad-brimmed Stutson hat." Stack, brought before the judge, asks him for mercy because of his old gray-haired mother and the "Stutson." The judge says he will have pity on him and gives him twenty-five years because of that "John

143

B. Stutson." The recurrent references to the Stetson hat place it at the center of the tragedy. But this Stetson is not the one that inspired the original song. It is not the specially made Stetson that the macks wore in St. Louis. This hat is the cowboy Stetson.

17

Blueswomen: Stagolee Did Them Wrong

By the 1920s, Prohibition had forced the transformation of the saloons into speakeasies.[1] Speakeasies were open to all segments of society, young and old, lower classes and upper classes—but not to blacks. Blacks had formed their own clubs, called black and tans. It was there that the blues version of Stagolee continued to be heard informally.

If white men could retell the story of Stagolee as a white outlaw, black blues singers surely had an even more legitimate claim to it. Blues recording started in February 1921, with Okeh Records' success with Mammie Smith singing "Crazy Blues." It reached a high-water mark in 1926, with $128 million in sales.[2] White record companies began making "race records," recording black singers for black consumers. During the decade, close to 15,000 race records were released, of which approximately 10,000 were blues titles, before the industry died in the early 1930s.[3] But it was black women from the legitimate minstrel circuit, not black men, who tended to make the recordings.

"The Mother of the Blues," as Ma Rainey was known, sang

ninety-three selections for Paramount Records between 1923 and 1928. One of these was called "Stack-o-Lee Blues," made in January 1926.[4] According to music scholar Norm Cohen, this was the first recording of Stagolee.[5]

As Cohen pointed out, however, the tune she sang was the tune to "Frankie and Johnny." Moreover, in her version, the lyrics also became confused with those of "Frankie and Johnny." There is no mention of Billy Lyons or of Stagolee's Stetson hat.

> Stack-o-Lee was a bad man
> Everybody knows
> And when they see Stack-o-Lee coming
> They give him the road.

> He was my man
> But he done me wrong
> Stack-o-Lee, Stack-o-Lee
> Was so desperate and bad
> He would take everything his woman
> And everything they had.[6]

Although Ma Rainey and other black women introduced blues to a wide audience, I am not convinced, as Hazel V. Carby apparently is, that by 1928 "the blues sung by blacks were only secondarily of folk origin" and that the "primary source for the group transmission of the blues was by phonograph which was then joined by the radio."[7] I believe the oral tradition of blues singing was the primary way the blues was transmitted from community to community. Black women had been singing the Stagolee song in prisons and fields and backyards for decades by the time Ma Rainey recorded it. When African-American singers were asked for material to sing, they drew on the songs they had heard, songs that were part of the oral tradition. In her "Stack-o-Lee Blues," Ma Rainey brought the oral tradition of the "bad man" ballads to a new technology. Her version is a folk blues adapted to the standards of the race music formula. Thus Ma Rainey mediated the "crucial transition from a rural folk blues to an urban popular blues."[8]

Ma Rainey knew how to express the black woman's abandon ment in the blues mood. She used the blue notes of traditional folk blues to build emotions that fall in a moan. But like other blues singers, she "also created specific innovations in blue note patterns." In her "Stack-o-Lee Blues" Ma Rainey moved from "a blue third note up to a major third note," blending folk blues with the emerging sound of New Orleans jazz.[9] Incorporating these two influences (early jazz in its instrumentation, blues in its arrangement), this recording by Ma Rainey crystallizes a transitional moment in the history of American black music.

In her recording session, Ma Rainey didn't sing the song to a live black audience, the traditional setting for a Stagolee performance. She sang to a microphone, and perhaps this is why she confused the lyrics of Stagolee with those of "Frankie and Johnny." Illiterate like most black singers, in the recording studio she composed while performing without a traditional audience, and so was not aware that her lyrics didn't make sense. A traditional audience would have corrected her.

Less than a decade later, when John Lomax was collecting songs in Alabama, his friend Ruby Pickens Tartt introduced him to Vera Hall, a tall, proud black woman, and they quickly became friends. In 1937 Hall sang for Lomax the most beautiful, soul-

ful version of the Stagolee ballad ever recorded.[10] Her voice was so
wonderful that Lomax arranged for her to give a concert in New
York City, which was a big success. When she died ten years later,
Lomax wrote a tender and thoughtful obituary.[11]

Hall's version has several elements that relate it to the archetype
discussed in Chapter 3. In it, Stagolee accuses Billy Lyons of stealing his hat ("You done stole my Stetson hat and I'm bound to take
your life"), and Lyons, in his plea for mercy, mentions three children, not two ("I got three little children and a dear little loving
wife"). But the most significant trait tying Hall's version to the basic type is the presence of a prostitute as female helper:

> Stagolee went to his woman and asked her how much change you
>   got.
> She ran her hand in her stocking feet and pulled out a hundred
>   dollar spot
> Stagolee's woman walked up to the "boss man"
> And asked him for some change
> "I got my baby in the station house
> And my business must be arranged."
> Stagolee's woman hustled a long time before she got forty
>   thousand dollars for bond.

In Ma Rainey's version the female speaker calls on Stagolee for
help, but in Hall's version the woman offers to help him and takes
an active part in getting him out of jail; she thinks nothing of ap-
proaching the "boss man" for a favor to help her man. This image of the black woman as a go-between remains a popular one in
African-American folk culture.

18

Bluesmen and Black Bad Man

When Margaret Walker (who later became famous as a novelist) went in 1937 to the house of one of her Chicago informants to take down memories of slavery, the old woman surprised her with a question: "Is ah evah telled you bout mah cousin, Yallah Hammuh?"

Before Walker could answer, the informant went on: "Well, man dat wuz one moah bad guy. Dat guy so bad de sharef scairt ta go nigh his house." The sheriff was afraid to go near his house. This had been said of Stagolee, too. But Walker simply listened and took notes, writing the story in the language that she heard.

> "Yalluh Hammuh!" [the sheriff called to him] an Yalluh
> Hammuh say, "Whut?" an de sharef say, "Dey wants you
> in town," an Yalluh Hammuh say, "Aw, all right, ahll be
> in attuh while. Gone back down dere an tell em ahm
> cummin." Das jes his jive, but de sharef know he healthy
> ta fergit Yalluh Hammuhs jive.
>
> Now dis heah town hwere Yalluh Hammuh live air a
> mill town. Evyting depen on de mill an de mill wattuh by
> powuh fum de canal. Dey drains de canal onct a week.
> Now you kin see how anybody kin git bumped off an

trowed ovah in dat dere canal an aint nobody know tell
de weeks ovsh an dey drains de canal.

Man, youghta see de peoples cum down te watch em
drain de canal and see ef any dey kinfokes done bin
bumped off in de canal, an ef not dey kin fokes, ta see
whosen is an whosen aint. Well, mos evhy week Yalluh
Hammuh done bump somebody off in de canal. Whut
dey do ta him? Aint ah tell ya? De sharef cum up clost ez
he dare an serve notice, an ef he wanta go, he go, an ef he
aint wanta go, he aint go. Dat is he aint go, tell dat time
cum whin Pick-Ankle-Slim aint gin Yalluh Hammuh no
choice. Now Yalluh Hammuh is a bad guy all right, but
dis Pick-Ankle-Slim pose ta be a badder guy. He a bad
bad guy. He so bad he real bad; bad as Stagolee.[1]

This story indicates that the legend of Stagolee as a bad man cir-
culated widely among the illiterate people of the Midwest as well as
the South. The usual distinction given Stagolee was not that he was
bad, but that he was badder than some other "bad nigger." In the
case described here, Yalluh Hammuh was bad, but Pick-Ankle-Slim
was badder still.

In a 1939 article titled "Ba-ad Nigger," H. C. Brearley began with
an example of the "ba-ad man." But he claimed that in "many
Negro communities . . . this emphasis upon heroic deviltry is so
marked that the very word *bad* often loses its original significance
and may be used as an epithet of honor." If a black wanted to use
the word with its usual meaning, he pronounced it as described in
the dictionary, but if he wished to describe "a local hero, he calls him
'ba-ad.' The more he prolongs the *a,* the greater is his homage."[2]

During the 1920s, the heavyweight boxer Jack Johnson was a symbol of the "bad nigger" for both blacks and whites. For whites,

Johnson was a man to be feared and dreaded. For blacks, he was somebody to be proud of, someone who would not stay in the "place" assigned him by white society.

As Kevin J. Mumford has pointed out, Johnson was a celebrity, legend, and symbol.[3] He was also a scapegoat and the victim of a racial and sexual system. In order to send a message to other black men that white women were forbidden, Congress in 1913 passed the White Slave Traffic Act. Using the provisions of this act, federal authorities alleged that Johnson had traveled across state lines for the purpose of prostitution with his former white girlfriend, Belle Schreiber. To escape prison, Johnson fled to Paris. Like Lee Shelton, Johnson had owned a social gathering place, the Café de Champion, which catered to a wealthy clique of Chicago sophisticates and where black/white couples socialized. Johnson's case may have been emblematic, but it was not unique: even before passage of the White Slave Traffic Act, black men across America were not only hounded but lynched for associating with white women, even if, as was the case with both of Johnson's wives, they were prostitutes.[4]

In a 1971 essay on Jack Johnson, William H. Wiggins Jr. discussed the definition of "bad nigger" as it applied to the famed boxer.[5] Johnson was his own man; he refused to allow anyone, white or black, to determine his place in society or the manner in which he should live. According to Johnson's biographer Finis Farr, "With Johnson, one never could be sure what he would say or do; and this from a Negro made white people nervous when it did not agree with them."[6] Johnson, Wiggins contended, was a "bad nigger" because he "welcomed and often instigated direct confrontations with white society's stereotype of the Negro's role and place in American life."[7]

Several critics of definitions of the "bad nigger" have established some clear criteria for membership in this category. Wiggins maintained that the traits that made Jack Johnson qualify were an utter disregard for death and danger; a great concern with sexual virility; great extravagance in cars, clothing, and the like; and an insatiable appetite for "a good time." The same criteria would have met the definition of a "bad nigger" among the black blues singers of the period.

Although most commercial blues singers were black women, some black men recorded blues songs. One of the two who sang about Bad Man Stagolee was Papa Henry Hull with his Down Home Boys. Hull and his Down Home Boys were thought to be from Mobile, Alabama. Although we know little about Hull, his playing style—a blend of ragtime and parlor guitar—is typical of songsters on race records. His "I'm Alabama Bound" was based on roustabout coonjinings.

In 1927 Hull and the Down Home Boys recorded "Original Stack O' Lee Blues." Hull's Stagolee is a "bully" who fights the policeman Billy Lyons.

> Stagolee was a bully
> He bullied all his life
> Well, he bullied two Chicago police down
> With a ten cent pocket knife.
> Stagolee said to Billy,
> "How can it be you can arrest a man
> Badder than me,
> but you won't arrest Stagolee."
> Oh, Bad man.

Hull's brilliant guitar picking bridges to the next stanza:

> Then Stagolee said to Billy
> "Don't you take my life

Well, all I got is nothing but I have two children
and a darling loving wife."
[Billy replies:]
"One is a boy and the other one is a girl.
You may see them again,
but it will be in the other world."[8]

Hull's Stagolee is a "bad" bully in the sense of "good." Even a bully
who fights a policeman—even a black policeman—is a hero.

Hull changes the traditional version both by having Stagolee talk
about his two children and by making Billy Lyons a policeman and
Stagolee his potential victim. This is an excellent example of how
a performer can turn a traditional motif to his own use in a particular situation. Billy is the policeman who tells Stagolee that if
Stagolee sees his children again it will be in the other world—that
is, after Billy has killed them. This switch in roles makes Billy the
cold-hearted killer.

The other bluesman who sang and recorded the "bad
man" version of Stagolee was Mississippi John Hurt. Born in Teoc,
Mississippi, in 1882, Hurt learned to play guitar by imitating local
songsters. He played for dances and parties in nearby Delta towns
for many years before he began recording in 1928. Hurt represented
an older, down-home style of blues and never associated with the
other bluesmen of his time. Unlike the classic blues singers, who recorded with a jazz band, Hurt usually accompanied himself on the
guitar.

After emancipation, poor blacks were pushed out of the church.
Outside the church, "black musical idioms" thrived through black

hobo musicians.[9] By living on the road and never having to work for a white man, hobo musicians were considered to have beaten the white man at his own game; they became a symbol of freedom and enjoyed a high status among blacks.

These traveling musicians became the prototype blues musicians. They and the blues musicians like Mississippi John Hurt became the carriers of the Stagolee tradition during the last half of the 1890s and up through 1910. Embodying aspects both of the antebellum "truth teller" black preacher and of the "trickster" and "bad man" from devil theology, traveling musicians were the black angels who had fallen out of heaven into the hell that was America, especially the American South.

In November 1934, in Austin, Texas, John and Alan Lomax recorded a version of Stagolee by Foe Gant, a white woman, that incorporates these elements.[10] Her Stagolee is riding freight trains. He shoots the light out of the brakeman's hand, saying, "Go on, Guy, keep pulling your train." Arrested and put in the county jail, Stagolee says, "I will be out before the sun goes down if my woman do not fail." At his instructions, his woman brings him his "colt forty one." He makes the jailer give him the keys, and he escapes. He goes through town in a cloud of smoke caused by his shooting.

At the end of the song, this outlaw/hobo Stagolee tells his mother, "better name my brother after me so that [when] I'm dead and gone, there'll still be a Stagolee."

The lyrics to Mississippi John Hurt's 1928 rendition of "Stack O'Lee Blues" are similar to Hull's version. Both are concerned with police brutality. The opening stanza runs:

> Police, officers, how can it be.
> You can arrest everybody but

Cruel Stagolee,
That bad man!
O, cruel Stagolee![11]

When Hurt recorded this, there was probably no place in the Jim Crow South—or indeed in most other parts of the country—where a white policeman was afraid of arresting, shooting, or killing a black man. If the officer was afraid, he could get help quickly. Lynch mobs seem to have been easier to form than any other public gathering. In one example in New Orleans, a mere altercation between two policemen and a black man, Robert Charles, turned into a race riot. When whites saw that there was a struggle between the police and a black man, they quickly joined in with the policeman.[12]

The image of a white policeman afraid of arresting this black man gives power to the hero, making him bigger and bolder than he was in reality. Stagolee is so bad that the police, in a world where the police arrest and kill blacks every day, are afraid of arresting him. But there is also here an implicit fantasized violence.

In the first stanza, Hurt's speaker addresses the police officers. In the next, he narrates Billy's speech to Stagolee:

Billy Lyons told Stagolee,
Please don't take my life,
I got two little babies and a darling, lovin' wife.
That bad man! Oh, cruel Stagolee.

There is no logical connection between these two stanzas. The officers are asked why they can't arrest Stagolee, yet apparently he has not yet committed the crime. The sequence itself implies that the world of Stagolee is one of illogical connections. And there is another possible explanation: as the transmitter of an oral text, Hurt may have assumed that his listeners already knew the legend and did not mind the lack of chronological order.

Stagolee replies dramatically that he cares nothing about Billy's children. From what we now know about the real Lee Shelton, this scenario may be close to the truth. The interdiction is strong and clear, and the poor soul who violates that interdiction is doomed. Stagolee informs Billy of the rules, unspoken but inevitable:

> What I care about your two little babies and darlin' wife
> You done stole my Stetson hat
> I'm bound to take your life.

Hurt has an ingenious way of narrating the story. He starts with a sound and, like a movie editor, cuts to its results: a dead man lying on the floor.

> Boom! Boom! Went a forty fo'
> When I spied Billy Lyons, he was lyin' on the flo'
> Oh that bad man! O, cruel Stagolee.

The narrator turns to the jury, as if he were standing right in front of them:

> Gentlemen of the jury
> What do you think of that?
> Staggerlee kill Billy
> For a five dollar hat
> Oh, that bad man, Oh, cruel Staggerlee!

Hurt chides the jury for not protecting the people from bullies like Stagolee. According to the unwritten "Negro law," a black man could kill another black man, but a white jury usually let him off with a token punishment.

In the next stanza Hurt gives Stagolee the highest praise: he paints an indelible image of a man meeting his end with dignity. As we shall see, this message, that even the most despised of black men could not be deprived of their dignity, continued to exert a strong attraction on other black singers of Stagolee and their audiences.

> Standing on the gallows
> Head way up high
> Twelve o'clock they killed him.
> They were all glad to see him die.
> Oh that bad man
> O cruel Stagolee.

In this down-home blues version, Hurt takes the point of view of the eyewitness/narrator, whereas earlier versions, such as those sung by blacks in Georgia, give the narration to Stagolee himself.

Like the "mean mate" and "shack bully" from the steamboat and the levee camp, Hurt's Stagolee is "cruel" and "bad." Hurt's guitar breaks emphasize the story line, and his voice imitates the sound of Stack's gun. He hums and plays for four measures, allowing the impact of the story to sink in.

The first black solo musicians, blues singers accompanied themselves on guitar, which "tends to support and imitate the voice." As blues scholar Ben Sidran notes, it was blues singers who started the trend of "including vocal technique as part of instrumental technique."[13] Hurt's technique conveyed intense personal passions that mirrored Stagolee's pain and resentment, a pain and resentment shared by the thousands of black people who formed his audience. His uses of the narrative and the music to present a man whom the white authorities fear support each other, inviting the audience to identify actively with both the hero and the narrator. His version is the classic example of the Stagolee bad-man ballad.

19

On the Trail of Sinful Stagolee

In the 1920s and 1930s some white folklorists, intrigued by the process of oral composition among blues singers, went looking for the unofficial culture underlying that process. As we saw in Chapter 14, blacks were generally reluctant to share their songs with whites; but there were a few exceptions to this rule, including Lawrence Gellert and John and Alan Lomax.[1] John Lomax and his son traveled through the South and Southwest, carrying a new recording machine issued by the Library of Congress, collecting versions of Stagolee and other songs in small towns, on farms, and in prisons. During this time, most black men in these regions were either in prison or eking out livings as sharecroppers.

By the early 1930s the country was sunk in the Great Depression. The young Richard Wright had just made it out of the South to Chicago and begun work on two novels and some short stories. By the end of the decade he had produced *Uncle Tom's Children* (1938) and *Native Son* (1938), both of them informed by the rural folklore he had imbibed during his Mississippi upbringing. For some black Americans, the New Deal had offered a ray of hope, but most remained mired in joblessness, poverty, and day-to-day racial harassment.

Late in the summer of 1934 the Lomaxes arrived at the Smithers Plantation in the Trinity River Bottoms near Huntsville, Texas.[2] They had contacted the plantation manager and explained that they were looking for "made-up," improvised songs, in contrast to "recorded music and . . . written-out songs."

The manager called in one of the black sharecroppers, "a stalwart fellow who went by the name of 'One-Eye Charley.'" While One-Eye stood just inside the door, his body taut as if he were ready to run and could scarcely control himself, sweating in an extremity of fear and embarrassment, the manager said, "One-Eye, these gentlemen want to hear some real, old-time nigger singin', not hymns, but some of the songs that you've sort of made up out in the field, choppin' cotton or plowin' with the mules."

The black man had strained his head up and away from the Lomaxes until it was impossible to catch his eye. John Lomax could see, through his patched and tattered shirt, the sweat bursting out and streaming down his chest.

"I ain't no kind of a songster myself, boss. 'Coase I do hum dese here sanctified hymns sometimes, but I'se a member of de chu'ch an' I done clean forgot all de wor'ly songs I ever knowed. Now over on de Blanton plantation, 'bout fo' mile down de road, dey used to be an old feller, name of Patterin', what could sho'ly pick a geetar an' sing dem made-up, 'sinful' songs you talkin' 'bout. He de man you ought to see. 'Coase, he might be daid; I ain't been over dere for a year or two."

The "sinful" songs that One-Eye distinguished from the "sanctified hymns" he sang in church were from the unofficial culture, and thus taboo under Jim Crow.

The sharecropper then "turned and started out," but the manager knew his man. "Wait a minute," he called out to him. "You lying black rascal you. You can sing an' you know it. These gentlemen have got a machine to make a record of your voice if you can sing them one of your made-up songs."

This prospect apparently interested One-Eye, who replied, "A recort like what you buy in de sto' in Huntsville?"

The magic of the recording machine drew a large part of the black community that evening. "When darkness had come up out of the bottom and settled over the whole plantation," John Lomax later wrote, "we lighted a little kerosene lamp inside the schoolhouse and found that the room was full of Negroes—old men peering at us out of the dim eyes; young men, hats cocked at a rakish angle, red bandannas high about their throats, sitting off away from the women; with babies; big-eyed children; young men, with their backs to the men, giggling." With the "embarrassment that is usual to a ballad-hunter when he breaks the ice," Lomax got up and asked if anybody could sing "Stagolee."

One man, called Blue, arose after someone in the crowd introduced him as "knowing mo' 'bout Stagolee dan ole Stag do hissef."

"Can you sing 'Stagolee'?" asked Lomax.

"Yessah, I knows old Stagolee, an' I'll sing it fuh you, ef you 'low me to sing 'nuther song fust."

"Is it a made-up song?" This question came from the plantation manager, who had accompanied the Lomaxes.

Blue replied, "Well, I reckon 'tis. Didn't I make it up dis aftahnoon in de fiel, special foh dese gen'lmuns? I reckon it's 'bout the made-up in es' song dey is. Turn on yo' machine, young mistah, 'cause I ain't gwine sing it but one time an' I want to git on yo' recort."

Although they recorded songs all evening, the Lomaxes were unable to get anybody to sing "Stagolee." They concluded that people hadn't wanted to sing it because the song was considered too "sinful."

After this experience the Lomaxes headed "straight for New Orleans, where we knew vice of all sorts flourishes, and where, accordingly, we hoped to record the songs and ballads that the country Negro was so reluctant to sing for us." Like many whites who visited the slums, they took a "brace of city detectives" with them to the dives and joints of New Orleans. But every time they entered a beer parlor, "a constrained silence would fall on the assembled men and women; and not long after, we four, with the bartender, would be the only ones left in the silent hall."

When Alan Lomax went back alone to one of these places the next morning, a peg-legged man came up to him and said: "Was you de jemmun huntin' foh songsters here las' night? You know when I see you come in wid de law, I didn't know how to trus' you— I been arrested once befo' an' sent to de pen when I hadn' been doin' nothin'."

Incredibly, the Lomaxes hadn't realized that blacks were not going to volunteer any information so long as there was a policeman or any other white authority figure present. Having failed with the police escort, Alan Lomax persuaded a pimp to lead him into the nightlife. While Lomax was paying the bill for his guide's losses at pool, he heard "a piano tinkling" in a "dim-lit, dirty room." Entering the room, he "saw a buck Negro playing; around him in various drunken attitudes some ten or fifteen Negro men and women. For the hundredth time I asked the question: 'Do you know the song about that bad man Stagolee?'"

This time Lomax was in luck. The pianist, who was "very young and very tight," said, "Wid a little mo' gin in me, I kin remember ev'ything that Stack did and make up some mo'. But what you want to hear dat song fer?"

Lomax told him that he was just interested in "old-timey songs," that he was collecting them, and that he wanted to put the pianist down on record. He showed him the typewriter he'd brought with him.

"Well," he said, "dat's diffunt. Yo makes a recort and we splits de profit. O.K., Jake, bring me some mo' gin. Dis white frien' of mine gonna pay de bill." After ordering a bottle, which he passed around to two girlfriends, the pianist sang a version of Stagolee.

> Stagolee he was a bad man, ev'body know
> He toted a stack-barreled blow-gun an' a blue-steel forty-fo'.
> Way down in New Orleans, dey call it de Lyon club,
> Ev'y step you walk in, you walkin' in Billy Lyon blood.

Not surprisingly, this retelling replaced St. Louis with New Orleans and St. Louis's Market Street with the local Rampart Street:

> "I go down to Rampart Street,
> I walk through water and mud and come to the Bucket of Blood."
> He shot him three times in de forehead an' two times in de side.
> Say "I'm gonna keep on shootin' till Billy Lyon die."
> Billy Lyon got glassy eye an' he gasp an' hung he head.
> Stack say, "I know by expression on his face dat Billy Lyon dead."
> Stack tole Mrs. Billy, "Ef you don' believe yo' man is dead,
> Come up to de bar-room an' see da hole I shot in his head."

As he described the quarrel between Billy Lyons and Stagolee, the singer began to fight with some other people in the room. When a drunken woman pushed him, he rose from the piano and shouted, "Goddam, let's git outta dis joint. Come on, white folks. I take you to a place where I got a friend that'll treat me right."

After driving through the back alleys of New Orleans, the singer and Lomax found "a narrow room, containing one battered piano, one feeble kerosene lamp high up on the wall, and a crowd of Negro men and women. We set at once to work, I on a milk-crate with my typewriter on my knees, my singer thumping the piano. The lamp had been brought down so that I could see my machine. The people in the place were crowded in a tight semicircle around me, looking over my shoulders." Soon the pianist crooned:

> Chief tol' his deputies, "Git yo rifles an' come wid me;
> We got to arres' dat bad nigger Stagolee."
> De deputies took dey shiny badges, an' dey laid 'em on de she'f.
> "Ef you wants dat nigger, go git him by yo own damn se'f."
> Chief Maloney say to de bartender, "Who kin dat drunk man be?"
> "Speak sof'ly," say de bartender, "it's dat bad man Stagolee."
> Chief Maloney touch Stack on the shoulder, say "Stack, why don't you run?"
> "I don't run, white folk, when I got my forty-one."

But Lomax didn't have time to finish writing the song down. At that point a man grabbed the lamp, put it back on its hook, and told them to get out.

By half past three that morning, they found a quiet house with a piano and "sent po' Stack to hell, after he had been shot eight times and hanged," thus:

> He had a three-hundred dollar fun'el an' a thousand dollar hearse,
> Satisfaction undertaker put him six feet in the earth.
> De Devil's little children went sc'amblin' up de wall,
> Saying, "Save us, papa, 'er Stack will kill us all."

As in the Faust myth, Stagolee makes a deal with the devil, selling his soul in return for luck at the gambling tables. The devil also grants him protection from the police so long as Stack wears his Stetsons. According to Onah Spencer, "Satan heard about Stack's weakness for Stetson hats, so he coaxed him into trading his soul, promising him he could do all kinds of magic and devilish things as long as he wore that oxblood Stetson."[3] In the classic legend of Faust, the man who sells his soul is subdued and victimized by the devil. But in the black versions of this myth, Stack victimizes the devil and takes over his territory.

> Stackolee took his big pistol an put it on de shelf
> Took de pitchfork from de devil an' say "I'm put in charge of hell myself.
> Stackolee (say), "Now, now Mr. Devil, if me an you have fun.
> You play the cornet, Black Betty beat de drum."[4]

Long before Robert Johnson sang "Me and the Devil Blues," blacks had called the blues "devil's music."[5] Many blacks didn't want to sing the blues because of this association. Eventually, to record "authentic" versions of Stagolee, the Lomaxes went to the prisons.

20

Stagolee in a World Full of Trouble

To help her friend John Lomax out in the 1930s, Ruby Pickens Tartt went looking for Jesse Harris, a singer and accordion player, blind from birth, who traveled through the southern countryside. She finally found him in a field near Shuqualac, Mississipi, sitting in the sun on the front porch of his tiny cabin. When Ruby told him that she had come to hear him play, he shuffled inside, brought out his "macordium," and unselfconsciously began to play and sing about Stagolee.[1]

On "that dark, stormy night" Billy and Stagolee had that "noble fight,"

> Stagolee says to Billy Lyons, "Come and drink with me.
> I'm in a world full of trouble and I'm out on a drinking spree."[2]

In the 1930s and 1940s the Lomaxes found this "world full of trouble" in the "Negro prison farms of the South," where they went hoping to "find that the Negro, away from the pressure of the churchly community, ignorant of the uplifting educational movement, having none but official contact with white men, dependent on the resources of his own group for amusement, and hearing no canned music, would have preserved and increased his heritage of secular folk-music."[3] Alan Lomax wrote about these experiences in the liner notes to a 1957 record album of prison songs.[4]

At Mississippi's Parchman Farm the Lomaxes gained a rare view inside a system that was "worse than slavery." Parchman Farm was simply a cotton plantation using convicts as labor. Like most southern prison farms, it perpetuated southern attitudes and traditions dating from the period of slavery. From the 1870s until the 1920s many southern states leased convicts, most of them black, to private companies. These convicts performed such heavy labor as timbering, turpentine extraction, mining, railroad work, and industrial farming, with no concern given to their safety, health, shelter, or clothing. Starved, half-clothed prisoners were forced to work from "can't see in the morning to can't see at night." Their sentences were never completed; the men were simply worked to death.[5]

Parchman Farm was built in 1904. It covered forty-six square miles. By 1915 the self-sufficient prison plantation was turning a profit for the state. In a history of the prison farm system, David Oshinsky wrote that Parchman "was divided into fifteen camps, each surrounded by barbed wire and positioned at least a half-mile apart." Though segregated by race and sex, the camps were not divided according to age and type of crime. "First offenders were caged with incorrigibles, and adults with juveniles, some as young as twelve and thirteen. Feeble-minded men were thrown in with ax-murderers."[6]

Much as in the levee camps decades earlier, each field camp had a sergeant, or overseer, and two assistant sergeants, or "drivers," supervising more than a hundred inmates. Parchman used the "trusty system," in which about 20 percent of "selected inmates, called trusty-shooters, watched over the regular convicts (known as gunmen, because they toiled under the guns of the trusties) . . . the trusty-shooters lived apart from the gunmen, wore vertical stripes instead of horizontal ones, and carried .30-.30 Winchesters on the job."[7]

The division between the two black male groups was strictly maintained: the shooters never talked to the gunmen to tell them how fast or how slowly to work. A driver on a mule did that. And in the fields one of the gunmen served as a caller, controlling the pace by shouting work chants, thus sustaining a practice that had been common in West Africa and in the antebellum American South.

The men rose before dawn and ran all the way to the fields, sometimes a distance of several miles, with their guards galloping along behind them on horseback. According to Alan Lomax, "The swiftest workers headed each gang, and the others were compelled to keep pace with them. Anyone who did not keep up or who objected was subject to severe punishment. I saw men who had worked so long and hard that their feet had turned into masses of pulpy bones."[8]

"The men worked to the caller's chanting tempo, the whole line moving as one," wrote Oshinsky. "The caller would sing his verse; a mighty chorus would respond. The power of that sound, said a visitor to Parchman, 'could almost take you off your feet.'" He also noted that the callers had nicknames describing their looks, their whereabouts, and the crimes that had put them away: "There were 'Fat Heat' and 'Bootmouth,' 'Burndown' (an arsonist), and '22' (serving twenty-two years)." This traditional use of nicknames has persisted through Lee Shelton's use of "Stack Lee" to today's rap musicians.[9]

The Lomaxes began collecting prison work songs in 1934. They found very few that could be dated back to slavery. What they found instead was a new musical genre and a repertoire that voiced the feelings and fantasies of the inmates and spoke tragically and ironically of the brutal conditions in the prisons. In every prison they visited, at least one work song was about Stagolee. Like the riverboat roustabouts decades earlier, the prisoners sang about Stagolee and the devil, who was a white man.

As Bruce Jackson notes about his own collection of Texas prison songs, the function of the work songs in the southern prison system was "to pace the men who hoed and chopped, to mediate between the strong and the weak, to pacify the prison bosses, to amuse, console, and dignify the men who worked every day from sun up to sun down under the eyes of armed guards." In every case, "The subject has to do with making it in Hell. The songs are sung outdoors. They are sung in daylight only. They do not exist in the dark. But it is darkness or absence or lostness or vacancy or deprivation that they are about."[10]

In 1947 Alan Lomax went back to Parchman with better equipment and recorded a caller named Bama, who had been a close friend of John Lomax for many years. Bama not only gave him a long work-song version of Stagolee but also explained the function of the caller. The quality or strength of the man's voice was unimportant. "It take the man with the most experience . . . to make the best leader in anything. You see, if you'd bring a brand new man here, if he had a voice where he could sing just like Peter could preach, and he didn't know what to sing about, well, he wouldn't do no good, see." The best singer would be someone one who could tie the themes of the songs to the workers' experience of the penal system. "Here's a fellow, he, maybe he ain't got no voice fer singin', but he been cooperating with the peoples so long an' been on the job so long till he know just exactly how it should go. And if he can just mostly talk it—why, and you understand how to work—well, it would go good with you."

"You mean the leader has to know about the timing?" Lomax asked.

"Yassuh. That's what it takes, the time that's all it is. You can just whistle and, if you know the time and can stay in time with the axes, you can whistle and do—cut just as good as you can if you were singin'. But you have to be done experienced."[11]

Bama's long version of the Stagolee ballad is a simple eight-bar blues. It is an obvious work song: each line ends with a "hunh!" as the worker brings his ax down. It begins with the traditional core stanzas:

Stackerlee, he was a bad man,
He wanted the whole round world to know,
He toted 32-20, and a smokeless 44.

Now Stackerlee, Lord, and Billy Lyons,
They was gamblin' early one day.
Stackerlee lost his money,
And he throwed the cards away.[12]

Bama did not, however, include the stanza that refers to the sheriff's being afraid to arrest him:

And them deputies took their pistols,
And they laid them on the shelf.
"If you want old Stackerlee,
Go arrest him by your own damn self."

This stanza was usually a favorite; according to Bruce Jackson, "Everywhere the singers seemed to relish the tale of an African American who killed for the joy of it and was so dangerous that even the police feared him."[13] Bama may have omitted it because he was singing the song in prison, a setting that demonstrated beyond doubt that there was no black man whom white men feared to arrest.

Stagolee often concludes with the hero's descent into hell, where he throws out the devil and takes charge himself. But Bama substituted some lines of his own devising:

Alberta, Lord, Alberta,
Baby don't you hear me callin' you?
But you three time seven, Alberta,
And you know what you want me to do.
I'm gonna call up the undertaker,
Lord, I'm gonna call up Mister Morgue,
What will Alberta's funeral cost?

Lomax commented on this change, noting that Bama, "who was a person of untrammeled imagination, here turns his aggressive fantasy on a girl who is resisting him. Laughing as he sings, he finishes his version with three violent and extravagant verses."[14] Once again the performer used the clichés of the bad man to express his own feelings.

In a version the Lomaxes collected from an unidentified convict in Arkansas, the sergeant kills Stagolee. Then comes a description of the funeral and its aftermath:

> The women come dressed in pink and they come dressed in red
> So glad to hear that bad man Stagolee was dead.
> They bought him a thousand-dollar casket and a million-dollar hearse
> And they lowered Stagolee six feet in the earth.
> They drove that poor boy up and down Murray Street.
> He was bloody from his head to his feet.
> The devil heard a rumbling. "I wonder who could it be?"
> I wouldn't talk back to the devil like that bad man Stagolee.
> "Come on, Stack boy, sit down on my knee.
> You too bad for the other world, but you're just right for me."[15]

For black men in a system "worse than slavery" a face-to-face conversation with the devil presented no threat; indeed, it offered a promise of salvation, or at least escape through death.

In another sense, a kind of inversion of the idea of the devil as a white man, the devil in hell represents a positive and procreative victory over the oppressive prison system. The Russian scholar Mikhail Bakhtin describes hell in the work of the Renaissance writer Rabelais as a "joyous recreation." "Carnival's hell," he wrote, "represents the earth which swallows up and gives birth: it is often transformed into a cornucopia; the monster, death, becomes pregnant."[16]

Given the conditions in which black Americans lived under Jim Crow, both inside and outside prisons, it is not surprising that the "Devil came to represent to the black culture not the perpetrator of original sin but a hero in evil, a Good/Bad figure."[17] Thus the black oral culture fused the two apparently contradictory notions of the devil as a white man and the devil as a "'bad nigger,' the free and independent black man who brought fear to the white culture through threat of physical and/or psychological violence." Associated with such men and their world was "devil music," the "good-time music that existed outside the church."[18] Significantly, in the white versions of Stagolee, the hero doesn't go to hell.

In most versions, Stagolee meets the devil after dying at the hands of white authorities or a member of Billy Lyons' family. But in a handful of versions Stagolee argues with the devil over his soul while still in his jail cell. In these there is no mention of Billy Lyons; instead, the devil becomes Stagolee's adversary. There may be a historical precedent for this motif. Folklorist Mary Wheeler, who researched Stagolee songs on the riverboats, reported a memory about a black man called Devil Winston who killed his wife with a razor and stuffed her remains in a suitcase. When the police apprehended him, he admitted to the crime. While Winston was in jail he became a preacher, seeking to convert other prisoners.[19] This may have been the source of the scene depicting the devil arguing with Stagolee in jail.

In the Jim Crow South, black Americans, and especially black men, lived in the straitjacket of a dual sense of guilt, imposed both by whites' racial hatred and discrimination, which denied them access to employment, and by being labeled criminals when, as a result, they were jailed for vagrancy. It was a condition from which there seemed no escape. This is the meaning of the lines "I'm in a world full of trouble."

In May 1936 an inmate at Florida's Raiford State Prison named Verna Flynn sang a version of Stagolee for John Lomax. Like most women in prison then, she may have been convicted of prostitution. Her version, like Bama's at Parchman years later, breaks into the traditional narrative with a plea for help that is clearly personal. She cries out to Stagolee to get her out of jail. In the first part of the song, Stagolee's adversary is again the devil:

> Stagolee told the devil
> Why don't you come and visit me
> I['m] in a world of trouble and I'm on my drinking spree.
> You can shoot me, you can try me, you can drive me from your do'
> Somebody got my gal and I hate to see her go
> Stagolee Ah, Stagolee, don't you hear me callin you?
> I'm in a world of trouble, tell me what you gonna do
> Don't the hearse look lonesome rolling up to your do'.[20]

"I'm in a world of trouble" would have conveyed to any black living in the South in the 1930s that the speaker was in jail.

21

From Rhythm and Blues to Rock and Roll: "I Heard My Bulldog Bark"

During the 1940s and 1950s, as in other decades, Stagolee existed in multiple forms. Sidney Bechet's 1950 jazz rendering of "Old Stack O' Lee Blues" is the most beautiful instrumental version ever recorded. Bechet's clarinet is like the lead singer on the work gang, wordlessly calling all the bluesy chorus into action. But the melody and the phrasing and tempo evoke the bordello, not the work gang. Bechet's version harkens back to the early jazz of New Orleans, of which he was a founding father.[1]

As the blues evolved into rhythm and blues from the 1930s through the early 1950s, and then crossed over into the white culture as rock and roll, Stagolee kept pace with the trends. There were three significant recordings of Stagolee during this period: a "good-feeling" version by Lucious Curtis and Willie Ford in 1940, a brilliant piano rhythm-and-blues version by Archibald Cox in 1950, and a 1959 version by Lloyd Price that became a rock-and-roll hit.[2]

Lucious Curtis was working in a Natchez, Mississippi, sawmill when John Lomax encountered him on October 19, 1940. With his partner Willie Ford, Curtis gave Lomax a happy, irresistibly danceable Stagolee.[3] According to Alan Lomax, both the melody and the traditional folk two-line stanzas "link his version to several others

172

later recorded by New Orleans pianists."[4] The first stanza has an eyewitness immediacy:

> It was late last night, I heard my bulldog bark.
> Stagolee and Billy Lyons, they was arguing in the dark.

Curtis then presents the devil theme:

> Stagolee, he told the devil, "Come on, let's have some fun.
> You get your pitchfork, I'm gonna get my forty-one."

He then returns to the "bad man" theme:

> Stagolee, he was a bad man; now boys, you don't know.
> Stagolee, he will get you, wherever you may go.

Next comes an eyewitness stanza about Stagolee and his "girls"— "girls" who may have been prostitutes:

> Now look, last night I was standing here when he come.
> He told his girls, "Come on, let's have some fun."

But Stagolee at once leaves his girls and runs to his mother with an odd "bad man" announcement:

> Stagolee went running to his mother, holding up his right hand.
> Said, "Looky here, mother, I got to kill me another man."

The scene shifts again, like a cut in a movie:

> Stagolee, he was a bad man, and he didn't live in town.
> Stagolee had a good woman, didn't 'low nobody 'round.

The final stanza celebrates Stagolee with a rhythm-and-blues beat:

> Come on now, people, let's go out to Stagolee's home.
> If you start this thing, I sure ain't gonna be here long.

Both Archibald Cox and Lloyd Price were influenced by big bands called "southwestern shouters." According to Leroi Jones (Imamu Amiri Baraka), the "Southwestern 'shouters' and big blues bands had a large influence on Negro music everywhere. The shouter gave impetus to a kind of blues that developed around the cities in the late thirties called 'rhythm & blues,' which was largely huge rhythm units smashing away behind screaming blues singers. The singers and their groups identified completely with performance, but they still had very legitimate connections with older blues forms."[5] Thus the function of the work-gang caller seems to have made its way beyond the barbed wire and into the black urban musical culture that thrived after World War II, when blacks' participation in the white "artistic" music world was still limited. In the still-segregated black community one could relax, let one's hair down, so to speak, and "shake that thing."

Archibald Cox, who played piano around New Orleans during the late 1940s and early 1950s, was born Leon T. Gross in 1912 in New Orleans. When he started playing at fraternity houses and wild parties in the 1930s, he was known as "Archie boy." He was significantly influenced by Burnell Santiago, the self-styled "King of Boogie," as well as by pianists such as Eileen Dufeau and Miss Isobel. According to music critic John Broven, a man named Stack-O-Lee taught him to play piano. After serving in the army during the war, Cox returned to New Orleans and was signed in 1950 by Al Young, the talent scout for Imperial Records. That year he recorded "Stackerlee," his first record and his only big hit. It held second place in the rhythm-and-blues charts for a year.[6]

According to Broven, Cox's "Stackerlee" "is one of the longest and most complete versions on record," probably because it was "performed in a black environment, where the audience's expectations of the narrative would have been different [from] those of

[an] audience in a white setting." The recording filled two sides of a disk, allowing Cox "plenty of scope to perform this old folk song."[7] A black audience would already have known long versions of the Stagolee narrative about the world of "sports" and pimps. This background undoubtedly helped structure Cox's interpretation of the narrative.

In 1970 Broven met Cox at a small party at his wooden one-story home on Fourth Street and made another recording of "Stackerlee." "He was suspicious," Broven reports, "but after passing a bottle of whiskey his confidence improved and he sat down at his battered piano and proceeded to give as good a show as one could wish for."[8]

On the piano, Cox's left hand brings up a wall of loud, rhythmically precise bass chords. His right hand improvises lucidly, leaping out of and then returning to the fixed rhythms of the upbeat tempo, as he sings:

I was standing on the corner
When I heard my bulldog bark
He was barking at two men
Who gambled in the dark
It was Staggerlee and Billy
Two men who gambled late
Staggerlee threw seven,
Billy swore that he threw eight
Staggerlee told Billy
I can't leave you go with that
You done won all my money
And my brand new Stetson hat!
Staggerlee went down that lonesome railroad track
I won't kill you but you better not be here when I get back!

Cox narrates the action from the viewpoint of a bystander, presenting Stagolee as an attractive gangster with mythic traits. In this he extends the griot tradition of singing praise of dead ancestors.

A younger musician, Lloyd Price, born in New Orleans in 1933, combined several careers: pianist, songwriter, record producer, club owner, and talent agent. Shortly after recording his first hit, "Lawdy Miss Clawdy," in 1952, he was drafted into the army. When he returned to New Orleans in 1956 and resumed playing rhythm and blues, his manager, Art Rupe, was busy with a new discovery, Little Richard. Price joined ABC's Paramount and recorded "Stagger Lee" early in 1959.[9] The song became a number-one hit.

Price's version is a work of sophisticated artifice compared with Cox's, and it presents only the core episode of the killing of Billy Lyons. A chorus offers encouragement with "Go, Stag, Go!" This chorus may have been added to compensate for the absence of a live black audience. John Broven didn't like the "female chorus with their machine-gun-like over dubbed shouts of 'dada dada'": he found it "horrible."[10] Even so, Robin D. G. Kelley calls "Stagger Lee" "the classic black baaadman narrative."[11]

Here is Price's recorded rendition. The cadenced beginning brilliantly anticipates the narrative line.

> The night was clear and the moon was yellow,
> And the leaves came tumbling down.
>
> I was standin' on the corner when I heard my bulldog bark.
> He was barkin' at the two men who were gamblin' in the dark.
> It was Stagger Lee and Billy, two men who gambled late.
> Stagger Lee threw seven, Billy swore that he threw eight.
>
> Stagger Lee told Billy, "I can't let you go with that.
> You have won all my money and my brand new Stetson hat."

Stagger Lee started off goin' down that railroad track.
He said, "I can't get you, Billy, but don't be here when I come
back."

Stagger Lee went home and he got his forty-four
Said, "I'm goin' to the barroom just to pay that debt I owe."
Stagger Lee went to the barroom and he stood across the barroom
door
He said, "Nobody move," and he pulled his forty-four.

Stagger Lee shot Billy, oh he shot that poor boy so bad
Till the bullet came through Billy and it broke the bartender's
glass.[12]

Cox accused Price of ripping him off, and in fact both the lyrics
and the music are very similar. But Price's white audience made his
rendition a rock-and-roll hit.

22

The Toast: Bad Black Hero of the Black Revolution

As the grip of Jim Crow began to loosen during the
late 1950s and early 1960s, the "white only" signs that had been
posted on all public facilities throughout the South gradually dis-
appeared, partly as a result of sit-ins by black and white students.
Uncle Lindsey, who had taught me Stagolee, never lived to see the
new days. I received the news of his death while I was a student at

Agricultural and Technical College in Greensboro, South Carolina, where I demonstrated against segregated lunch counters. An automobile driven by the young white son of the justice of the peace in our small town had killed him.

During the early 1960s, Stagolee finally became fully visible. Black musicians such as James Brown, Wilson Pickett, and the Isley Brothers recorded versions of Stagolee that expressed a newly acquired sense of power among black males. At the same time, in the black inner-city culture, a form of storytelling called the "toast," which had probably been around for several decades, became far more popular. Young black men began telling the story of Stagolee without musical accompaniment. In reciting the Stagolee toast, the speaker "performed" Stagolee, taking on the hero's character along with the role. The toast became an instrument enabling young black men to assert themselves as bullies and bad men, and thus to be powerful and charismatic.[1]

A toast is a narrative, two to ten minutes long, in rhyming couplets. It is organized around the line, the couplet, and the themes, or episodes. The line has four strong stresses. The narrator identifies with the hero and pretends that the hero's deeds are his own. It is a form of boast. In this regard, the toast looks back to the ballad and forward to rap music.

This Stagolee toast begins:

> Back in '32 when times was hard
> I had a sawed-off shotgun and a crooked deck of cards
> Pin-striped suit, fucked-up hat
> T-model Ford, didn't even have a payment on that
> Had a cute little broad, she throwed me out in the cold
> I asked her why, she said, Our love is growing old

So I packed all my little rags, took a walk down Rampart Street
That's where all the bad motherfuckers went down to meet
I walked through water and I waded through mud
Come to a little hole-in-the-wall, they call the "Bucket of Blood."[2]

Next come several lines on the theme of "Don't you know who I am?"[3] This is an African-American insult ritual designed to tell the other person who he is in relationship to the speaker. It is the way of asserting one's rank and status in the male world, and hence in the black community. We have already seen these repudiations of authority and assertions of hostility and arrogance in the black roustabouts and the "trusties" on the Parchman prison farm.

Now Stagolee asks for something to eat:

I walked in and asked the bartender
Dig, Chief, can I get something to eat?
He threw me a stale glass of water
And flung me a fucked-up piece of meat
I said, Raise, motherfucker, do you know who I am?
He said, Frankly, motherfucker, I just don't give a damn

I knowed right then that chickenshit was dead
I threw a thirty-eight shell through his motherfucking head.

Now consider this toast, collected from a Negro prisoner in the Virginia state penitentiary on December 2, 1974. Like many of the tellers of Stagolee, he is nameless.

Stag come to a crib they call the Buck o' Blood
He called to the bartender for something to eat
Bartender gave 'im a muddy glass o' water and a stale piece o'
	meat

He say, Bartender, bartender, you don't realize who I am!

Bartender say, Frankly speaking, Mister, I don't give a good
goddamn

But just then (the bartender hadn't realized what he had said)

Stag had pumped two forty-five slugs in his motherfucking head.[4]

In this performance the teller gives the tale a chilling psychological turn, as the bartender realizes too late that he has said the
wrong thing to the wrong man. The power and flexibility of the
Stagolee toast are particularly evident here: a good teller can make
the incident play with the tensions of a movie scene.

In yet another performance of this crucial episode, it is Stagolee's
instinctive behavior that causes him to kill the bartender almost in-
advertently:

I asked the bartender for something to eat,

he give me a muddy glass a water and a fucked-up piece of meat.

I said, "Mister," I say, "you must not know who I am."

He say, "Frankly, son, I don't give a damn."

Before I realized what I had did,

I had shot him six times through his motherfucken head.[5]

The protagonist of the toast is invariably a "bad nigger." As a
"bad nigger," the toast hero is remorseless.

The toast differs from the ballad or blues tradition in introduc-
ing many more characters, especially the bartender. The bartender
is never friendly to Stagolee, and in the toast version it is the bartender, not Billy Lyons, who becomes Stagolee's first victim.

The bartender is the guardian of the threshold who is keeping
the intruder, the stranger, Stagolee, from entering the inner sanc-
tum. A bartender figured in performances of Stagolee as early as

1897; Will Starks, an informant interviewed by John Lomax in 1935, recalled that about 1914 he heard the lines "Stagolee shot Billy so bad / that he broke the bartender's glass." References to this poetic shard in so many toasts have helped preserve the family resemblance through the decades. The presence and role of the bartender in the folk culture map blacks' experience of continuing exclusion when they migrated to cities—in this case, St. Louis—during Reconstruction.

The toast also introduced a new relationship between Stagolee and Billy Lyons' mother. In "Stacklee in Hell," after Stagolee shoots "Lion" between the eyes, he goes to Billy's mother, "Sister Lou."

> The other night I thought I heard a dog bark,
> But that was Stackolee and Billy Lion gamblin' in the dark.
> Stackolee says, "Now, Billy Lion, you stay here in this shack,
>   and I don't want to see you move your motherfucken ass till I get
>   back."
> Stackolee went home and got two smokin' forty-fives,
> he came back and placed 'em between Billy Lion's eyes.
> Billy Lion said, "Oh, Stackolee, don't take my life.
> I got four cross-eyed kids and a cripple-assed wife."
> He said, "I don't want your four cross-eyed kids or your cripple-
>   assed wife,"
> Said, "All I want's your cocksucken life."
> Shot him five times right through the head,
> Left him on the floor quivering till he's dead.
> Then he went and told Sister Lou just what he'd done,
> Said, "Say, Sister Lou, I just killed your no-'count cocksucken
>   son."
> She said, "Well, Stackolee, you know that's not true.

Hell, you and Billy been friends for a year or two."
He said, "Look, bitch, if you don't think he's dead,
Go down and count those five fucken holes I just put in his
head."[6]

In this version, Sister Lou takes revenge, much as we can imagine
Marie Brown, Billy Lyons' mother, would have wanted to.

Stackolee went walkin' down the track
And Sister Lou snuck up behind him and shot him in the back.
He shit, farted, stumbled, fell on his face
Right down in front of Joe's place.
Stackolee's wife come runnin' out the door hollerin'
"Stackolee, Stackolee! Somebody killed my Stackolee."
He rolled over and said, "Look, bitch, when I die don't dress me in
black,
'Cause if hell don't suit me I'm comin' back."

The toast form allows the speaker to add other episodes, and
here is an example. We have already encountered the devil motif in
the ballads collected from the prisons during the 1930s. Now those
motifs are thrown into the toasts:

There was a rumble in the earth and a roar in the ground,
That was Stackolee changin' hell around.
He said, "I want tables over here and the chairs over there,
And don't a motherfucker move while I comb my hair."
The devil said, "Look, Stackolee, I heard you's a pretty bad man in
that upper land,
But you know you're down here and met another bad man."
Said, "Okay, Devil, you get your pitchfork and let me get two
smokin' forty-ones,

And us two bad motherfuckers'll have us some fun."
The Devil got his pitchfork and Stackolee got two smokin' forty-
    ones,
And those two bad sonofabitches did have some fun.
Stackolee shot the devil right through the heart
And he lit up like a human torch.

The toasts allow room for the bawdy scenes that had always been a property of barroom ballads:

Caught the old lady bent over shovelin' coal,
Put twelve inches up her hole.
Four little devils runnin' around,
Hollerin, "Mother, mother, stop him 'fore he fucks us all."
Well he fucked St. Peter and he fucked St. Paul,
He'll be a fuckin' motherfucker ['til] the roll is called.

By highlighting the performative role of the first-person speaker (as opposed to a singer), the toast set the stage for the appearance of rap music in 1980 with the release of the Sugar Hill Gang's "Rapper's Delight" and Grandmaster Flash's "The Message." Shedding its musical line, Stagolee became the basic form used by the first hip-hoppers. During the 1980s, the first rhymers of rap took Stagolee to a new level, using its framework for their own personal narratives.

23

Folklore/Poplore: Bob Dylan's Stagolee

As part of the folk revival movement of the late 1950s, two excellent white singers, Tom Rush and Dave Van Ronk, sang versions of Stagolee. Rush, a middle-class youngster with an Ivy League education, recorded "Stackerlee" in 1959. Van Ronk, who had worked as a merchant marine, sang versions of the ballad with several New Orleans bands before turning up in New York's Greenwich Village and recording "Stackalee" in 1962.[1] In 1959 Harry Oster recorded a folklore version called "Stagolee" in the Angola State Penitentiary in Louisiana, performed by Hogman Maxey.[2]

About a hundred years after Stagolee was first sung as a ballad in a St. Louis Negro saloon, Bob Dylan recorded Frank Hutchinson's version of "Stack A Lee" in a New York City studio. The production values of the album, *World Gone Wrong*, are poor, and when critics collect Dylan's lyrics, they seldom mention "Stack A Lee." Yet it is one of the most interesting songs Dylan has sung in his long career.

On a dark night in an alley
Billy Lyons and Stack A Lee had a terrible fight
All about that John B Stetson hat.
Stack A Lee went into the bar, ordered a beer

184

Turned around and saw Billy Lyons
Look around and saw Billy, "What are you doin' here?"[3]

Stagolee accuses Billy of stealing his Stetson hat, and Billy Lyons
begs for his life, referring to his three children. Then

Stack A Lee shot him Billy Lyons, shot him right through the
head
Only took one shot to kill him dead

Stagolee is "on the gallows, about to hang," yet in the final stanza
the incorrigible escapes punishment, returning to our midst:

In an alley, about an hour ago
He's a bad man, they let him right back again.

In the liner notes, Dylan elaborates: "Stack's in a cell, no wall
phone. He is not some egotistical degraded existentialist Dionysian
idiot, neither does he represent any alternative lifestyle scam (give
me a thousand acres of tractable land & all the gang members that
exit & and you'll see the Authentic alternative lifestyle, the Agrarian
one)."

Is this recording an African-American song? Is it a white version
of an African-American song? Critics and scholars are not quite
sure what to call a performer who is not himself a member of the
group whose songs he sings. Is he merely an entertainer? Does Bob
Dylan express Stagolee for whites? For blacks?

W. T. Lhamon Jr. places Dylan's "Stack A Lee" in the blackface
tradition. He maintains that Dylan's "insistent recordings during
the 1990s of extraordinary old songs from that muddy terrain between folk and pop—'Delia,' 'Stack A Lee'—show how much the
weight presses on contemporary repertoires, but lurks mostly un-

acknowledged by either those who perform or those who listen."⁴ In Lhamon's view Bob Dylan is a link between low blues culture and the high culture—the kind of link that T. S. Eliot claimed to desire—and in his treatment of Stagolee Dylan mediates between black and white cultures.⁵

But tradition has another definition, one that implies the notion of balance between individual and collective expression. This notion of tradition reminds Eugene Bluestein of what Walt Whitman "liked to call the 'I and the en-masse.'" Bluestein calls this aspect of tradition "the imaginary anthropology . . . a state of nature [in which] the individual and the group were in perfect balance. But after the fall (due to varieties of original sinning) the balance is undone. We are left in our current state of disequilibrium, and tradition is the trace of that primitive movement."⁶ Modern thinkers overemphasize the "function of individualism" and "become victims of elitist arguments that overlook the continuing power of the folk imagination."⁷ But the American folk tradition does not involve the "submission" of individuals to culture; "rather, creative individuals use folk styles to make major changes in cultural materials."⁸ The development of Stagolee can be seen as an example of a folk tradition that depends on a balance between the individual and the group. Yet conservative folklorists do not recognize Stagolee as an important contribution to American folk music. And while rap music also depends on the creativity of the individual and the group, most white thinkers would not give it credit for creativity.⁹

If Stagolee cannot be African-American folklore, then what is it? What has happened to Stagolee as an oral performance? The cultural sites where Stagolee was performed—the riverboat gangplank, the levee camp, the road gangs, the prison work farms, the jook joint, all the places where field recordings were made—are gone. The conditions that produced the oral Stagolee are gone. Nevertheless, as we have seen, Stagolee survives into the twenty-first century not only as a Bob Dylan song but also in hip-hop and gangsta rap. Stagolee's insistence upon acknowledgment of his dignity, and his liquidation of those who insult him, survive in the hip-hop heroes.

Is Bob Dylan a folk artist or a popular entertainer? Eugene Bluestein argues that he is somewhere in between oral and electric culture. "Folklore means essentially oral narrative styles. Folklore is the deepest level of a people's culture." To characterize the use of folk oral forms in a more modern popular medium by performers like Dylan, Bluestein has come up with the term *poplore*. "If you listen to Dylan," Bluestein observes, "you realize that he has been listening to and using traditional material but in his own creative way. That's the big difference between folklore and poplore."[10] The performer no longer performs to an audience face to face; the message is copyrighted and produced for profit to a mass audience; yet that message may derive from or be closely tied to folklore.

Most people think of folklore as something antiquated and as having sprung from an anonymous group of people. Yet as we have seen, individuals with specific identities created the Stagolee folklore. And as Richard Bauman points out, in the past twenty years folklorists have tended "to turn away from viewing the folk as an 'anonymous collectivity' and to focus more on 'the individual performer.'"[11]

Alan Dundes has defined folk culture as "any group of people whatsoever who share at least one common factor. It does not matter what the linking factor is—it could be a common occupation, language, or religion—but what is important is that a group formed for whatever reason will have some traditions which it calls its own."[12] Bluestein adds the ingredient of creativity to Dundes' definition. Creativity, he argues, is what binds any group together. "Folk represents the way all ordinary people are creative—creative in pottery, in music, in song, and in dance," he told me in an interview. "Anyone who looks at American culture watches the way black people make up a dance every week. You know, if you live in a black area, you see new black dances every week. Black people come home every week with a new dance step. Pretty soon everyone is doing it. Black dances are created by the folk," he said, "but they are appropriated by whites." This creates a "terrible crazy paradox that people in America can't live without black music or black dance. They just don't want to live with black people."[13]

Taking Pete Seeger (and indirectly Woody Guthrie) as his role model, the young Bob Dylan lived a vagabond existence and steeped himself in black culture, mainly the blues culture. Dylan correctly saw the blues as expressing the perspective of poor blacks, and that out of their suffering they had forged an art form that could lift them out of their misery. Dylan saw that for African Americans, daily life was "transcended by an attitude of secret but ineradicable rebellion against [American] society." According to Maurice Capel, "it was this attitude that attracted Dylan to the blues."[14] Many of Dylan's own ballads were based on news accounts of black victims of racism.[15] In his attraction to outlaw ballads, whose heroes were marginal characters, Betsy Bowden perceives someone who sees himself as a hero "that American popular culture creates over and over—Stagolee, Billy the Kid, Capone, Bogart, Dylan."[16]

Dylan's identification with an outlaw figure resembles Walter Benjamin's flaneur, who is looking for hidden truths, the traces of an invisible world. Like the flaneur, Dylan seeks to express the viewpoint of silent, unnoticed victims.

In choosing Frank Hutchinson's version of Stagolee, Dylan identified himself with Hutchinson's musical heritage, both lyrically and musically, producing a kind of hillbilly blues. Like Hutchinson, Dylan learned the blues from black men and used it to say something about the society we live in, becoming in effect a white Negro. Like Hutchinson, Dylan seized on the implications of Stagolee's Stetson hat as a commodity capable of influencing events, even producing murder.

III

Mammy-Made: Stagolee and American Identity

24

The "Bad Nigger" Trope
in American Literature

"A gang of Negroes were laying a road south of Jackson, Mississippi. They were breaking rocks. Their picks clanged heavily, monotonously," begins a story written by a southerner in 1931, describing a gang of convicts working on a Mississippi road.[1]

"Then something happens," continues the story. "One of the Negroes suddenly breaks forth, rips open his shirt and bursts into a savage scream. He flings his muscular arms high above his upthrust head and utters a savage, booming cry.

"YOW-OW. YOW-OW-W-W."

The cry—a challenge and a prayer—splits open the sky. "Big Black was six feet and five inches tall. He was prodigiously, repulsively ugly . . . His shoulders and arms are gargantuan; his laugh is 'Rabelaisian.'"

When the convict gang retires after quitting time, Big Black wanders about the fields. Finding a young white girl bathing in a swamp river, he attacks her and then, disgusted with his actions, "throws the girl into the middle of the river and runs away. He realizes that the whites will be after him, and he jumps into the middle of the stream that takes him away."

The next time we see Big Black, he is laying road on another chain gang, this one in Savannah, Georgia. When he spits some tobacco onto a pile of rocks and sees the "brown stream of tobacco juice trickling over their white surface . . . a picture flashed sickeningly into his mind of a black hand . . . gripping the white face of a girl!" This memory of the rape causes him to tear "his blue shirt open to the waist, arch his huge black chest, fling his sweating arms above his head, and utter a savage, booming cry."

When Tennessee Williams wrote "Big Black: A Mississippi Idyll," he was only twenty years old. The story was never published during his lifetime, a fact that is a credit to his judgment. He must have known that a story about a black rapist was too stereotypical to publish. But although its subject matter is taboo, the story is well written. It shows, moreover, how deeply the "bad nigger" archetype had penetrated the white southern mentality and imagination.

Williams' handling of the details saves the story from being merely a pulp fiction about racial stereotypes. A good example is his passage about the effect of Big Black's song on the other convicts: it "knock[ed] them out of their torpor. It was a huge, towering cry, beginning upon a deep growling note and veering flame-like into an ululating peak, high enough and sharp enough, it seemed, to split open the sky."

This is accurately observed. Williams is describing the relationship between the lead caller on the chain gang and his fellow convicts. The caller's job is to get the other convicts singing and working. His cry and their song make the pains go away: "The aching of their backs and arms, the soreness of their feet, were less acute. Their miseries seemed to have found expression in Big Black's vast utterance and to be accordingly relieved. In a few moments they had caught up a song."

In Williams' story the black man is a rapist with animal lust for a white woman. His cry is a symbol of his inability to articulate his pain and desire.

The story fails when Williams attempts to imagine a black man's psychology. His description of Big Black's self-hatred is unconvincing: "His eyes fastened upon his Black Hand clasping the white, terrified face of the girl . . . He stared with fierce loathing at that black hand of his, and he muttered bitterly to himself. 'You big black devil! you big—black—devil!'"

For a convincing interpretation of a "bad nigger's" psychology, we had to wait for Richard Wright. Five years after Williams wrote his story, Wright published "Big Boy Leaves Home," a story with a similar theme. In Wright's story, four black boys, naked in a watering hole, are surprised by a white woman. In Wright's story as in Williams', black men and white women are contrasted sexually. However, in Williams' story the black man is a rapist, lusting after white flesh; in Wright's it is the white woman who lusts after the boys. She gazes at their nakedness, and when they try to cover themselves, she stands between them and their clothes.

Then the woman screams, and a white man comes with a gun. He kills two of the youngsters before Big Boy grabs the rifle from him. "The white man released the rifle, jerked Bobo to the ground, and began to batter the naked boy with his fists. Then Big Boy swung, striking the man in the mouth with the barrel . . . Breathing hard, the white man got up and faced Big Boy. 'Give me that gun, boy!' Big Boy leveled the rifle and backed way. The white man came at Big Boy. 'Ah'll kill you!' said Big Boy.'"[2]

In Big Boy, Wright may have created the first literary version of Stagolee. Big Boy grabs the gun from the white man and fights back. His own survival demands that he act as he does. This response was undoubtedly new to American readers; usually African Americans had been portrayed so sentimentally that there was no reason to associate them with real people. Unlike Williams' Big Black, who succumbs to the role and image assigned him by white society, Wright's Big Boy fights back and then escapes. Later, while waiting for his buddy Bobo to join him, he watches a mob lynch Bobo.

Both stories are about encounters between black men and white women at swimming holes. Since Williams' story was never published, it is doubtful that Wright read it. And since Wright's story was not published until 1936, it is doubtful that Williams was influenced by it. Rather, there is a common source for both stories: the oral folklore tradition of the "bad nigger."

Both Williams and Wright had access to the oral tradition. One of Williams' early nurses was a black woman who told him many folktales. He was so influenced by black speech that his mother was afraid he would go through life talking like a Negro.[3]

Richard Wright, James Baldwin, Ralph Ellison, and Ernest Gaines are only a few of the writers who have portrayed this "bad nigger" hero of oral folklore, but because of prevailing restrictions in publishing, they were not the first. The first published writers to use Negro folk elements were white.[4]

In his 1922 novel, *Rainbow Round My Shoulder,* the folklorist Howard Odum used a character called Stacker Lee and showed his long-held interest in black folk speech and dialects. His Stacker Lee thinks to himself, "One time I went to one dance, jes' meanness in me an' notin' else. I drunk jes' 'nough whisky to make me smell like I was dead drunk an' took thirty-eight special with me. Well, they had fine dance an' 'anjo music an' was going mighty fine. So I stalk right through room with gun I borrowed in my han', run right through middle of room, steppin' on folks' toes, hollerin' that I ain't gonna have no mo' playin' there that night, an' tellin' 'em they can put me out if they don't like it."[5]

White writers discovered that "the American Negro is rich in folk culture, and it is only natural that those who try to portray his life should make large use of the folk element."[6] But these early white writers did not recognize the profundity of the Stagolee myth, even when making allusions to him as the archetypal "bad nigger."

With the exception of Langston Hughes and Sterling Brown, black writers of the Harlem Renaissance did not use the "bad nigger" trope. Folklore, full of associations with ignorant, backward, superstitious ex-slaves, was an embarrassment to these writers from the aspiring middle class. And there is no "bad nigger" character in Zora Neale Hurston's fiction, although *Their Eyes Were Watching God* draws deeply on folklore. The closest she came to presenting a rebellious character was in "Mules and Men," a 1935 tale about a black man, High John De Conquer, who sells his soul to the devil. Not until years later would Margaret Walker write a poem about Stagolee. Here the voice is not that of an eyewitness, but of the community, at some distance in time:

> That Stagolee was an all-right lad
> Till he killed a cop and turned out bad,
> Though some do say to this very day
> He killed more'n one 'fore he killed that 'ofay.
> But anyhow the tale ain't new
> How Stagolee just up and slew
> A big policeman on 'leventh Street
> And all he knowed was tweet-tweet-tweet.
> Oh I 'speck he'd done some too bad dirt

Wid dat blade he wore underneaf his shirt
(And it ain't been said, but he coulda had
A dirk in his pocket 'cause he sho was bad.)
But one thing's certain and two things is sho
His bullets made holes no doc could cyo.
But the funniest thing about that job
Was he never got caught by no mob
And he missed the lynching meant for his hide
'Cause nobody knows how Stagolee died.
Bad man Stagolee ain't no mo
But his ghost still walks up and down the sho
Of Old Man River 'round New Orleans
With her gumbo, rice, and good red beans![7]

Walker presents Stagolee as a good boy who got into some trouble. The venue is different, and there is no reference to the traditional Stagolee as pimp, gambler, or cold-blooded murderer. But
the fact that Walker's Stagolee kills a policeman with a pocket knife
ties it in, at least indirectly, with the theme of police brutality.

If we compare Hull's traditional, oral Stagolee with Walker's literary version, the difference becomes clear. Although it was recorded in a studio (as a race record) in 1927, Hull's version is close
to one that was probably sung by wandering hoboes along the Mississippi levee. It makes concrete what life was like for blacks under
Jim Crow.

Stack O' Lee was a bully, he bullied all his life.
He bullied two, three coppers down
With a ten-cent pocket knife
Well, it's cruel Stack O' Lee.[8]

Stack O' Lee's strength lies in his ability to do the nearly impossible: he can take a pocket knife and keep three policemen away. He is a hero for many of the people who would like to do the same thing. Consequently, the stock phrase "cruel Stack O' Lee" (the apparent meaning) begins to take on a more implicit meaning: "courageous Stack O' Lee." People belonging to the culture of the black levee workers would have understood the intended and implicit meanings of this ballad in ways that Brooks's version cannot capture or convey.

In 1932 the poet and essayist Sterling Brown explored the devil motif in "The Devil and the Black Man."[9] The hero, Slim, is like Stagolee in every respect, and the episodes in Brown's poem are structurally similar to episodes from the oral tradition. Brown used traditional motifs to make the point that, because of racism, "hell" for the black lower classes was exactly where they were then living—in the Jim Crow South.

Brown's awareness of the Stagolee tradition is apparent, as when he has St. Peter send Slim down to hell.[10] In the folktale "Black Angel in Heaven," the angel is kicked out of heaven and given a parachute over Alabama. Similarly, Brown sends Slim to hell, where he sees many things that disillusion him about "them"—that is, whites.[11]

> Took him in a room
> Where Slim see De preacher wid a brownskin
> On each knee.
> Showed him giant stills,
> Goin' everywhere,
> Wid a passel of devils
> Stretched dead drunk there.

Den he took him to de furnace
Dat some devils was firin',
Hot as Hell, an' Slim start
A mean prespirin'.
Threw black devils on;
Slim thought he'd better
Be gittin' along.
An' he say—"Dis makes
Me think of home—
Vicksburg, Little Rock, Jackson,
Waco, and Rome."
Den de Devil gave Slim
De big Ha-Ha.
An' turned into a cracker,
Wid a sheriff's star.
Slim ran fo' his wings,
Lit out from de groun'
Hauled it back to Saint Peter,
Safety-boun'.

St. Peter puts Slim out of heaven because he is too stupid to know that "Dixie"—the American South from the black man's perspective—is hell. Anybody who deserves to be in heaven should know what hell really is.

Saint Peter said, "Well,
You got back quick.
How's de Devil? An' what's
His latest trick?"
An' Slim say, "Peter,
I really cain't tell,

The place was Dixie
That I mistook for Hell.
Then Peter say, "You must
Be crazy, I vow,
Where'n hell dja think Hell was,
Anyhow?
Git on back to de earth,
Cause I got de fear,
You's a leetle too dumb,
Fo' to stay up here."[12]

The white racist sheriff down in Mississippi is the devil in hell. Slim didn't know that because he has failed to see the world as it really is. Brown's poem is a direct reprise of the devil episode in Stagolee, as several of the field recordings quoted in earlier chapters demonstrate.

Unable to express admiration for the "bad nigger" in literature, black Americans turned to toasts. These short narratives, usually obscene and usually composed of rhymed couplets, are recited in pool halls, on street corners, in barbershops, and wherever else groups of black men assemble.[13] Daryl Dance links them to the tales of the "bad nigger." "The heroes are all 'bad,'" she writes. "They claim the virtues of courage, physical strength, clarity and coolness of mind, and knowledge of the rules of the game and ways of the world. They explicitly reject respect for the law, romantic love, pity and gratitude, chivalry or special consideration for women."[14] According to H. Nigel Thomas, "the protagonists of the toasts are the quintessential Bad Niggers," "sociopathic" figures who make "violence . . . a virtue."[15]

Both Bigger Thomas in Richard Wright's *Native Son* and Marcus

Payne in Ernest Gaines's *Of Love and Dust* are "bad niggers." As Gaines's novel opens, Marcus, a young black man accused of murder, is released to work on a plantation in Louisiana. The white overseer has arranged the release so that "he could use this Bad Nigger" to kill a rival overseer. H. Nigel Thomas sees the device of making the "Bad Nigger . . . a tool of whites" as something new.[16] Yet the folklore tradition had preceded Gaines's achievement; as we have seen, in the politics of St. Louis, Lee Shelton as a "bad nigger" may also have been used as a tool by whites.

Richard Wright recognized the significance of toasts, also known as "the dozens" or "the dirty dozens." He used the dozens at the beginning of his short story "Big Boy Leaves Home":

Yo mamma don wear no drawers . . .
Ah seena when she pulled em off . . .
N she washed em in alcohol . . .[17]

He also wrote one of the first scholarly essays on the subject.[18] "Out of the folk songs of the migrant Negro," he began, "there has come one form of Negro folklore that makes even Negroes blush a little among themselves when it is mentioned. These songs, sung by more adult Negroes than would willingly admit it, sum up the mood of despairing rebellion. They are called The Dirty Dozens." Wright found the origins of the dozens "obscure but their intent is plain and uninhibited. They jeer at life; they leer at what is decent, holy, just, wise, straight, right, and uplifting. I think that it is because from the Negro's point of view, it is the right, the holy, the just, that crush him in America."[19]

The dozens express the point of view of "a vast mass of semi-literate people living amidst the most complex, the most highly industrialized, nation on earth" and who are "trying to understand these contradictions: When the Negro turns his eyes from his unpainted wooden shack and sees the painted homes of whites, he seems to say to himself, 'Well, if what is happening to me is right, then, dammit, anything is right.'" In his bitterness, the Negro uses the dirty dozens to "extol incest, celebrate homosexuality; even God's ability to create a rational world is naively but scornfully doubted."[20] Brent Ostendorf sees a relationship between the dozens and "the adverse effects which a racial class system has on kinship structure and behavior: promiscuity, illegitimacy, and on the stigma such as extreme ugliness, Blackness, or filthiness." He views these urban subculture rituals as "institutionalized forms of rebellion, but rebellion turned inward."[21]

The dozens say all the bad things that the white man thinks about blacks, but the white part is assigned to one of the members of the group itself. This verbal analogue to burning the ghettos (Martin Luther King called rioting the "language of the unheard") has carried over into all black speech and may be felt in black poetry today, which accordingly seems jarring, exaggerated, and burdened with jive to unaccustomed ears. Urban folklore takes an unromantic, cynical view of American life; as the need for humorous camouflage disappears, humor evaporates with it. The alternatives are simple: win or lose.

Like Wright, Ellison recognized the rich oral tradition of the African American: "the places where a rich oral literature was truly functional," he writes of the small town in Oklahoma where he grew up, "were the churches, the school yards, the barbershops, the cotton-picking camps; places where folklore and gossip thrived." However, whereas Wright devoted over twenty pages to "the dozens," Ellison limited his discussion of this phenomenon to only one sentence: "I was impressed by expert players of the 'dozens' and certain notorious bootleggers of corn whiskey."[22]

In his essay "How Bigger Was Born," Richard Wright explained that he had based his novel *Native Son* on the "bad nigger" types of black men he had grown up with in the South. Wright called a black character who resented the way whites treated him the "Bigger Thomas type."[23] He then sketched seven subtypes of Bigger Thomas, which might have been a typology of Stagolee.

Wright discovered the inner life of Bigger Thomas when he compared the lives of oppressed Russians with the black lives he saw around him every day. He recalled

> reading an interesting pamphlet telling of the friendship of Gorky and Lenin in exile . . . Lenin and Gorky were walking down a London street. Lenin turned to Gorky and, pointing, said: "Here is their Big Ben." "There is their Westminster Abbey." "There is their library." And at once, while reading that passage, my mind stopped, teased, challenged with the effort to remember, to associate widely disparate but meaningful experiences in my life. For a moment nothing would come, but I remain convinced that I had heard the meaning of those words sometime, somewhere before. Then, with a sudden glow of satisfaction of having gained a little more knowledge about the world in which I lived, I'd end up by saying: "That's Bigger. That's the Bigger Thomas reaction."[24]

This is precisely the view that Stagolee has of the world. And it was the view that black men wanted Stagolee to represent for them.

Stagolee and Bigger Thomas shared a deep sense of exclusion. The feeling of looking at things with a painful and unwarrantable nakedness was an experience, Wright learned, that transcended national and racial boundaries. "It was this intolerable sense of feeling and understanding so much, and yet living on a plane of social reality where the look of a world which one did not make or own struck one with a blinding objectivity and tangibility, that made me grasp the revolutionary impulse in my life and the lives of those about me and far away."[25]

Wright remembers reading a passage in a book dealing with old Russia which said, "We must be ready to make endless sacrifices if we are to be able to overthrow the Czar. And again I'd say to myself: 'I've heard that somewhere, sometime before.' And again I'd hear Bigger Thomas, far away and long ago, telling some white man who was trying to impose upon him: 'I'll kill you and go to hell and pay for it.'"[26] This battle cry was already a part of the oral tradition. In the lyrics of Stagolee, one often heard the hero say,

> "I'll kill anybody big enough to die
> I'm on my drinking spree."

"While living in America," Wright said, "I heard from far-away Russia the bitter accents of tragic calculation of how much human life and suffering it would cost a man to live as a man in a world that denied him the right to live with dignity."[27]

In his criticism of Wright's Bigger Thomas, James Baldwin said that *Native Son* fails because Bigger doesn't love himself and his people; Bigger doesn't understand his history, his own oral culture. Bigger doesn't understand the "nigger" in himself. "His kinsmen are quite right to weep and be frightened, even to be appalled: for it is not his love for them or for himself which causes him to die, but his hatred and his self-hatred; he does not redeem the pains of a despised people, but revels, on the contrary, in nothing more than his own fierce bitterness at having been born one of them."[28]

Thomas maintains that Wright didn't allude to the toast form in the novel because such folklore would have humanized Bigger and made him sympathetic; Wright wanted him to be a "total monster." This thesis demonstrates literary critics' lack of interest in folklore as a criterion by which to judge black fiction. "The fact is not that the Negro has no tradition," lamented Baldwin, "but that there has yet arrived no sensibility sufficiently profound and tough to make this tradition articulate."[29] More than any other writer of his generation, Baldwin was aware of the connection between African-American oral traditions like Stagolee and African-American literature.

25

James Baldwin's "Staggerlee Wonders"

During the summer of 1982 I visited James Baldwin in the south of France. He was busy writing poems. One of these poems was "Staggerlee Wonders," which was published in his 1985 collection, *Jimmy's Blues*. During that visit, Baldwin read to me from the poem with great humor and laughter. He liked the folk character Stagolee so much that he had also begun a novel about him.

While a red sun set over the Provençal hills, Baldwin loved to sit with his guests around "the welcoming table" in his garden and entertain them with stories. It was on one of those evenings, about seven or eight, after dinner, that we first discussed Stagolee.

At that time we didn't have the facts before us, as I have now. We didn't know that Lee Shelton was the original, yet we accepted the legend. We speculated about who Stagolee was, because we knew that oral tradition depends on memory. Baldwin's version of

Stagolee draws strongly upon the traditional tale as he heard it, respecting the significance of folk memory.

David Leeming, Baldwin's lifelong friend and biographer, claimed that my discussions with Baldwin inspired the final shape of the poem.[1] If that was so, then I accept the credit, though I am sure that Baldwin had given much thought to the legend and myth of Stagolee long before he met me. The inspiration for his Stagolee poem may have been Bobby Seale, the founder and leader of the Black Panther party.

In 1978 Baldwin visited with Bobby Seale in jail.[2] During one of their visits, Seale asked Baldwin to write a foreword to his autobiography.[3] When Baldwin wrote that foreword, titled "Stagolee," he knew that by the 1970s Stagolee had become a powerful archetype, a "bad nigger" cultural hero. For many lower-class blacks, especially southern blacks, Stagolee was now identified with dignity and pride.

Baldwin wrote that Seale's generation had access to more useful heroes than his own: "Our most visible heroes were Father Divine and Joe Louis—we, in the ghetto then, knew very little about Paul Robeson. We knew very little about anything black, in fact, and this was not our fault. Those of us who found out more than the schools were willing to teach us did so at the price of becoming unmanageable, isolated, and, indeed, subversive."[4]

The heroes offered to Baldwin's generation had been sports figures such as Joe Louis and evangelistic figures such as Father Divine, figures that seemed to embody the white society's view of black culture. Figures like Stagolee, who represented forces that whites found disreputable or downright threatening, were unavailable.

What was missing in figures like Louis and Father Divine was militancy. Stagolee was a hero who fought back against the system. Stagolee was a hero for people existing at the margins of the larger society; their heroic figures were celebrated in the spoken or sung, not the written, word.

For Seale's generation "the beacon had been lit in 1956, in Montgomery, Alabama, by an anonymous black woman, who elicited an answering fire from all the wretched, all over the earth, and signaled the beginning of the end of the racial nightmare—for it will end, no lie endures forever—and helped Stagolee, the black folk hero Bobby takes for his model, to achieve his manhood. For, it is that tremendous journey which Bobby's book is about: the act of assuming and becoming oneself."[5] The black folk hero provided a way for black men like Bobby Seale to gain perspective on their own situation and thus to become themselves. The black folk hero Stagolee was a model for achieving manhood.

Baldwin endowed this model with a first-person immediacy in his poem "Staggerlee Wonders."[6] As Leeming notes, the poem "assumes an African-American understanding of reality to which racism makes the oppressor essentially blind" through "the voice of the black tall-tale trickster character, Staggerlee (Stagolee—'the baddest nigger that ever lived')."[7] It begins:

> I always wonder
> what they think the niggers are doing
> while they, the pink and alabaster pragmatists
> are containing
> Russia
> and defining and re-defining and re-aligning
> China.

Baldwin foregrounds Staggerlee's struggle against a racist doctrine that, unless it is stopped, will destroy the world.

Baldwin's Staggerlee is a thinker. Like Brer Rabbit among the wolf and the fox, his life depends on his being mentally alert. And what is he thinking? About what the white man is thinking about what black people are doing while the white man is thinking about them.

Why does Staggerlee think of whites? A few lines later, he tells us:

> I would not think of them,
> one way or the other,
> did not they so grotesquely
> block the view
> between me and my brother.

Baldwin felt that black men in America, as the most obvious targets of white oppression, had to love each other, to warn each other, and to communicate with each other if they were to escape being defined only in reaction to that oppression. They had to seek and find in their own tradition the human qualities that white men, through their unrelenting brutality, had lost.

Staggerlee ridicules the power structure in a series of snapshots of the "pink and alabaster pragmatists":

> and, as for Patty, heiress of all ages
> . . . she had the greatest vacation
> of any heiress, anywhere:
> Golly-gee, whillikens, Mom, real guns!
> and they come with a real big, black funky stud, too:
> oh, Ma! he's making eyes at me!

In 1978 Patty Hearst, granddaughter of Randolph Hearst, founder of the newspaper empire, was kidnapped by the Symbionese Liberation Army, a black revolutionary group. Apparently she became a member of this group, and apparently, too, she was raped by all the men. The mention of Hearst captures the world of interracial sex that provided the original St. Louis context of Stagolee.

Baldwin presents these snapshots with a satiric humor that belongs to the marketplace, to the slaves and their descendants. Whites are wishing, Staggerlee is saying, that blacks would disappear, that some "old sweet chariot" would carry them "home," that is, to death. But Staggerlee is not about to die. On the contrary, although Staggerlee is a common man, he is also a conjurer and a trickster, with uncommon insight into other men's minds.

> For, I have seen,
> in the eyes regarding me,
> or regarding my brother,
> . . .
> a flame leap up, then flicker and go out,
> alone in that cave
> which every soul remembers.

What is this "cave which every soul remembers"? It is the plantation where blacks were enslaved by oppressive ignorance. There, as in Plato's cave, one sees only flickering shadows, mistaking them for reality. It is a dreadful place, from which Staggerlee "staggers" out "into the healing air," to

> fall flat on the healing ground,
> singing praises, counseling
> my heart, my soul, to praise.

Once he is revived, he asks himself: "What is it that this people cannot forget?" Whites cannot believe that their "crimes are original."

There is nothing in the least original
About the fiery tongs to the eyeballs,
The sex torn from the socket,
The infant ripped from the womb.

Staggerlee links these crimes to the myth of manifest destiny:

Manifest Destiny is a hymn to madness
feeding on itself, ending
(when it ends) in madness.

Staggerlee, like Jonah, is able to save himself and his people, but he is not able to save the white man. He ends by saying good-bye to him and wishing him good luck. What else can he do?

Godspeed.
The niggers are calculating
from day to day, life everlasting
and wish you well:
but decline to imitate the Son of the Morning,
and rule in Hell.

Baldwin's poem adds to the tradition of the folk hero and gives him a new dimension. Like all Baldwin's heroes, Staggerlee embodies the qualities that the black man can use as a model for action against attempts to degrade and defame black people and their culture.

26

Stagolee as Cultural and Political Hero

In this long battle, a battle by no means finished, the unforesee-
able effects of which will be felt by many future generations, the
white's motive was the protection of his identity; the black man
was motivated by the need to establish an identity.

—JAMES BALDWIN, "STRANGER IN THE VILLAGE," 1955

Eldridge Cleaver, the author of *Soul on Ice*, was one of
the most famous figures in black freedom struggles of the 1960s.
When I got to know him, in the early 1990s, he and I often talked
about Stagolee. Cleaver told me that during the early days of the
Black Panther party, Bobby Seale often recited a Stagolee toast at
social gatherings. He gave me Seale's telephone number, and in
April 1998 I called him. We arranged to meet in Oakland in mid-
May, along with Eldridge, who was planning to come up from Los
Angeles. But Eldridge Cleaver died on May 1, 1998. On May 7 Bobby
Seale and I met at his house in North Oakland.

We were driving in Bobby Seale's big Cadillac. When the batteries
in my tape recorder ran down, we stopped at the Safeway to pick up
some more. As he drove, we talked about Stagolee. Bobby had first

heard about Stagolee back in the 1960s when he took a music course and heard somebody play the Stagolee ballad on a record. "By 1969," he said, "my need to reference Stagolee had sort of subsided. Actually, my research about Stagolee in terms of blues music, or the history of it, was part of my early research on African/African American studies." But the Stagolee character impressed him. At that time he was becoming acquainted with Huey P. Newton, who was always haranguing about the "lumpen proletariat." Seale gave me his own definition of the term as "that particular group of people, or brothers and sisters, in some underdeveloped area where they have been colonialized and oppressed by some white racism, who get together. And they will band together and move at a point to oppose their oppressors. But largely, until they become politically hip, they are a band of roving illigit." Putting this idea into context, Seale continued: "Now I transformed Stagolee, more or less in my own mind, into brothers standing on the block and all of the illegitimate activity. In effect, they were the lumpen proletariat in a high-tech social order, different from how 'lumpen' had been described historically." In short, as Newton had told him, the lumpen proletariat was the average brother in the street.

Raised on the streets of Oakland, Huey P. Newton earned a Ph.D. and wrote a book with Erik Erikson. A charismatic person, he would qualify as a "political" Stagolee. Seale discussed Frantz Fanon's book *The Wretched of the Earth* with Newton, and described what he brought away from the experience: "My point is this; that Malcolm X at one time was an illegitimate hustler. Later in life, Malcolm X grows to have the most profound political consciousness as far as I'm concerned. To me, this brother was really getting ready to move. So symbolically, at one time he was Stagolee . . . To me, Stagolee was the true grassroots."

Seale saw Stagolee and Huey as heroic brothers on the street. Every day in America, police attack black men, beat them, and sometimes kill them. When these black men realize what is happening to them, they become politicized. In the Rodney King incident, a videotape of officers beating a black man shocked the nation. Many blacks called for an end to "police profiling." This is what Seale called an "unorganized nigger" who becomes "organized."

It was this image of Stagolee as a hero of the working class that inspired Seale to perform him as a toast at Black Panther political parties to get young brothers to relate to their cause. When his wife delivered a baby boy, Seale wanted to name the baby Stagolee.

"Why Stagolee?" Artie, his wife, asked. "Because Stagolee was a bad nigger off the block and didn't take shit from nobody. All you had to do was organize him, like Malcolm X, make him politically conscious. The nigger's name is Malik Nkrumah Stagolee Seale."[1]

Seale obviously saw the folk hero as an "unorganized nigger," similar to such political figures as Malcolm X and Kwame Nkrumah. "Nkrumah was a bad motherfucker and Malcolm X was a bad nigger," he said. At the time, of course, Seale knew nothing of the real Lee Shelton whose life the legend was based on. He didn't know that Stagolee had a political origin, and he laughed when I told him about Lee Shelton's background.

Seale talked to me about how he had started the Black Panther party right there in that house, right there around that kitchen table. But he never forgot Stagolee. In a documentary film made about Seale while he was in prison, Bobby talked about Stagolee, expressing admiration for him as a folk hero.

From the written history of the years between 1890 and 1930, a period that parallels the development of Stagolee, black Americans developed what David Gordon Nielson calls a "Black Ethos." "The ethos of the black community, however, was shaped by the over-whelming majority of the black population that still formed a more-or-less homogeneous mass at the bottom of the social struc-ture."[2] Stagolee came to personify the collective feeling of blacks at the bottom of society, and it was in this sense that Stagolee became a symbol of the black community.

This process seems to repeat itself. By retrieving the older cliché, the black ethos seems to retrieve other clichés, which become sur-vival traditions. According to Sterling Stuckey, this process has been going on since slavery: "slaves were able to fashion a lifestyle and set of values—an ethos—which prevented them from being im-prisoned altogether by the definitions which the larger society tried to impose. This ethos was an amalgam of Africanisms and New World elements which helped slaves, in Guy Johnson's words, 'feel their way along the course of American slavery, enabling them to endure.'"[3] As an expression of a new ethos, Stagolee enabled blacks to use it as a charter for survival.

Once a narrative has been conceived in the form of a ballad, it may serve as a paradigm to "inform the action of important politi-cal leaders."[4] The Stagolee paradigm, rather than the life of the real Stagolee, becomes the basis for so many renditions of "Stagolee." After the social drama of the killing, any reference to that incident, however much it can be disguised, is used by the members of the African-American community to justify their actions.

Black folklore can take a hero like Stagolee and apply his ethos to that of living figures. This can be seen in the identification of po-litical figures such as Adam Clayton Powell Jr., Huey P. Newton, and Malcolm X with the "bad nigger." All three men, coming from very different backgrounds, came to be political representations of the Stagolee figure in African-American culture.

In the film *Malcolm X* (1993), we discover in one of the early scenes that Malcolm X was a pimp called "Detroit Red." We "discover" this by his behavior and what his conduct implies about "reputation" on the street. He walks into a Harlem bar wearing a flashy suit and a large hat. When someone insults him, he hits the man on the head with a bottle. This act wins him the admiration of the other gangsters in the bar, including the man he assaulted. Such violent behavior establishes his reputation. When others hear about what he has done, he becomes powerful, both culturally and politically—culturally, because he represents black men's attitudes toward street representation; politically, because he becomes conscious of the historical context in which his representation takes place. As a figure identified in the black community, he is powerful in his resistance to white oppression.

Al Freeman Jr., who played the role of Elijah Muhammed in the film *Malcolm X,* believed that only a black director could have articulated the connection between Stagolee and Malcolm X's political development. "I'm not saying that a white director couldn't have done a sensitive job about a black person; however, I do believe that with those frames of reference of our folkloric culture that belong to us, they are certainly more accessible to those of the group."

Clearly, Stagolee as signifier of the "bad nigger" has continued to shape African-American culture in both literature and politics.

27

Stagolee and Modernism

We have followed Stagolee's career from Lee Shelton's murder of Billy Lyons in St. Louis to the role of the Stagolee myth in literature, politics, and culture. Now it is time to take a broad, final look and draw some conclusions.

Some white Americans admire what they see as black Americans' rich and special sense of life. That special quality is tightly bound up with the black oral tradition, which was brought to America from Africa. That tradition was interwoven with music, even when the music was reduced solely to rhythm. Whites, relying on literacy as a way to view the world, were unable to strip the oral tradition of its layered meanings, including its "double-voiced" expressions of yearning for freedom.[1]

Other scholars believe that blacks have a special view of life because of their oral traditions. Eric A. Havelock goes further, saying that they have a special consciousness. If we use the term "lower class," we are missing the point. It is the oral traditions of the lower classes that make the difference.

The "oral personality" perceives time differently from the literate personality. As Eric Havelock observes, "Whereas paper and ink are the medium of the literate man, oral communication is immediate.

That is, oral communication is free from intervention of a medium."[2]

Because of its foundation in the oral tradition, black oral narrative is easily misunderstood by critics who specialize in literate rather than oral forms. One of the misunderstandings of literate culture has to do with the black concept of rhythm. As Ben Sidran makes clear, the "black approach to rhythm, being a function of the greater oral approach to time, is more difficult to define in writing." The complexity of the rhythmic approach is due to the value placed on "spontaneity and the inherently communal nature of oral improvisations."[3]

As in the oral culture derived from Africa, in the African-American oral culture there is no distinction between the artist and the audience, even though individual talent is admired. Music, an integral part of the social life, helps integrate the individual into "the society at such a basic level of experience."[4]

Rhythm is a way to "transmit a description of experience" in an emotional and not an abstract way. It is more than a metaphor; it is a physical experience as real as any other. Because the "rhythmic freedom of black music was immediately restricted upon the institution of slavery," its gradual return is the "reemergence of the black ego." Sidran believed that on this basis black music can be seen as a "source for black social organizations." The process of communication is, he claimed, "the process of community."[5]

With emancipation, blacks regained "rhythmic freedom." Blacks used rhythm to create cathartic release. As Sidran pointed out, "Tension released through rhythm is strongly associated with the sexual act. To Western man, Afro-American rhythms have often been particularly associated with this act."[6]

We have seen how the Stagolee narrative has been associated

with the pimp and the prostitute, beginning with ragtime music. But blacks "use rhythm as a cultural catharsis" to release pent-up energy brought on by both slavery and modern life. Rhythm is the expression of the black "cultural ego."

As an integral part of the black oral tradition, black music was "underground" in the slaves' work songs. Music becomes not just something to do, but a *way* to do it and an attitude toward life. Black music did not have the same "sanctimonious behavior" that was associated with white music. Black music had the responsibility of carrying the spirit, the history, and the story of black people.

Havelock thinks that the psychological relationship between the reciter and his hero is positive. By "psychology" he refers to the "shift in the ratio of the senses." Psychology, in this sense, has an essential function in any healthy society. It involves rhythm, morality, and narrative. As Havelock says, "Narrative along with rhythm had been the necessary means of supporting the oral memory."[7]

What is missing from the scholarship on African-American oral narrative folklore is an oral theory. From oral theory one can find inspiration in the work of Eric Havelock, Albert Lord, Isadore Okpewho, Amin Sweeney, and Walter Ong. Much can be learned from classical scholars such as Richard P. Martin.[8] Sweeney and Havelock have suggested that orality is a different state of mind from that of literacy.[9] That orality has carried through from the first reciter of Stagolee to the electronic rapper.

What is also missing is Benjamin's definition of modernism. One of the reasons the rag-picker was a favorite image for Benjamin is that the rag-picker not only picks up the usable; he also takes the old and discarded and turns it into something new. Young rappers such as Too Short continue to put this principle into practice.

As Americans, black men and white men share a lot of the same ideas about masculinity. Both are competitive and are fascinated with conquest metaphors. Yet there are significant ways in which they are different. White men have the mass media through which to express their heroes. Many of those media were closed to African Americans and remain so today. The one sure instrument that black men have of recreating themselves is the oral narrative tradition.

Masculinity represents power, which white men have historically been unwilling to allow to black men. Kevin Mumford argues that "Black manhood is conflicted with the norms of masculinity because the codes 'imply power, control, and authority,' which were 'denied to black men since slavery.'" He believes that black men respond to this contradiction by assuming an air of "coolness."[10]

This is the point that Richard Wright and James Baldwin made about Stagolee as a black hero. As we have seen, Baldwin and Wright saw Stagolee as a defiant, angry revolutionary, a figure consistent with his reputation from the St. Louis streets of the last century. These authors recognized the essential character of Stagolee as a symbol of protest.

Mumford closes his lectures with this reminder: "an understanding of Negro expression cannot be arrived at without a constant reference to the environment which cradles it." If the Negro moves into the "main stream of American life," Negro literature "as such" "might actually disappear."[11]

In the development of rap music and hip-hop culture, Stagolee's influence is very clear. We have seen Stagolee as a type of oral performance that influenced other performance forms such as the "Signifying Monkey," "Dolomite," "Shine," and the "dozens." Although some rappers did perform versions of "Signifying Monkey" (Rapper Schooly D, for example), most were influenced by the form of Stagolee as an oral performance. Stagolee's influence persists in rap music in the use of the first-person narrator, the performers' adoption of nicknames, the social drama, the humor, and participation in the commodity culture.

The use of the "I" as a signifying practice in "Stagolee" is similar to the "I" in dramatic monologue. From the 1930s to the 1950s, most reciters of Stagolee told the story from the third person. After the rise of the toasts tradition in the 1960s, most reciters told the story from the first person. In both Stagolee and the dramatic monologue, the narrator creates a character who gives the audience a look into his special world. The audience sees through the eyes of the character the rapper creates. It is the "I" that makes the bridge between the "I" of the rapper and the "I" of the character.

Writing about the "social realism" of "gangsta" rap, Robin D. G. Kelley concluded that the "first-person" is one of the essential ingredients in the rap narrative.[12]

A reciter of Stagolee associates himself with the hero, but he also makes it clear that he is not Stagolee too. He can effectively change himself in the eyes of his spectators and listeners. In gangsta rap, the performers are acting out the life of the criminal in an effort to dispel the criminal out of their midst, as a way to get rid of the negative energy.[13]

More than half of the entire corpus of Stagolee is delivered from the "intrusive 'I'" stance. In using the "I," a performer is willingly placing himself in the role of the projected hero. In this position, the reciter becomes active. In the role of the active reciter of the narrative, the speaker is, like the flaneur, actively participating in the world around him.

When rap music became popular during the 1970s and 1980s, reciters had developed "epithets" who told the story from their point of view. This shift to the first person allowed any rapper to use the form and to fill in the character sketched which the epithet provides with some "authentic" details. Some rappers' nicknames—Ice T, Ice Cube, Vanilla Ice—convey coldness, lack of feeling, the remorselessness of the "bad nigger" toward his victim. Some epithets pick out a quality that is persona.

Stagolee's third influence on rap music is the use of the formula, or cliché. As we have noted, Stagolee is composed of cliché lines that are easy to remember. In rap music, performers found it necessary to use such clichés to keep the rap going.

The black oral imagination mapped the hustling world of the St. Louis Stagolee onto the new rap narratives.

Roger D. Abrahams identified the gang as the suitable context for the toast. The toast was, in fact, situated in the gang. The gang was the conduit between the toast and the rap, a conduit facilitated by the gang leader, who spoke in rhythm and rhyme. When Ice T, one of the first gangsta rappers, started rapping, he had already known and performed many toasts.

This gang rhyme is midway between the Stagolee form and the rap narrative. Just as in Stagolee, somebody violates the bad man's interdiction. By refusing to recognize the bad man's "law," the speaker draws the bad man's wrath. The word 'crip' is taken from the larger leaning of a menacing way that gang members walked, just as "Stagolee" is a form of "staggering"—a term that describes how the stevedores could carry a load many times their weight by staggering it from one carrier to another.

The fourth influence that Stagolee had on rap was participation in commodity culture. In the 1890s, the Stetson became a symbol of black male status; in the late 1990s, baggy pants became a signifier of status.

In *The Body in Late-Capitalist USA,* Donald M. Lowe shows how "lifestyles consumption" reconfigures racism in our society. Because blacks are no longer needed to work the fields and factories as they were during the 1890s and until recently, the old Marxist analysis cannot be used, argues Lowe.[14] Lifestyle consumption becomes more important, and blacks are subjugated to it in ways whites are not. "The new lifestyle consumption reconfigures racism in several ways," Lowe writes. "In general, those with less income and education are more vulnerable to the packaging, marketing, and advertising, i.e. the semiotics, of new commodities."[15] Liquor stores are targeted for the ghetto population. Seagram's owns Universal Studios, which distributes rap records, CDs, and movies. Big money has a vested interest in profiting from black lifestyle consumption. Too Short's career is a retrieval from the life of the hustler, which has had an unbroken line from the early slums of the nineteenth century until now.

Middle-class whites also buy into the consumer society. But lower-class blacks are less able to understand that they are being exploited, or why. As in earlier generations, ghetto blacks fight back against white appropriation through weird dress (like baggy pants). To be able to purchase the commodities, ghetto youth resort to hustling, as their parents and grandparents did.

Too Short's life exemplifies the hustler ethic. From the point of view of people left out of the American Dream, life was a hustle. They couldn't afford to believe that a nine-to-five job would solve their problems, because they could never get those jobs. Too Short uses the elements of his lifestyle—cars, clothes, girls—as signifiers of success and wealth. He scraps the old cliché of the ghetto hustler with a slick suit and a truckload of hot goods for the new archetype of the rapper.

The term and the concept of the "mack" are a retrieval of the old cliché of the St. Louis mack that Lee Shelton once embodied. The new archetype turns the older cliché of the pimp like Iceberg Slim into a cult figure, and the stories of pimps' lives into classic urban myth. The worldview of the red-light district in St. Louis, which had been scrapped in the 1930s, is retrieved by rappers like Too Short. It is not just the mack who is revived, but the women who will do anything for him, including selling their bodies. The girls Too Short speaks of in his raps are whores, or "hos," just as they were back in the pre-industrial ballads of Stagolee. The mack is based on the French concept of sexual manipulation that was the essence of Lee Shelton's Stagolee. Too Short began our interview talking about the influence the blaxploitation film *The Mack* (1971) had on his music. In several of his raps, he makes reference to characters in *The Mack,* in addition to using the musical themes from it.

Walter Benjamin is right: the destructive character leads to liberation. T. S. Eliot is right: the poet must address those who can neither read nor write. Albert Goldman is right: the roots of the counterculture are rooted in the criminal culture. The white projects his own sense of criminality onto the black and views the black as the prototypical criminal.

The black uses his ritual performance to dispel this projection and in the process to create a form by which the white can emulate. This emulation becomes a style, a hip form to immunize the white. This process happened at the end of the last century, and it is happening at the end of this century. It is the essence of what it means to be an African American. In spite of the glamorization of violence in gangsta rap, there is hope because rap music and hip-hop have provided a model of survival for the African American in the twenty-first century.

As an oral performance, Stagolee has influenced a new art form in rap music and hip-hop. As an invisible hero, Stagolee is an image of a man who can find dignity in his own country, which seeks to disgrace him. Members of the hip-hop generation have learned from this legacy. As a form, hip-hop has opened the discussion to everybody. And this discussion is still evolving.

Stagolee is looking at the world, but he is not visible; these facts account both for his "hidden" social history and for the persistence of the myth, for Stagolee is antimyth, the discontinuous, the speech act, and the blues aesthetic. Stagolee becomes the allegory of the "player," the mack, who never can be destroyed because his existence is conditioned on his not being noticed. He is the shadow. Everybody has a shadow: when you don't have you, you have become shadow. Stagolee's story is the secret history extending from the steamboat to the electronic age in the American twenty-first century.

Stagolee creates "reality." He is an allegory of the oral black man who traveled from the mechanical world and now lives in an electronic information world. I am using the word *allegory* in the sense of a narrative in which parts of the story are hidden. By this definition, the narrative Stagolee is an allegory of a murder that took place in 1895. But the story of the murder is more than just that murder; it contains a host of meanings.

Walter Benjamin saw the commodity as an allegory, too. According to scholar Graeme Gilloch, "For Benjamin, the commodity both exhibits charcteristics similar to the allegorical—it is 'hollow'— and the object of the allegorical gaze—as a result of which, it becomes a ruin." Both commodities and allegory are empty of use-value and exchange-value; "hollowed out and barren, the commodity is revealed as nothing other than a ruin."[16]

Paradoxically, the ruins afford an opportunity to see the new. "Allegory unmasks the ever-new (of fashion) as always the same and the timeless as temporary." Thus, "one of the strongest impulses [of allegory] is an appreciation of the 'transience of things, and the concern to rescue them for eternity.'"[17]

As rappers like Too Short see it, the world is reduced to fragments and rubble. The marginal people of a city have to take the scraps and fragments and put them together to make a whole cloth. Rap music takes its name from the verb "to rap," which is short for "rhapsodize," which in Greek means "to stitch a song together." African Americans have a tradition of stitching bits of narrative together, and when they stitched together songs about police brutality, they produced gangsta rap.

Blues scholar William Barlow has noted the similarities between ragtime and rap, both drawing on the process of making something new out of already-existing music. "Ragtime was derived from the African-American practice of 'ragging' popular European melodies," and "ragging [rapping] was in essence the age-old West African practice of separating the melody from the basic time scheme by positioning notes slightly ahead of or behind the groundbeat."[18] Rappers have gone one step further, separating song and melody, recreating themselves through chanted narratives that are strongly reminiscent of the toast.

Stagolee is the viewing subject, who looks but is never himself seen. Is he the representation of modernism? Yes. Stagolee is the flaneur of the information age, for he possess the two qualities that fit him for this title (to use Michel Foucault's expression): "discontinuity and dandyism."[19]

Like Stagolee, the African-American male is always a stranger in his own native land. In St. Louis during the 1890s, European whites could arrive and have better opportunities than the Negro, who had been native born. Stagolee keeps a trace of this history when he asks the "bartender" for something to eat and gets a "dirty glass of water and a stale piece of meat." This is all that is left of a reality that kept the black man in virtual slavery.

Stagolee is, therefore, the allegory, or symbol, of the black man as the person who is the inverse of a stranger. According to the famous sociologist Georg Simmel, "The stranger is thus a foreigner who becomes like a native."[20] But Stagolee is the inverse of that: *he is the native who becomes like a foreigner.*

It is this status of being both the viewing subject and the subject incapable of being viewed that creates the powerful energy known as the African-American male. Thus, Stagolee is a perspective, a point of view. Like the flaneur who roamed the streets of nineteenth-century cities, Stagolee's view penetrates cyberspace and turns the plastic space into urban streets.

Stagolee becomes, ultimately, a form of postmodernity. Throughout the performance of Stagolee, one can take the myths created by the city and "create a reality" through representing the fragmented subject matter in a new way. Discourse is what Stagolee's performers insist on. They recall an old reality through words that have previously been used and from this they create a new reality.

The 1890s provide the archeological site for unearthing the meaning of Stagolee. More than a century later, there is evidence of his resurgence. Stagolee is alive, but the condition of his vibrancy is that he remains unseen, hidden, and unreadable. Yet it is his view on which we all depend, for without him we cannot be who we are as Americans.

On weekends, I meet with my nephew Lionel, who is ten. Once he overheard me talking about Stagolee and asked me about him. I recited a few stanzas of the toast. His eyes lit up with excitement. I found myself reciting as many stanzas as I could remember.

The next weekend, not long after his arrival, he again asked me about Stagolee. When I pretended I didn't know what he was talking about, he said, "You know, can you tell me the poem about Stagolee?" A few weekends later, he brought his buddy Matthew along. When he introduced me to Matthew, he said, "This is my uncle. He knows about Stagolee!"

Then I recited the toast for them. In their youthful eyes, I saw myself when I was hearing the toast for the first time. In their excitement I felt my own at the story of the "ba-ad" black hero who strutted into the bar and said, "Don't you know who I am? I'm Stagolee."

Thus Stagolee continues his progress by word of mouth from one generation to the next.

Notes

Bibliography

Index

Notes

INTRODUCTION

Epigraphs: Richard Wright Reader, ed. Ellen Wright and Michael Fabre (New York: Harper and Row, 1978), 39; Bob Dylan, "Stack A Lee," *World Gone Wrong,* Columbia Records, New York, 1993.

1. Archie Green, *Only a Miner: Studies in Recorded Coal-mining Songs* (Urbana: University of Illinois Press, 1972), 32.
2. Greil Marcus, "Sly Stone: The Myth of Staggerlee," in *Mystery Train,* 3d ed. (New York: Dutton, 1990), 65.
3. William Barlow, *Looking Up at Down: The Emergence of Blues Culture* (Philadelphia: Temple University Press, 1989), 19.
4. Lawrence Levine, *Black Culture and Black Consciousness* (London: Oxford University Press, 1977), p. 413.
5. Hogman Maxey, "Stagolee," *Angola Prisoner's Blues,* Arhoolie Records, El Cerrito, Calif., 1959.
6. Harry Osler, liner notes, *Angola Prisoners' Blues.*
7. David C. Rubin, *Memory in Oral Traditions: The Cognitive Psychology of Epic, Ballads, and Counting-out Rhymes* (Oxford: Oxford University Press, 1995), 258.
8. Quoted in ibid., 17.
9. I am greatly indebted to Richard Bauman, *Story, Event, and Performance: Contextual Studies of Oral Narrative* (Cambridge: Cambridge University Press, 1986), for the terms *narrative event, narrated event,* and *narrative text.* Roman Jakobson's "Shifters, Verbal Categories,

and the Russian Verb," in *Selected Writings* (The Hague: Mouton, 1971), 2: 130-147, has also been helpful.

10. Victor Turner, *From Ritual to Theater: The Human Seriousness of Play* (New York: PAJ, 1992).

11. Turner summarizes Van Gennep's schema in ibid., 24.

12. John W. Roberts, "Stackolee and the Development of a Black Heroic Idea," *Western Folklore* 13 (July 1983): 179.

13. John Lomax and Alan Lomax, *American Ballads and Folk Songs* (New York: Macmillan, 1934), 93-95.

14. Ibid., p. 93.

15. Paul Oliver, *Songsters and Saints: Vocal Tradition on Race Records* (Cambridge: Cambridge University Press, 1984), 241.

16. Cited in John R. David, "Tragedy in Ragtime: Black Folktales from St. Louis" (Ph.D. diss., St. Louis University, 1976), 167.

17. Frederick William Turner III, "Badmen, and Black and White: The Continuity of American Folk Traditions" (Ph.D. diss., University of Pennsylvania, 1965), 305.

18. John W. Roberts, *From Trickster to Badman* (Philadelphia: University of Pennsylvania Press, 1989), 1, n. 1.

19. John David's dissertation has been a font of ideas and suggestions. I am grateful to his widow, Judith Ann David, who allowed me to look at some of her late husband's research sources.

20. Kevin J. Mumford, *Interzones: Black/White Sex Districts in Chicago and New York in the Early Twentieth Century* (New York: Columbia University Press, 1997).

21. Albert Harry Goldman, *Grassroots: Marijuana in America Today* (New York: Harper and Row, 1979), 7.

22. Jack Johnson is a "bad nigger," according to folk tradition and scholarship. See William H. Wiggins Jr., "Jack Johnson as Bad Nigger: The Folklore of His Life," *Black Scholar* 5 (January 1971): 35-46.

23. Randee Dawn, "Sex and Thugs and Bulletholes," *New Musical Express,* December 1994.

24. Greil Marcus, "Stagger Lee," *Mojo* 25 (January 1996): 7.
25. Robin D. G. Kelley, *Race Rebels: Culture, Politics, and the Black Working Class* (New York: Free Press, 1994), 66.
26. Arnold Rampersad, *Jackie Robinson: A Biography* (New York: Knopf, 1997), 21.
27. Barlow, *Looking Up at Down,* 250.
28. Mumford, *Interzones,* 20.
29. Barlow, *Looking Up at Down,* 251.
30. Mumford, *Interzones,* xii.
31. Ibid., xviii.

1. STAGOLEE SHOT BILLY

Epigraphs: Jelly Roll Morton, "Levee Man Blues," *Library of Congress Recordings, Vol. 1,* reissued by Rounder Records, Cambridge, Mass., 1991; Onah L. Spencer, "Stackalee," *Directions* 4 (Summer 1941): 17, quoted in John R. David, "Tragedy in Ragtime: Black Folktales from St. Louis" (Ph.D. diss., St. Louis University, 1976), 200.

1. David A. Jasen and Trebor Jay Tichenor, *Rags and Ragtime: A Musical History* (New York: Dover, 1978), 79.
2. *St. Louis Post-Dispatch,* February 21, 1891.
3. Ibid.
4. David, "Tragedy in Ragtime," 74.
5. Account by Henry Crump, transcript 576, Lyons inquest, copy given to me by John David's widow, Judith Ann David. Unless otherwise noted, all eyewitness accounts quoted in this chapter are from this transcript.
6. This fictional description is based on a composite of factual sources given in Arna Bontemps and Jack Conroy, *Anywhere but Here* (New York: Hill and Wang, 1966). Another source is Nathan B. Young's "Transgressions: Death, Legends, and Music of Bad Man Stackolee," Manuscript M2, St. Louis University Archives, 1983.
7. Theodore Dreiser, *A Book about Myself* (New York: Boni and Liveright, 1922).

8. *St. Louis Sunday Star-Sayings,* December 29, 1895.

9. The account of the inquest is in ibid.

10. David, "Tragedy in Ragtime," 186.

11. Ibid.

12. *St. Louis Globe-Democrat,* January 4, 1886, 11.

13. *St. Louis Globe-Democrat,* June 26, 1896.

14. Anonymous, quoted in David, "Tragedy in Ragtime," 282.

15. James Neal Primm, *Lion of the Valley: St. Louis, Missouri* (Boulder: Pruett, 1990), 391.

16. D. K. Wilgus Collection, Folklore Archives, University of North Carolina at Chapel Hill.

17. *St. Louis Globe-Democrat,* August 26, 1897.

18. "Stackalee," *The Mirror,* January 3, 1919.

19. David, "Tragedy in Ragtime," 178.

20. Ibid., 196.

21. Ibid.

22. Ibid., 198.

23. Victor Turner, *From Ritual to Theater: The Human Seriousness of Play* (New York: PAJ, 1992), 69, 70–71.

24. Nathan B. Young, "Some Basic Cultural Developments," in *Ain't but a Place,* ed. Gerald Early (St. Louis: St. Louis Historical Society, 1999), 339.

2. LEE SHELTON

1. Lee Shelton, prison records, Missouri State Penitentiary, Jefferson City; copy in John R. David's collection, provided by Judith Ann David.

2. Al Rose, *Storyville, New Orleans* (Tuscaloosa: University of Alabama, 1974), 135.

3. John R. David, "Tragedy in Ragtime: Black Folktales from St. Louis" (Ph.D. diss., St. Louis University, 1976), 183.

4. In 1895 few blacks worked as carriage drivers. In his study of blacks in Philadelphia in the 1890s, Roger Lane found that "private

coachmen were an . . . elite group, even more likely than hotel waiters to be chosen for their bearing in uniform." Coachmen earned twice as much as butlers, about 400 dollars a year, and far more than "laborers." Blacks made up 46.3 percent of the "unskilled" labor force, compared with 14.4 percent of whites. In St. Louis as in Philadelphia, most blacks were shut out of the factory or industrial jobs. They were also barred from the better-paying heavy construction associated with city contracts; such jobs were reserved for the Irish. Most blacks who had such prestigious jobs as coach drivers used their positions as a front for more profitable "hustles." See Roger Lane, *Violent Death in the City: Suicide, Accident, and Murder in Nineteenth-Century Philadelphia* (Cambridge, Mass.: Harvard University Press, 1979), 23.

5. Stephen Longstreet, *Storyville to Harlem: Fifty Years in the Jazz Scene* (New Brunswick, N.J.: Rutgers University Press, 1986), 27.

6. Kevin J. Mumford, *Interzones: Black/White Sex Districts in Chicago and New York in the Early Twentieth Century* (New York: Columbia University, 1997), 23.

7. William Barlow, *Looking Up at Down: The Emergence of Blues Culture* (Philadelphia: Temple University Press, 1989), 255.

8. *St. Louis Star-Sayings,* December 25, 1895.

9. Mumford, *Interzones,* 141.

10. Lawrence Oland Christensen, "Black St. Louis: A Study in Race Relations, 1865–1916" (Ph.D. diss., University of Missouri, 1972), 15, 198, 205.

11. Selwyn K. Troen and Glen E. Holt, eds., *St. Louis* (New York: New Viewpoints, 1977), 83.

12. John Lomax and Alan Lomax, *American Ballads and Folk Songs* (New York: Macmillan, 1934), 99.

13. *St. Louis Star-Sayings,* December 29, 1895.

14. Shields McIlwaine, *Memphis down in Dixie* (New York: E. P. Dutton, 1948), 200.

15. Lomax and Lomax, *American Ballads and Folk Songs,* 93–94; Alan

Lomax, liner notes, *Prison Songs,* Rounder Records, Cambridge, Mass., 1997.

16. Richard E. Buehler, "Stacker Lee: A Partial Investigation into the Historicity of a Negro Murder Ballad," *Keystone Folklore Quarterly* 12 (Fall 1967): 187.

17. McIlwaine, *Memphis down in Dixie,* 201.

18. Garnett Laidlaw Eskew, "Coonjine in Manhattan" (1939), p. 9, American Life Histories: Manuscripts from the Federal Writers' Project, 1936–1940, Library of Congress. According to folklorist Nathan B. Young, "The Negro roustabout . . . invented the fine art of jostling heavy cotton bales and toting fabulous weights by balancing and synchronizing their bodies and muscles into a dancing trot called 'coonjinin'"; "Some Basic Cultural Developments," in *Ain't but a Place,* ed. Gerald Early (St. Louis: St. Louis Historical Society, 1999), 341.

19. Eskew, "Coonjine in Manhattan."

20. This version is now in the W. K. Wilgus Collection, Folklore Archives, University of North Carolina at Chapel Hill.

21. See Mumford's excellent chapter "'New Fallen Women': Black/White Prostitution," in *Interzones,* esp. p. 38.

22. Ibid., pp. 39, 101, 14.

3. THAT BAD PIMP OF OLD ST. LOUIS

1. Quoted in Graeme Gilloch, *Myth and Metropolis* (London: Polity), 6.

2. I found the 1903 version in Los Angeles in 1995, in the files of W. K. Wilgus, whose widow kindly let me look through his Stagolee collection. On my copy is a note saying: "sent to D. R. W. by [the folklorist] G. Legman, 1955." Wilgus' collection is now in the Folklore Archives, University of North Carolina at Chapel Hill.

3. This version was given me by Alan Dundes, from the Folklore Archives, University of California at Berkeley.

4. Most Stagolee ballads that show him as a pimp are never printed except in private editions for men only or as erotic material.

5. The concept of hidden history is developed by Robin D. G. Kelley,

Race Rebels: Culture, Politics, and the Black Working Class (New York: Free Press, 1994), 77–100, as "hidden transcripts."

6. From the files of folklorist Robert W. Gordon, University of California at Berkeley, sent on January 11, 1924, from Salt Lake City by "R. E. M." The same lines occur in Charles Finger, ed., *Frontier Ballads Heard and Gathered* (New York: Doubleday Page, 1927), 90.

7. See Vladimir Propp, *Morphology of the Folktale* (Austin: University of Texas Press, 1990), 39–40.

8. Account by Officer Falvey, transcript 738, Lyons inquest, copy given to me by Judith Ann David.

9. Tom Rush, "Stackalee," *Tom Rush,* Fantasy Records, Berkeley, Calif., 1959.

10. *The Compact Edition of the Oxford English Dictionary,* vol. 2 (Oxford: Oxford University Press, 1971), s.v., I.d.

11. Kevin J. Mumford, *Interzones: Black/White Sex Districts in Chicago and New York in the Early Twentieth Century* (New York: Columbia University, 1997), 102.

12. S. J. Duffield to Robert Gordon, September 30, 1925, published by Gordon in his magazine, *Adventure,* in 1927; reprinted in Sigmund Spaeth, *Weep Some More My Lady* (Garden City, N.Y.: Doubleday, 1927), 131–133.

13. Alan Dundes, "From Etic to Emic Units in the Structural Study of Folktalkes," *Journal of American Folklore* 75 (1962): 69. Langston Hughes and Arna Bontemps collected several of the ballad's allomotifs in 1941, published in *The Book of Negro Folklore* (New York: Apollo, 1958), 363. Another well-known allomotif of the gravesite motifeme, collected by Robert Gordon in Georgia in 1924, has the dead Stagolee attended by "one hundred macks"; Robert W. Gordon Collection, American Folklore Center, Library of Congress. For a fuller discussion of allomotifs and Stagolee, see Cecil Brown, "From Shack Bully to Culture Hero" (Ph.D. diss., University of California, Berkeley; UMI Dissertation Services, Ann Arbor, Mich., no. 9430407).

4. "POOR BILLY LYONS"

1. Richard E. Buehler, "Stacker Lee: A Partial Investigation into the Historicity of a Negro Murder Ballad," *Keystone Folklore Quarterly* 12 (Fall 1967): 187–191.

2. Cited in ibid., 183.

3. Lawrence Oland Christensen, "Black St. Louis: A Study in Race Relations, 1865–1916" (Ph.D. diss., University of Missouri, 1972) 173.

4. John R. David, "Tragedy in Ragtime: Black Folktales from St. Louis" (Ph.D. diss., St. Louis University, 1976). Then as now, it was not unusual for urban black Americans to hold more than one job.

5. Harold Courlander, *Negro Folk Music, USA* (New York: Columbia University Press, 1970), 178–179.

6. Billy Martin, collected October 7, 1937, by John Lomax, American Folklore Collection, Library of Congress.

7. David C. Rubin, *Memory in Oral Traditions: The Cognitive Psychology of Epic, Ballads, and Counting-out Rhymes* (Oxford: Oxford University Press, 1995).

8. 1926, Robert W. Gordon Collection, American Folklore Center, Library of Congress.

9. David, "Tragedy in Ragtime," 193.

10. Ibid., 16.

11. Alan Lomax and John A. Lomax, *American Ballads and Folk Songs,* 2d ed. (New York: Macmillan, 1960), 97.

12. Tale 32, in Daryl C. Dance, *Shuckin' and Jivin': Folklore from Contemporary Black Americans* (Bloomington: Indiana University Indiana Press, 1978), 224.

13. Theodore Dreiser, *Journalism,* ed. T. D. Nostwich (Philadelphia: University of Pennsylvania Press, 1988), 94.

14. Richard Collins, *St. Louis Globe-Democrat,* June 28, 1933.

15. "Murder in a Crap Dive," *St. Louis Globe-Democrat,* September 12, 1902.

16. Informant: John Drum, age twenty-two, Norfolk, Va., 1958.
17. D. K. Wilgus, 1955, Western Kentucky Folklore Archive, Bowling Green.
18. David, "Tragedy in Ragtime," 195.
19. Howard W. Odum, "Folk-Songs and Folk-Poetry as Found in the Secular Songs of the Southern Negroes," *Journal of American Folklore* 24 (1911): 256.
20. No. 245, American Folklore Collection, Library of Congress.
21. *A Box of Rain: Collected Lyrics of Robert Hunter* (New York: Viking, 1990), 56.

5. NARRATIVE EVENTS AND NARRATED EVENTS

1. Victor Turner, *From Ritual to Theater: The Human Seriousness of Play* (New York: PAJ, 1982), 73.
2. Walter Burkert, *Structure and History in Greek Mythology and Ritual* (Berkeley: University of California Press, 1979), 23.
3. Richard Bauman, *Story, Performance, and Event: Contextual Studies of Oral Narrative* (Cambridge: Cambridge University Press, 1986), 2. I am indebted to Bauman for the reference to Roman Jakobson's article "Shifters, Verbal Categories, and the Russian Verb," in *Selected Writings,* vol. 2 (The Hague: Mouton, 1971), 130–147.
4. Walter Benjamin, *Reflections: Essays, Aphorisms, Autobiographical Writings* (New York: Schocken, 1978), 87.
5. Bauman, *Story, Performance, and Event,* 1–10.
6. Burkert, *Structure and History,* 18.
7. For a discussion of interdictions and responses to their violation, see Vladimir Propp, *Morphology of the Folktale* (Austin: University of Texas Press, 1990), 27–38.
8. Dundes and Lévi-Strauss agree on the general principle but differ in their application of this principle. See Alan Dundes, "Typography of North American Indian Tales," in *The Study of Folklore,* ed. Dundes (Englewood Cliffs, N.J.: Prentice-Hall, 1965), 206–215; Claude Lévi-Strauss, "The Structural Study of Myth," in *Structural Anthropology* (New York: Doubleday, 1986).

9. Alex Olrik, "Epic Laws of Folk Narrative," in Dundes, *The Study of Folklore,* 129–141.

10. John R. David, "Tragedy in Ragtime: Black Folktales from St. Louis" (Ph.D. diss., St. Louis University, 1976), 201. The following references are all taken from David, 195–201.

11. Account by Frank Boyd, transcript 576, Lyons inquest, quoted in ibid., 171.

12. "Stackerlee," *The Mirror,* January 3, 1919, 11.

13. Quoted in ibid., 282.

14. Lawrence Oland Christensen, "Black St. Louis: A Study in Race Relations, 1865–1916" (Ph.D. diss., University of Missouri, 1972), 213.

15. *St. Louis Star,* April 1916, 84A.

16. Ibid.

17. Gary R. Kremer, *James Milton Turner and the Promise of America: The Public Life of a Post–Civil War Black Leader* (Columbia: University of Missouri Press, 1991), 177; Christensen, "Black St. Louis," 213.

18. 1903 version, W. K. Wilgus Collection, Folklore Archives, University of North Carolina at Chapel Hill.

19. *St. Louis Globe-Democrat,* May 5, 1931; also Necrology Scrapbook, 130, Missouri State Historical Society, St. Louis.

20. Ben Scott appears in several variants, such as the one printed in Sigmund Spaeth's *Weep Some More My Lady* (Garden City, N.Y.: Doubleday, 1927), p. 131:

    Ben Scott sent for the police
    And they came on the run;
    The bar boy up and told them
    What Stackalee dun done,
    That bad, that bad man Stackalee.

    The version quoted in the text is in ibid., 131–133.

21. Langston Hughes and Arna W. Bontemps, eds., *The Book of Negro Folklore* (New York: Dodd, 1983), p. 361.

22. Interview with Dorothy Todd, St. Louis, summer 1992.

6. STAGOLEE AND POLITICS

1. Lawrence Oland Christensen, "Black St. Louis: A Study in Race Relations, 1865-1916" (Ph.D. diss., University of Missouri, 1972), 209.
2. George B. Vashon, "Progress of Negroes in Their Efforts to Free Themselves from Republicanism," *St. Louis Republic,* August 4, 1901, 3.
3. Christensen, "Black St. Louis," 21l.
4. Ibid.
5. Vashon, "Progress of Negroes."
6. William Barlow, *Looking Up at Down: The Emergence of Blues Culture* (Philadelphia: Temple University Press, 1989), 250.
7. John R. David, "Tragedy in Ragtime: Black Folktales from St. Louis" (Ph.D. diss., St. Louis University, 1976), 55.
8. Howard Odum, *The Negro and His Songs* (Chapel Hill: University of North Carolina Press, 1925).
9. David, "Tragedy in Ragtime," 78.
10. Ibid., 79.
11. Vashon, "Progress of Negroes."
12. David, "Tragedy in Ragtime," 78.
13. Vashon, "Progress of Negroes."
14. Addison Burnett, interview with John David, St. Louis, 1977.
15. Vashon, "Progress of Negroes," 6.

7. UNDER THE LID

1. Arna Bontemps, *God Sends Sunday* (New York: Harcourt, Brace, 1931), 80-81.
2. Ibid., 85.
3. Robert W. Gordon Collection, American Folklore Center, Library of Congress, from about 1927.
4. Handy discusses in detail how he combined the vocalized songs of blacks with ragtime to make the "St. Louis Blues" in *Father of the Blues* (New York: Da Capo, 1985), 142-143.

5. Shane White and Graham White, *Stylin': African American Expressive Culture from Its Beginnings to the Zoot Suit* (Ithaca: Cornell University Press, 1998), pp. 160–161.

6. Ibid., p. 161.

7. From Paul Oliver, *The Blues Fell This Morning: The Meaning of the Blues* (New York: Cambridge University Press, 1984), 175.

8. Robin D. G. Kelley, *Race Rebels: Culture, Politics, and the Black Working Class* (New York: Free Press, 1994), 40.

9. See Adrienne M. Seward, "The Black Pimp as a Folk Hero" (Master's thesis, University of California, Berkeley, 1974).

10. Timothy J. Gilfoyle, *City of Eros: New York City, Prostitution, and the Commercialization of Sex* (New York: W. W. Norton, 1992), 115.

11. Attacks by brothel bullies departed in several ways from the earlier forms of pre-industrial collective violence, but like the earlier forms, their sprees were drunken displays of egalitarianism.

12. Seward, "Black Pimp as Folk Hero," 54, 64.

13. Both references are quoted by Kevin J. Mumford, *Interzones: Black/White Sex Districts in Chicago and New York in the Early Twentieth Century* (New York: Columbia University Press, 1997), 146–148.

14. Dreiser, *Newspaper Days* (Philadelphia: University of Pennsylvania Press, 1991), 338.

15. Karl Marx, *The Eighteenth Brumaire of Louis Bonaparte,* trans. Joseph Weydemeyer (New York: International Publishers, 1963), section V, paragraph 4.

16. Graeme Gilloch, *Myth and Metropolis: Walter Benjamin and the City* (New York: Polity, 1996), pp. 148, 15.

17. Stanley A. Lawrence, ed., *Rap: The Lyrics* (New York: Penguin, 1992), 150.

8. THE BLACK SOCIAL CLUBS

1. Susan Curtis, *Dancing to a Black Man's Tune: A Life of Scott Joplin* (Columbia: University of Missouri Press, 1994), 78, 82.

2. Edward A. Berlin, *King of Ragtime: Scott Joplin and His Era* (Oxford: Oxford University Press, 1994), 42, 43.

3. Kevin J. Mumford, *Interzones: Black/White Sex Districts in Chicago and New York in the Early Twentieth Century* (New York: Columbia University Press, 1997), 71.

4. Berlin, *King of Ragtime,* 41.

5. Ibid., 43.

6. Ibid., 44.

7. Ethel M. King, *Reflections of Reedy: A Biography of William Marion Reedy of Reedy's Mirror* (Brooklyn: Gerald J. Rickard, 1961), 16.

8. Curtis, *Dancing to a Black Man's Tune,* 87.

9. Nell Kimball, *Her Life as an American Madam: By Herself,* ed. Stephen Longstreet (New York: Macmillan, 1970), 259.

10. Jelly Roll Morton, "Aaron Harris Blues," in *Kansas City Stomp, Library of Congress Recordings, Vol. 1,* reissued by Rounder Records, Cambridge, Mass., 1993.

9. HATS AND NICKNAMES

1. Howard W. Odum, "Folk-Songs and Folk Poetry as Found in the Secular Songs of the Southern Negro," *Journal of American Folklore* 24 (1911): 288–289.

2. Howard W. Odum, *Negro Workaday Songs* (Chapel Hill: University of North Carolina Press, 1926).

3. Robin D. G. Kelley, *Race Rebels: Culture, Politics, and the Black Working Class* (New York: Free Press, 1994), 16.

4. Nathan B. Young, "The Saga of Stackerlee" (manuscript, St. Louis University, n.d.), 157.

5. Michael Harrison, *The History of the Hat* (London: Herbert Jenkins, 1960), 68.

6. Young, "The Saga of Stackerlee," 68.

7. Sigmund Freud, "A Connection between a Symbol and a Symp-

tom," *Character and Culture,* ed. Philip Reiff (1916; reprint, New York: Collier, 1963), 156.

8. Louis Armstrong, *Satchmo: My Life in New Orleans* (New York: Da Capo, 1986), 164.

9. Mae Irwin, "Bully of the Town," in *Paramount Old Time Tunes (20s and 30s),* Arhoolie Records, El Cerrito, Calif., 1983.

10. Lafcadio Hearn, "Levee Life," in *Selected Writings of Lafcadio Hearn,* ed. Henry Goodman (1904; reprint, New York: Citadel, 1949), 117.

11. Lafcadio Hearn called the red-light district in the New Orleans levee "Buck Town"; the implication is that a man residing there or a patron of the bordellos was a buck, or sexual stud. "Levee Life," 117.

12. Quoted in Mel Watkins, *On the Real Side . . .* (New York: Simon and Schuster, 1994), 142.

13. Kevin J. Mumford, *Interzones: Black/White Sex Districts in Chicago and New York in the Early Twentieth Century* (New York: Columbia University Press, 1997), 61, 28, 152.

14. One example was Dan the Dude's Old Stag Café in New York City; Ashbury Herbert, *The Gangs of New York* (Garden City, N.Y.: Garden City Publishing, 1928).

15. Geneva Smitherman, *Talkin and Testifyin: The Language of Black America* (Boston: Houghton Mifflin, 1977), 52.

16. Nell Kimball, *Her Life as an American Madam: By Herself,* ed. Stephen Longstreet (New York: Macmillan, n.d.), 70.

17. George B. Vashon, "Progress of Negroes in Their Efforts to Free Themselves from Republicanism," *St. Louis Republic,* August 4, 1901.

18. Thomas L. Clark, *Dictionary of Gambling and Gaming* (New York: Cold Spring, 1987), 215.

19. Onah Spencer, "Stackalee," *Directions* 4 (Summer 1941), reprinted in Benjamin A. Botkins, *Treasury of American Folklore* (New York: Crown, 1944), 17.

20. Botkins, *Treasury,* 123.

10. RAGTIME AND STAGOLEE

1. John R. David, "Tragedy in Ragtime: Black Folktales from St. Louis" (Ph.D. diss., St. Louis University, 1976), 202.

2. Nathan B. Young, "Madam Babe: St. Louis' Golden Bordello Idyll" (manuscript, St. Louis University, 1987), unpaginated.

3. Nathan B. Young, "The Father of the Jazz Age," in *Ain't but a Place,* ed. Gerald Early (St. Louis: St. Louis Historical Society, 1999), 345; David, "Tragedy in Ragtime," 202.

4. Howard W. Odum, *Negro Workaday Songs* (Chapel Hill: University of North Carolina Press, 1926).

5. See Young, "Madam Babe."

6. Orrick Johns, *Times of Our Lives: The Story of My Father and Myself* (New York: Octagon, 1937), 97. In "Madam Babe," Young recreates a performance of Mama Lou's "obscene" songs and their lyrics. They are quite bawdy on the page, but I suspect that the audience's reaction at an actual performance would be one of hilarity. Much of what seems obscene in a bordello may not be when experienced in the context of a social drama.

7. William Barlow and Thomas L. Morgan, *From Cakewalks to Concert Halls: An Illustrated History of African-American Popular Music from 1895 to 1930* (Washington, D.C.: Elliot and Clark, 1992).

8. W. C. Handy, *The Father of the Blues* (New York: Da Capo, 1985), 118.

9. This account of May Irwin is taken from Young's "Madam Babe." The Reedy quotes in the following paragraph are not cited spepcifically, but Young claims they are from Reedy's *Sunday Sayings.*

10. Isaac Goldberg, *Tin Pan Alley: A Chronicle of American Popular Music* (New York: Ungar, 1961).

11. James Weldon Johnson, *The Black Manhattan* (Salem, N.H.: Ayer, 1988).

11. THE BLUES AND STAGOLEE

1. William Barlow, *Looking Up at Down: The Emergence of a Blues Culture* (Philadelphia: Temple University Press, 1989), 251.
2. W. C. Handy, *Father of the Blues* (New York: Da Capo, 1985), 142.
3. G. Malcolm Laws Jr., *Native American Balladry: A Descriptive Study and a Bibliographical Syllabus* (Philadelphia: American Folklore Society, 1964), 83.
4. Nathan B. Young, "The Father of Jazz," in *Ain't but a Place,* ed. Gerald Early (St. Louis: St. Louis Historical Society, 1999), 345.
5. Laws, *Native American Balladry,* 83–84.
6. Ibid., 87.
7. Ibid., 94.
8. This was how Robert Gordon described this quality in a letter to another collector, dated August 21, 1924, Robert Gordon Collection, Oregon State University.
9. William Barlow and Thomas L. Morgan, *From Cakewalks to Concert Halls: An Illustrated History of African-American Popular Music from 1895 to 1930* (Washington, D.C.: Elliot and Clark, 1992), 8.
10. Ibid., 9.
11. Ibid.
12. Eileen Southern, *The Music of Black Americans: A History* (New York: W. W. Norton, 1971), 184.
13. Barlow, *Looking Up at Down,* 18, 19.
14. Ibid., 20.
15. Reported to me by a reader of the manuscript.
16. Giles Oakley, *The Devil's Music* (Milwaukee: Miller Freeman, 1998), 183, 184.
17. Ibid., 188.
18. John R. David, "Tragedy in Ragtime: Black Folktales from St. Louis" (Ph.D. diss., St. Louis University, 1976), 199.
19. Cecil Brown, "Stagolee: From Shack Bully to Culture Hero" (Ph.D. diss., UMI Dissertation Services, Ann Arbor, 1993), 156.

20. This episode is similar to the bawdy Irish ballad "Finnegan's Wake," in which several friends of the dead Finnegan carry on a drunken brawl; the song was popular during the 1890s and was considered lowbrow entertainment. Clearly, James Joyce saw such ballads as the basis for high art.

12. JIM CROW AND ORAL NARRATIVE

1. S. J. Duffield to Robert Gordon, September 30, 1925; Lt. F. Rorschach to Robert Gordon, 1927; Nice to Gordon, February 14, 1927, all in Letters of Robert W. Gordon, Library of Congress.
2. Leon Litwack, *Trouble in Mind: Black Southerners in the Age of Jim Crow* (New York: Alfred A. Knopf, 1998), xiv.
3. Ibid.
4. Anders Stephanson, *Manifest Destiny: American Expansion and the Empire of Right* (New York: Hill and Wang, 1995), 144.
5. Nathan B. Young, "Transgressions: Death, Legends, and Music of Bad Man Stackolee," Manuscript M2, St. Louis University Archives, 1983, 3.
6. Isidore Okpewho, ed., *The Oral Performance in Africa* (Ibadan, Nigeria: Spectrum, 1990), 57.

13. RIVERBOAT ROUSTER AND MEAN MATE

1. Gerald Early, ed., *Ain't but a Place* (St. Louis: St. Louis Historical Society, 1999) 340.
2. Garnett Laidlaw Eskew, "Coonjine in Manhattan" (1939), American Life Histories: Manuscripts from the Federal Writers' Project, 1936–1940, Library of Congress.
3. Ibid.
4. Eskew's account is drawn from ibid.
5. Paul Oliver, *Screening the Blues* (New York: Da Capo, 1968), 38.
6. Mary Wheeler, "Stacker Lee No. 3," in *Steamboatin' Days* (Baton Rouge: Louisiana State University Press, 1944), 100.

14. WORK CAMPS, HOBOES, AND SHACK BULLY HOLLERS

1. John L. Matthews, *Remaking the Mississippi* (Boston: Houghton Mifflin, 1909).

2. John Cowley, *Shack Bullies and Levee Contractors: Studies in the Oral History of a Black Protest Song Tradition* (Los Angeles: University of California at Los Angeles, 1980), 182–192, quotation p. 183.

3. John A. Lomax, *Adventures of a Ballad Hunter* (New York: Macmillan, 1947), 33.

4. Cowley, *Shack Bullies and Levee Contractors*, 25. Around July 11, 1933, the Lomaxes discovered and recorded Henry Truvillion, a foreman working for the Wier Lumber Company, in Wiergate, Texas. Truvillion recalled several songs from his Mississippi past of twenty years before and one of the songs was "Shack Bully Holler," which contains the first known reference to a white family of levee contractors—the Lorentz brothers.

5. Mary Wheeler, "Stacker Lee No. 1," in *Steamboatin' Days* (Baton Rouge: Louisiana State University Press, 1944), 100.

15. WILLIAM MARION REEDY'S WHITE OUTLAW

1. "Stackerlee," *The Mirror,* January 3, 1919, 11.

2. Charles J. Finger, *Frontier Ballads: Heard and Gathered* (New York: Doubleday, Page, 1927), 90.

3. Ibid., 21.

4. Max Putzel, *The Man in the Mirror: William Marion Reedy and His Magazine* (Cambridge, Mass.: Harvard University Press, 1963), 11, 3–4. For more on Reedy, see also Ethel M. King, *Reflections of Reedy: A Biography of William Marion Reedy of Reedy's Mirror* (Brooklyn: Gerald J. Rickard, 1961).

5. Nathan B. Young, "Madam Babe: St. Louis' Golden Bordello Idyll" (manuscript, St. Louis University, 1987), unpaginated.

6. Arna Bontemps and Jack Conroy, *Anywhere but Here* (New York: Hill and Wang, 1966), 115.

7. James Neal Primm, *Lion of the Valley: St. Louis, Missouri* (Boulder: Pruett, 1990), 319, 14, 23–25.

8. Putzel, *The Man in the Mirror,* 30.

9. Ibid., 47.

10. See Kevin J. Mumford, *Interzones: Black/White Sex Districts in Chicago and New York in the Early Twentieth Century* (New York: Columbia University Press, 1997), esp. chap. 8, "Slumming."

11. Putzel, *The Man in the Mirror,* 30.

12. Ibid., 51, 52.

13. Ibid., 30.

16. COWBOY STAGOLEE AND HILLBILLY BLUES

1. Art Burton, *Black, Red, and Dangerous* (Austin, Tex.: Eakin Press, 1991), 2.

2. Thomas L. Morgan and William Barlow, *From Cakewalks to Concert Halls: An Illustrated History of African American Popular Music from 1895 to 1930* (Washington, D.C.: Elliott and Clark, 1992), 12, 13.

3. For more on Gordon's methods of collection, see Debora Kodish's informative biography, *Good Friends and Bad Enemies* (Urbana: University of Illinois Press, 1986).

4. S. J. Duffield to Robert Gordon, September 30, 1925, Letters of Robert Gordon, Library of Congress.

5. Gordon to Duffield, October 18, 1925, ibid.

6. Duffield to Gordon, October 24, 1925, ibid.

7. Lt. F. Rorschach to Gordon, December 7, 1927, ibid.

8. Nice to Gordon, February 14, 1927, ibid.

9. Gordon to Nice, February 18, 1927, ibid.

10. Tony Russell, liner notes, *Frank Hutchinson: Complete Recorded Works in Chronological Order, Volume 1926–1929,* Document Records, Vienna, Austria.

11. Ibid.

12. Fruit Jar Guzzlers, "Stack-O-Lee," Paramount Old Time Tunes, New York, 1928.

17. BLUESWOMEN

1. See Kevin J. Mumford's *Interzones: Black/White Sex Districts in Chicago and New York in the Early Twentieth Century* (New York: Columbia University Press, 1997).

2. William Barlow, *Looking Up at Down: The Emergence of Blues Culture* (Philadelphia: Temple University Press, 1989), 130, 133.

3. William Barlow and Thomas L. Morgan, *From Cakewalks to Concert Halls: An Illustrated History of African American Popular Music from 1895 to 1930* (Washington, D.C.: Elliot and Clark, 1992), 127.

4. Barlow, *Looking Up at Down,* 131.

5. Norm Cohen, *Minstrels and Tunesmiths: The Roots of American Music, 1902–1923* (Los Angeles: John Edwards Memorial Foundation, 1983), 13.

6. Ma Rainey, "Stack-o-Lee Blues," *Ma Rainey's Black Bottom,* Yazoo Records, New Jersey, 1981.

7. Hazel Carby, "It Just Be's Dat Way Sometime: The Sexual Politics of Women's Blues," *Radical America* 20, no. 4 (1999): 9–22.

8. Barlow, *Looking Up at Down,* 140.

9. Ibid., 141.

10. Virginia P. Brown and Laurella Owens, *Toting the Lead Row: Ruby Pickens Tartt, Alabama Folklorist* (Mobile: University of Alabama Press, 1981), 20; Vera Hall, "Stagolee," no. 1323, American Folklore Collection, Library of Congress.

11. John Lomax, "The Passing of a Great Singer—Vera Hall," *Sing Out* 14, no. 3 (1964): 30–31.

18. BLUESMEN AND BLACK BAD MAN

1. Mary Brown, transcribed by Margaret Walker (1939), American Life Histories: Manuscripts from the Federal Writers' Project, North Carolina, Library of Congress.

2. H. C. Brearley, "Ba-ad Nigger" (1939), in *Mother Wit from the Laughing Barrel,* ed. Alan Dundes (Jackson: University of Mississippi Press, 1972), 581.

3. Kevin J. Mumford, *Interzones: Black/White Sex Districts in Chicago and New York in the Early Twentieth Century* (New York: Columbia University Press, 1997), 3. Biographies of Jack Johnson include Robert H. DeCoy, *The Big Black Fire* (Los Angeles: Holloway House, 1969); Randy Robert, *Papa Jack: Jackson and the Era of White Hopes* (New York: Free Press, 1983); and Finis Farr, *Black Champion: The Life and Times of Jack Johnson* (New York: Scribner, 1964).

4. Mumford, *Interzones,* 10–12.

5. William H. Wiggins Jr., "Jack Johnson as Bad Nigger: The Folklore of His Life," *Black Scholar* 5 (January 1971): 35.

6. Farr, *Black Champion,* 36.

7. Wiggins, "Jack Johnson as Bad Nigger," 35.

8. Papa Henry Hull, "Original Stack O' Lee Blues," *The Songster Tradition (1927–1925),* Document Records, Vienna, Austria, 1991.

9. Ben Sidran, *Black Talk* (New York: Holt, Rinehart and Winston, 1971).

10. No. 61, American Folklore Collection, Library of Congress.

11. Mississippi John Hurt, "Stack O'Lee Blues," *1928 Sessions,* Yazoo Records, Newton, N.J., 1990.

12. Ida B. Wells-Barnett, "Robert Charles and His Fight to the Death," in *Mob Rule in New Orleans* (New York: Arno, 1969), 12.

13. Sidran, *Black Talk,* 23.

19. ON THE TRAIL OF SINFUL STAGOLEE

1. Lawrence Gellert, *Negro Songs of Protest,* vol. 2: *Cap'n, You're So Mean,* Rounder Records, Somerville, Mass., 1936.

2. This account is taken from Alan Lomax, "Sinful Songs of the Southern Negro," *Southwest Quarterly* 19 (1934): 105–131.

3. Onah L. Spencer, "Stackalee," *Directions* 4 (1941): 15.

4. "Stagolee," in John Lomax and Alan Lomax, *American Ballads and Folk Songs* (New York: Macmillan, 1934), 93–99.

5. Robert Johnson, "Me and the Devil Blues," *King of the Delta Blues Singers,* Columbia Records, New York, 1998.

20. STAGOLEE IN A WORLD FULL OF TROUBLE

1. Virginia P. Brown and Laurella Owens, *Toting the Lead Row: Ruby Pickens Tartt, Alabama Folklorist* (Mobile: University of Alabama Press, 1981), 20.

2. Recorded by John Lomax in Livingston, Alabama, July 1937, no. 1320, American Folklore Collection, Library of Congress.

3. Alan Lomax, "Sinful Songs of the Southern Negro," *Southwest Quarterly* 19 (1934): 131.

4. Alan Lomax, liner notes, *Prison Songs: Historical Recordings from Parchman Farm, 1947–48,* Rounder Records, Cambridge, Mass., 1957.

5. Ibid.

6. David M. Oshinsky, *Worse than Slavery: Parchman Farm and the Ordeal of Jim Crow Justice* (New York: Free Press, 1966), 136.

7. Ibid., 134.

8. Lomax, liner notes, *Prison Songs.*

9. Oshinsky, *Worse than Slavery,* 136. See also Cecil Brown, "Homer and Rap Music," *San Francisco Examiner Sunday Magazine,* December 19, 1998.

10. Bruce Jackson, *Wake Up Dead Man: Afro-American Work Songs from Texas Prisons* (Cambridge, Mass.: Harvard University Press, 1975), xvii, xvi.

11. Lomax, liner notes, *Prison Songs.*

12. Alan Lomax, *Negro Prison Songs from the Mississippi State Penitentiary,* Tradition Record Notes, Music Division, Library of Congress, 1975.

13. Jackson, *Wake Up Dead Man,* 7.

14. Lomax, liner notes, *Prison Songs.*

15. Ibid.

16. Pam Morris, ed., *The Bakhtin Reader: Selected Writings of Bakhtin, Medvedev, Voloshinov* (New York: Edward Arnold, 1994), 209.

17. Nathan B. Young, "Transgressions: Death, Legends, and Music of Bad Man Stackolee," Manuscript M2, St. Louis University Archives, 1983.

18. Ben Sidran, *Black Talk* (New York: Holt, Rinehart and Winston, 1971), 21.

19. Mary Wheeler, *Steamboatin' Days* (Baton Rouge: Louisiana State University Press, 1944), 100.

20. American Folklore Collection, no. 699, Library of Congress.

21. FROM RHYTHM AND BLUES TO ROCK AND ROLL

1. Sidney Bechet, "Old Stack O' Lee Blues," *The Best of Sidney Bechet,* Blue Note Records, New York, 1994.

2. David Toop, *The Rap Attack 2* (Bridgend, Wales: Serpent's Tail, 1991), 2, 30.

3. October 19, 1940, American Folklore Recordings, Library of Congress, reissued in *Deep River Song: Mississippi, Saints and Sinners: From before the Blues and Gospel,* Rounder Records, Cambridge, Mass.

4. Alan Lomax, liner notes, *Deep River Song.*

5. Imamu Amiri Baraka, *Blues People* (New York: Morrow, 1963), 168.

6. John Broven, *Walking to New Orleans: The Story of New Orleans Rhythm and Blues* (Bexhill-on-Sea: Flyright Records, 1977), 10, 12. I have not been able to find any information about such a pianist in New Orleans.

7. Ibid., 11.

8. Ibid., 12.

9. Ibid., 39.

10. Ibid., 40.

11. Robin D. G. Kelley, *Race Rebels: Culture, Politics, and the Black Working Class* (New York: Free Press, 1994), 187.

12. Lloyd Price, "Stagger Lee," *Personality Price,* Specialty Records, New York, 1986.

22. THE TOAST

1. In 1964 Roger D. Abrahams published his pathbreaking study of black oral narrative, *Deep Down in the Jungle* (1964; reprint, Chicago: Aldine, 1970). Along with other folklorists, such as Daniel J. Crowley (*I Could Talk Old-Story Good: Creativity in Bahamian Folklore* [Berkeley: University of California Press, 1966]) and Bruce Jackson (*"Get Your Ass in the Water and Swim like Me": Narrative Poetry from Black Oral Tradition* [Cambridge, Mass.: Harvard University Press, 1974]), Abrahams established a new theory of oral narrative folklore. These professors-turned-folklorists embodied what one scholar has called the "socio-psychological approach" (see Bengt Holbek, *The Interpretation of Fairy Tale: Danish Folklore in a European Perspective* [Helsinki: Academia Scientiarum Fennica, 1987], 390). But if collectors of Stagolee from the 1900s and 1920s could be accused of taking a colonialist perspective, then the next major collectors, Abrahams and Jackson, may be accused of doing much the same in seeking to measure Stagolee against the yardstick of psychopathology. Abrahams looked at Stagolee in the context of black gang leaders; Jackson, who followed Abrahams, concentrated on the black pimp and reached the conclusion that Stagolee is a "sociopath"; *"Get Your Ass in the Water,"* 30.
2. Jackson, *"Get Your Ass in the Water,"* 136.
3. Brazilian culture has a similar expression, "Voce sabe com quem esta falando?" Roberto Damatta observes that it has "overtones of vexing authority, hostility, and arrogance"; *Carnivals, Rogues, and Heroes* (Notre Dame, Ind.: Notre Dame University Press, 1991), 137. This brilliant book reveals how a ritual expression can embody a self-image that helps the individual survive in the group.
4. Daryl C. Dance, *Shuckin' and Jivin': Folklore from Contemporary Black Americans* (Bloomington: Indiana University Press, 1978), 376.
5. Jackson, *"Get Your Ass in the Water,"* 43, collected at the Ramsay, Texas, prison in 1965.
6. Ibid., 44, collected at Jefferson City, Missouri.

23. FOLKLORE/POPLORE

1. Tom Rush, "Stackerlee," *Tom Rush,* Fantasy Records, Berkeley, California, 1959; Dave Van Ronk, "Stackalee," *Van Ronk,* Fantasy Records, Berkeley, Calif., 1962.

   I met Dave Van Ronk in Berkeley in 1998 in the dressing room of the Freight and Salvage folk club, right after a performance. He told me that somebody had given him a newspaper clipping about Lee Shelton. Van Ronk was said to have over five hundred versions of Stagolee, though when I asked him about that he laughed and said it was all folklore. He did know several versions, and he sang me a couple.

2. Hogman Maxey, "Stagolee," *Angola Prisoner's Blues,* Arhoolie Records, El Cerrito, Calif., 1959.

3. Bob Dylan, "Stack A Lee," *World Gone Wrong,* Columbia Records, New York, 1993.

4. W. T. Lhamon Jr., *Raising Cain: Blackface Performance from Jim Crow to Hip Hop* (Cambridge, Mass.: Harvard University Press, 1998), 160.

5. T. S. Eliot wrote: "I believe that the poet naturally prefers to write for as large and miscellaneous an audience as possible, and that it is the half-educated and ill-educated, rather than the uneducated, that stand in the way. I myself should like an audience which could neither read nor write"; quoted in Gene Bluestein, *The Voice of the Folk* (Amherst: University of Massachusetts Press, 1972), 142.

6. Eugene Bluestein, *Poplore: Folk and Pop in American Culture* (Amherst: University of Massachusetts Press, 1994), 89.

7. Telephone conversation with Eugene Bluestein, July 3, 2001.

8. Bluestein, *Poplore,* 91.

9. Imbalance is established by such events as the emergence of the jazz musician. The metaphor of the jazzman illustrates the relationship better than any analogy we have seen to this point. Jazz values improvisations, personal vision, and assault on the conventional modes of musical expression, but it will not allow the individual to forget what he owes to tradition—not the tradition of a

great man, but the legacy shaped by a whole people. Most folklorists' work has been weighted in favor of the force of tradition, according to Bluestein, "not so much because the concept seemed to correct extreme individualism but because it underscores the anonymity of 'authentic' folk expression"; *The Voice of the Folk*, 223. But, as Richard Bauman has pointed out, over the past twenty years folklorists have tended "to turn away from viewing the folk as an 'anonymous collectivity' and to focus more on 'the individual performer'"; *Story, Performance, and Event: Contextual Studies of Oral Narrative* (Cambridge: Cambridge University Press, 1986), 231. Much of new folklore is identifiable, but "the unwillingness of folklorists to acknowledge [it] has denied us an adequate definition of folk styles in our society." The folklore process must account for the contribution of known individuals to the folk legacy.

10. Bluestein, *Poplore*, 91.
11. Bauman, *Story, Performance, and Event*, 231.
12. Alan Dundes, *Interpreting Folklore* (Bloomington: Indiana University Press, 1980), 7.
13. Telephone conversation with Bluestein, July 3, 2001.
14. Maurice Capel, "The Blessing of the Damned," in *The Dylan Companion*, ed. Elizabeth Thomason and David Gutman (London: Da Capo), 107.
15. David Hajdu, *Positively Fourth: The Lives and Times of Joan Baez, Bob Dylan, Mimi Baez Farina, and Richard Farina* (New York: Farrar, Straus and Giroux, 2001), 92.
16. Betsy Bowden, *Performed Literature* (New York: University Press of America, 2001), 140.

24. THE "BAD NIGGER" TROPE IN AMERICAN LITERATURE

1. Tennessee Williams, *Collected Stories*, 26–31.
2. Richard Wright, "Big Boy Leaves Home," in *Uncle Tom's Children* (New York: Harper & Row, 1940), 27.
3. Lyle Leverich, *Tom: The Unknown Tennessee Williams* (New York: Crown, 1995), 118.

4. Guy B. Johnson, "Folk Values in Recent Literature on the Negro," *Folk-Say: A Regional Miscellany* 2 (1930): 359–372, does not mention a single African-American writer.

5. Howard W. Odum, *Rainbow round My Shoulder: The Blue Trail of Black Ulysses* (Indianapolis: Bobbs-Merrill, 1925), 82–83.

6. Johnson, "Folk Values," 360.

7. Margaret Walker, "Stagolee," *Anthology of Negro Poets,* Folkways Records, 1954; originally published in Walker, *For My People* (New Haven: Yale University Press, 1942), 35.

8. Papa Harvey Hull, "Stack O' Lee Blues," *The Songster Tradition, 1927–1935,* Document Records, Vienna, Austria, 1982.

9. Sterling A. Brown, "The Devil and the Black Man," *Folk-Say* 4 (1932): 246–256, esp. 248–254.

10. See Ralph Ellison's "Flying Home," in *Calling the Wind,* ed. Clarence Majors (New York: HarperCollins, 1993), 135; and Brendt Ostendorf, *Black Literature in White America* (Sussex: Harvester, 1982), 133–144.

11. See Richard Hoggart, *The Uses of Literacy* (New Brunswick, N.J.: Transaction, 1955).

12. Brown, "The Devil and the Black Man," 251.

13. H. Nigel Thomas, *From Folklore to Fiction: A Study of Folk Heroes and Rituals in the Black American Novel* (New York: Greenwood, 1988), 33.

14. Quoted in ibid.

15. Thomas, *From Folklore to Fiction,* 71–79.

16. Ibid., 71, 75–76.

17. Wright, "Big Boy Leaves Home," 17.

18. Richard Wright, "The Literature of the Negro in the United States," in *White Man, Listen!* (Garden City, N.Y.: Doubleday, 1957), 105–149.

19. Wright, *White Man, Listen!* 92.

20. Ibid., 93.

21. Ostendorf, *Black Literature in White America,* 211.

22. Ralph Ellison, *Shadow and Act* (New York: Vintage, 1972), 203.

23. Richard Wright, "How Bigger Was Born," *Saturday Review,* June 1,

1940, 4–5, 17–20, reprinted in *Early Works of Richard Wright,* ed. Arnold Rampersad (New York: Library of America, 1991), 854.

24. Ibid., 865–866.
25. Ibid., 866.
26. Ibid., 867.
27. Ibid., 868.
28. James Baldwin, "Many Thousand Gone," in *Collected Essays* (Washington, D.C.: Library of America, 1998), 30–31.
29. Ibid., 28.

25. JAMES BALDWIN'S "STAGGERLEE WONDERS"

1. David Lemmings, *James Baldwin: A Biography* (New York: Alfred A. Knopf, 1998), 358.
2. Ibid., 293.
3. Bobby Seale, *A Lonely Rage* (New York: Times Books, 1978).
4. James Baldwin, "Stagolee," foreword to Bobby Seale, *A Lonely Rage* (New York: Times Books, 1978), xii.
5. Ibid.
6. James Baldwin, "Staggerlee Wonders," in *Jimmy's Blues: Selected Poems* (New York: St. Martin's, 1985), 7–23.
7. Lemmings, *James Baldwin,* 359.

26. STAGOLEE AS CULTURAL AND POLITICAL HERO

Epigraph: James Baldwin, "The Negro at Home and Abroad," in *Collected Essays of James Baldwin* (New York: Library of America, 1998), 603.

1. Bobby Seale, *Seize the Time: The Story of the Black Panther Party and Huey P. Newton* (New York: Random House, 1970), 4.
2. David Gordon Nielson, *Black Ethos: Northern Urban Negro Life and Thought, 1890–1930* (Westport, Conn.: Greenwood, 1989), 1.
3. Sterling Stuckey, "Through the Prism of Folklore: The Black Ethos in Slavery," in *American Negro Slavery: A Modern Reader,* ed. Allen Weinstein and Frank Otto Gatell (New York: Oxford University Press, 1973), 135.

4. Victor Turner, *From Ritual to Theater: The Human Seriousness of Play* (New York: PAJ, 1982), 10.

27. STAGOLEE AND MODERNISM

1. Quoted in Brent Ostendorf, *Black Literature in White America* (Sussex: Harvester, 1982), 1. References to Sidran in the following discussion are from this source.
2. Eric Havelock, *The Muse Learns to Write* (Cambridge, Mass.: Harvard University Press, 1986), 30.
3. Ben Sidran, *Black Talk* (New York: Holt, Rinehart and Winston, 1971), 3.
4. Ibid., 9.
5. Ibid., 11.
6. Ibid., 30.
7. Havelock, *The Muse Learns to Write*, 28, 29.
8. Richard P. Martin, *The Language of Heroes: Speech and Performance in the Iliad* (Ithaca, N.Y.: Cornell University Press, 1989).
9. See Akin Sweeney, *A Full Hearing* (Berkeley: University of California Press, 1987), 83.
10. Kevin J. Mumford, *Interzones: Black/White Sex Districts in Chicago and New York in the Early Twentieth Century* (New York: Columbia University Press, 1997), 68.
11. Ibid., 135, 136.
12. Robin D. G. Kelley, *Race Rebels: Culture, Politics, and the Black Working Class* (New York: Free Press, 1994), 194. Linguists Wlad Godzich and Jeffrey Kittay offer helpful ideas on how black signifying practices use language in oral performance. As the vehicle of language, the speaker is the means whereby language institutes itself in the concreteness of the here and now of a certain audience. To the extent that the ritual is successful, the divine will make itself present. See Wlad Godzich, *The Culture of Literacy* (Cambridge, Mass.: Harvard University Press, 1994); and Jeffrey Kittay and Wlad Godzich, *The Emergence of Prose: An Essay in Prosaic* (Minneapolis: University of Minnesota Press, 1987).

13. The second function of ritual is its protocol. It prescribes specific actions and lays down rules by which they are to be followed. When the ritual is displaced by the performance of a singer of a tale, we can see that the "criterion of success of the performance is not some objective efficacy, some production other than represented action."

14. Donald Lowe, *The Body in Late-Capitalist USA* (Durham, N.C.: Duke University Press, 1995), 109.

15. Ibid., 111.

16. Graeme Gilloch, *Myth and Metropolis: Walter Benjamin and the City* (New York: Polity, 1996), 135.

17. Ibid., 137.

18. William Barlow, *Looking Up at Down: The Emergence of Blues Culture* (Philadelphia: Temple University Press, 1989), 82.

19. Quoted in Keith Tester, *The Flaneur* (London: Routledge, 1994), 53.

20. Quoted in ibid., 68.

Bibliography

PUBLISHED SOURCES

Aarne, Antti, and Sith Thompson. *The Types of the Folktale.* 2d rev. ed. Helsinki: Suomalainen Tiedeakatemia, 1961.

Abrahams, Roger D. "Black Talk in the Street." In *Explorations in the Ethnography of Speaking.* Edited by Dell Hymes. Cambridge: Cambridge University Press, 1982.

—— *Deep Down in the Jungle.* 1964; reprint, Chicago: Aldine, 1970.

—— "The Enactment-Centered Theory." In *Frontiers of Folklore.* Edited by William Bascom. Boulder: Westview, 1977, pp. 79–120.

—— "The Negro Stereotype, Negro Folklore and the Riots." *Journal of American Folklore* 83 (1970): 228–249.

—— *Singing the Master: The Emergence of African American Culture in the Plantation South.* New York: Pantheon, 1991.

Abrahams, Roger D., and John F. Szwed, eds. *After Africa.* New Haven: Yale University Press, 1983.

Adams, Edward C. L. *Tales of the Congaree.* 1928; reprint, Chapel Hill: University of North Carolina Press, 1987.

Armstrong, Louis. *Satchmo: My Life in New Orleans.* New York: Da Capo, 1986.

Baer, Florence. *Sources and Analogues of the Uncle Remus Tale.* Helsinki: Academia Scientiarum Fennica, 1980.

Baker, Houston A. *Blues, Ideology, and Afro-American Literature: A Vernacular Theory.* Chicago: University of Chicago Press, 1984.

—— *Long Black Song.* Chicago: University of Chicago Press, 1972.

Bakhtin, Mikhail. "The Hero, and the Position of the Author with Regard to the Hero, in Dostoevsky's Art." In *Problems of Dostoevsky's Poetics.* Edited by Caryl Emerson. Minneapolis: University of Minnesota Press, 1984, pp. 47–77.

—— *Rabelais and His World.* Translated by Helene Iswolsky. Bloomington: Indiana University Press, 1984.

Bal, Mieke. *Narratology.* Toronto: University of Toronto Press, 1988.

Baldwin, James. *Jimmy's Blues.* New York: St. Martin's, 1985.

—— *Notes of a Native Son.* Boston: Beacon, 1984.

—— "Stagolee." Foreword to Bobby Seale, *A Lonely Rage.* New York: Times Books, 1978.

Baraka, Imamu Amiri (LeRoi Jones). *Blues People.* New York: Morrow, 1963.

——, ed. *Black Fire: An Anthology of Afro-American Writing.* New York: Morrow, 1968.

Barlow, William. *Looking Up at Down: The Emergence of Blues Culture.* Philadelphia: Temple University Press, 1989.

Barlow, William, and Thomas L. Morgan. *From Cakewalks to Concert*

Halls: An Illustrated History of African American Popular Music from 1895 to 1930. Washington, D.C.: Elliot and Clark, 1992.

Bascom, William. *Shango in the New World.* Austin: University of Texas, African and Afro-American Research Institute, 1972.

Bateson, Gregory. *Naven: The Culture of the Latmul People of New Guinea as Revealed through the Study of the "Naven" Ceremonial.* Stanford: Stanford University Press, 1958.

Bauman, Richard. *Story, Performance, and Event: Contextual Studies of Oral Narrative.* Cambridge: Cambridge University Press, 1986.

Beck, Robert. *Pimp: The Story of My Life, by Iceberg Slim.* Los Angeles: Holloway House, 1967.

Bedient, Calvin. *He Do the Police in Different Voices: The Waste Land and Its Protagonist.* Chicago: University of Chicago Press, 1986.

Benjamin, Walter. *Gesammelte Schriften.* Edited by Rolf Tiedemann and Hermann Schweppenhäuser. 4 vols. Frankfurt am Main: Suhrkamp Verlag, 1972–1977.

—— *Illuminations.* Edited by Hannah Arendt. Translated by Harry Zohn. New York: Schocken, 1969.

—— *Reflections: Essays, Aphorisms, Autobiographical Writings.* Translated by Edmund Jephcott. New York: Schocken, 1978.

Benveniste, Emile. *Problems in General Linguistics.* Translated by Mary Elizabeth Meek. Miami: University of Miami Press, 1971.

Bergonzi, Bernard. "Eliot's Cities." In *T. S. Eliot at the Turn of the Century.* Edited by Marianne Thorahlen. Lund: Lund University Press, 1994.

Berlin, Edward A. *King of Ragtime: Scott Joplin and His Era.* Oxford: Oxford University Press, 1994.

Blacking, John. *How Musical Is Man?* Seattle: University of Washington Press, 1973.

Bluestein, Eugene. *Poplore: Folk and Pop in American Culture.* Amherst: University of Massachusetts Press, 1994.

—— *The Voice of the Folk.* Amherst: University of Massachusetts Press, 1972.

Bontemps, Arna. *God Sends Sunday.* New York: Harcourt, Brace, 1931.

Bontemps, Arna, and Jack Conroy. *Anywhere but Here.* New York: Hill and Wang, 1966.

Bourdieu, Pierre. *Outline of a Theory of Practice.* Cambridge: Cambridge University Press, 1972.

Bowden, Betsy. *Performed Literature.* New York: University Press of America, 2001.

Brearley, H. C. "Ba-ad Nigger" (1939). In *Mother Wit from the Laughing Barrel.* Edited by Alan Dundes. Jackson: University of Mississippi Press, 1972, pp. 578–585.

Broven, John. *Walking to New Orleans: The Story of New Orleans Rhythm and Blues.* Bexhill-on-Sea: Flyright Records, 1977.

Brown, Sterling A. "The Devil and The Black Man." *Folk-Say* 4 (1932): 246–256.

Brown, Virginia P., and Laurella Owens. *Toting the Lead Row: Ruby Pickens Tartt, Alabama Folklorist.* Mobile: University of Alabama Press, 1981.

Buck-Morss, Susan. *The Dialectics of Seeing: Walter Benjamin and the Arcades Project.* Cambridge, Mass.: MIT Press, 1997.

Buehler, Richard. "Stacker Lee: A Partial Investigation into the Historicity of a Negro Murder Ballad." *Keystone Folklore Quarterly* 12 (Fall 1967): 187–191.

Burkert, Walter. *Structure and History in Greek Mythology and Ritual.* Berkeley: University of California Press, 1979.

Byrum, Jack. *The Daemon in the Woods.* Cambridge: Cambridge University Press, 1960.

Carby, Hazel. "It Just Be's Dat Way Sometime: The Sexual Politics of Women's Blues," *Radical America* 20, no. 4 (1999): 9-22.

Charnas, Dan. "Ice Cube—A Gangsta's World View." *The Source: The Voice of the Rap Music Industry* 3, no. 4 (1991): 20-22.

Christensen, Lawrence Oland. "Black St. Louis: A Study in Race Relations, 1865-1916." Ph.D. diss., University of Missouri, 1972.

Cohen, Norm. *Long Steel Rail: The Railroad in American Folksong.* Urbana: University of Illinois Press, 1981.

—— *Minstrels and Tunesmiths: The Roots of American Music, 1902–1923.* Los Angeles: John Edwards Memorial Foundation, 1983.

Conard, Howard, and William Hyde, eds. *Encyclopedia of the History of St. Louis.* St. Louis: Southern History, 1899.

Connelly, Bridget. *Arab Folk Epic and Identity.* Berkeley: University of California Press, 1986.

Courlander, Harold. *Negro Folk Music, USA.* New York: Columbia University Press, 1970.

Cowley, John. *Shack Bullies and Levee Contractors: Studies in the Oral History of a Black Protest Song Tradition.* Los Angeles: University of California at Los Angeles, 1980, pp. 182-192.

Cross, Brian. *It's Not about a Salary.* New York: Verso, 1993.

Curtis, Susan. *Dancing to a Black Man's Tune: A Life of Scott Joplin.* Columbia: University of Missouri Press, 1994.

Dance, Daryl C. *Shuckin' and Jivin': Folklore from Contemporary Black Americans*. Bloomington: Indiana University Press, 1978.

David, John R. "Tragedy in Ragtime: Black Folktales from St. Louis." Ph.D. diss., St. Louis University, 1976.

DeCoy, Robert H. *The Big Black Fire*. Los Angeles: Holloway House, 1969.

Detweiler, Frederick G. *The Negro Press in the United States*. Chicago: University of Chicago Press, 1922.

Devereux, George. *From Anxiety to Method in the Behavioral Sciences*. Paris: Mouton, 1967.

Dorsey, William. *Philadelphia and Ours*. New York: Oxford University Press, 1999.

Dorson, Richard. *American in Legend: Folklore from the Colonial Period to the Present*. New York: Random House, 1973.

—— *American Negro Folktales*. Greenwich, Conn.: Fawcett, 1967.

Douglass, Ann. *Terrible Honesty Mongrel Manhattan in the 1920*. New York: Noonday Press/Farrar, Straus and Giroux, 1995.

Dreiser, Theodore. *Journalism*. Edited by T. D. Nostwich. Philadelphia: University of Pennsylvania Press, 1988.

Dundes, Alan. *Analytic Essays in Folklore*. Paris: Mouton, 1975.

—— "From Etic to Emic Units in the Structural Study of Folktales." *Journal of American Folklore* 75 (1962): 69.

—— *Mother Wit from the Laughing Barrel*. Jackson: University of Mississippi Press, 1991.

—— *Parsing through Customs*. Madison: University of Wisconsin Press, 1987.

—— *The Study of Folklore*. Englewood Cliffs, N.J.: Prentice-Hall, 1965.

Early, Gerald, ed. *Ain't but a Place.* St. Louis: St. Louis Historical Society, 1999.

Eisley, Loren. *Darwin's Century.* Garden City, N.Y.: Doubleday, 1961.

Ellison, Ralph. *Shadow and Act.* New York: Vintage, 1972.

Epstein, Dena J. *Sinful Tunes and Spirituals: Black Folk Music to the Civil War.* Urbana: University of Illinois Press, 1977.

Erdoes, Richard, ed. *Tales from the American Frontier.* New York: Alfred A. Knopf, 1991.

Evans, David. *Big Road Blues: Tradition and Creativity in the Folk Blues.* New York: Da Capo, 1982.

Fernandez, James. "Edification by Puzzlement." In *Modes of Thought.* Tübingen: J. C. B. Mohr, 1985, pp. 44–60.

Fillmore, Charles. *Frames and Semantics of Understanding.* Bologna: Società editrice de Mulino, 1982.

Fine, Elizabeth. *The Performing Text.* Austin: University of Texas Press, 1977.

Finnegan, Ruth. *Oral Literature in Africa.* Oxford: Oxford University Press, 1970.

Finger, Charles J. *Frontier Ballads: Heard and Gathered.* Garden City, N.Y.: Doubleday, Page, 1927.

Floyd, Samuel A. *The Power of Black Music: Interpreting Its History from Africa to the United States.* New York: Oxford University Press, 1995.

Freud, Sigmund, and D. E. Oppenheim. "A Connection between a Symbol and a Symptom." In *Character and Culture.* Edited by Philip Reiff. 1916; reprint, New York: Collier, 1963, pp. 55–56.

—— "Psychoanalysis." In *Character and Culture*. Edited by Philip Reiff. New York: Collier, 1963, pp. 230–251.

—— *Dreams in Folklore*. New York: International Universities Press, 1958.

Galoob, Debra. *"Back in '32 When the Times Was Hard" Riata*. Austin: University of Texas Press, 1965, pp. 15–30.

Gates, David. "The Rap Attitude." *Newsweek*, March 19, 1990, pp. 56–63.

Gates, Henry Louis, Jr. *Signifying Monkey: A Theory of Afro-American Literature*. New York: Oxford University Press, 1988.

Gellert, Lawrence. *Negro Songs of Protest*. Arranged for voice and piano by Elie Siegmeister, illustrated by Hugo Gellert. American Music League, New York, 1933.

—— *Negro Songs of Protest*. Vol. 2: *Cap'n, You're So Mean*. Rounder Records, Somerville, Mass., 1936.

Genette, Gérard. *Narrative Discourse: An Essay in Method*. Ithaca: Cornell University Press, 1987.

Gilbert, Douglass. *Lost Chords: The Diverting Story of American Popular Story of American's Popular Songs*. Garden City, N.Y.: Doubleday, 1942.

Gilfoyle, Timothy J. *City of Eros: New York City, Prostitution, and the Commercialism of Sex*. New York: W. W. Norton, 1992.

—— "Strumpets and Misogynists: Brothel Riots and the Transformation of Prostitution in Antebellum New York City." *New York History*, January 1987, pp. 45–65.

Gilloch, Graeme. *Myth and Metropolis: Walter Benjamin and the City*. New York: Polity, 1996.

Gilroy, Paul. *The Black Atlantic: Modernity and Double Consciousness.* Cambridge, Mass.: Harvard University Press, 1993.

Godzich, Wlad. *The Culture of Literacy.* Cambridge, Mass.: Harvard University Press, 1994.

Goldberg, Isaac. *Tin Pan Alley: A Chronicle of American Popular Music.* New York: Ungar, 1961.

Goldman, Albert Harry. *Grass Roots: Marijuana in America Today.* New York: Harper and Row, 1979.

Goody, Jack. *The Domestication of the Savage Mind.* Cambridge: Cambridge University Press, 1978.

Grant, Douglas. *Mark Twain.* New York: Grove, 1962.

Green, Archie. *Calf's Head and Union Tail.* Urbana: University of Illinois Press, 1996.

——— "Industrial Lore: A Bibliographic-Semantic Query." *Western Folklore* 37 (1978): 213–244.

——— *Only a Miner: Studies in Recorded Coal-Mining Songs.* Urbana: University of Illinois Press, 1972.

Greenberg, Kenneth S. *Honor and Slavery.* Princeton: Princeton University Press, 1996.

Greenway, John. *American Folksongs of Protest.* New York: Perpetura, 1953.

Hajdu, David. *Positively Fourth Street.* New York: Farrar, Straus and Giroux, 2001.

Haley, Alex. *The Autobiography of Malcolm X.* New York: Ballantine, 1990.

Handy, W. C. *The Father of the Blues.* New York: Da Capo, 1985.

Harris, Trudier. *Fiction and Folklore: The Novels of Toni Morrison.* Knoxville: University of Tennessee Press, 1991.

Harrison, Michael. *The History of the Hat.* London: Herbert Jenkins, 1960.

Hasse, John Edward, ed. *The History of Ragtime: Its History, Composers, and Music.* New York: Schirmer, 1985.

Havelock, Eric Alfred. *The Muse Learns to Write: Reflections on Orality and Literacy from Antiquity to the Present.* New Haven: Yale University Press, 1986.

—— *Preface to Plato.* Cambridge, Mass.: Harvard University Press, 1963.

Hearn, Lafacadio. "Levee Life." In *Selected Writings of Lacadio Hearn.* Edited by Henry Goodman. 1904; reprint, New York: Citadel, 1949, pp. 215–233.

Hegel, G. W. F. "The Phenomenology of the Spirit." In *The Philosophy of Hegel.* Edited by Carl J. Friedrich. New York: Modern Library, 1954.

Henderson, Stephen. *Understanding New Black Poetry: Black Speech and Black Music as Poetic Reference.* New York: William Morrow, 1973.

Hendricks, W. C., ed. *Bundle of Trouble and Other Tarheel Stories.* Durham: Duke University Press, 1943.

Henry, Charles. *Jesse Jackson: The Search for Common Ground.* Oakland, Calif.: Black Scholar Press, 1991.

Herskovits, Melville J. *Dohenyan Narratives.* Evanston: Northwestern University Press, 1985.

—— "Some Comments by Professor Herskovits." *South Atlantic Quarterly* 39 (1940): 350–351.

Herzfeld, Michael. *The Poetics of Manhood: Contest and Identity in a Cretan Mountain Village.* Princeton: Princeton University Press, 1985.

Hoggart, Richard. *The Uses of Literacy.* New Brunswick, N.J.: Transaction, 1955.

Holbek, Bengt. *The Interpretation of Fairy Tale: Danish Folklore in a European Perspective.* Helsinki: Academia Scientiarum Fennica, 1987.

Holloway, Joseph E., ed. *Africanisms in American Culture.* Bloomington: Indiana University Press, 1991.

Huggins, Nathan. *Black Odyssey: The Afro-American Ordeal in Slavery.* New York: Viking, 1979.

Hugill, Stan. *Shanties and Sailors' Songs.* New York: Praeger, 1969.

Hunter, Robert. *A Box of Rain: Collected Lyrics of Robert Hunter.* New York: Viking, 1990.

Hurston, Zora Neale. *Jonah's Gourd.* London: Virago, 1990.

—— *Mules and Men.* New York: Perennial Library, 1990.

Huxley, Martin. *Eminem: Crossing the Line.* New York: St. Martin's Griffin, 2000.

Immortalia. N.p., 1927, pp. 23–33.

Irele, Abiola. *The African Experience in Literature and Ideology.* Bloomington: Indiana University Press, 1981.

Irvin, Mae. "The Bully." In *Minstrels and Tunesmiths: The Roots of American Music, 1902–1923.* Los Angeles: John Edwards Memorial Foundation; Arhoolie Records, El Cerrito, Calif., 1983.

Jackson, Bruce. "Circus and Street: Psychosocial Aspects of the Black Toast." *Journal of American Folklore* 85 (1972): 123–139.

—— *"Get Your Ass in the Water and Swim like Me": Narrative Poetry from Black Oral Tradition.* Cambridge, Mass.: Harvard University Press, 1974.

—— "Wake Up Dead Man." In *Black Convict Worksongs from Texas Prison.* Rounder Records, Somerville, Mass., 1966.

—— *Wake Up Dead Man: Afro-American Work Songs from Texas Prisons.* Cambridge, Mass.: Harvard University Press, 1975.

Jahn, Janheinz. *Muntu: An Outline of the New African Culture.* London: Faber and Faber, 1961.

Jakobson, Roman. 1971. "Shifters, Verbal Categories, and the Russian Verb." In *Selected Writings.* Vol. 2. The Hague: Mouton, 1971, pp. 130–147.

Jameson, Fredric. *The Political Unconscious: Narrative as a Socially Symbolic Act.* Ithaca: Cornell University Press, 1981.

Jasen, David A., and Trebor Jay Tichenor, *Rags and Ragtime: A Musical History.* New York: Dover, 1978.

Jobes, Gertrude. *Dictionary of Mythology, Folklore and Symbols.* New York: Scarecrow, 1972.

Johnson, Guy B. "Folk Values in Recent Literature on the Negro." In *Folk-Say: A Regional Miscellany.* Vol. 2. Norman, Okla., 1930, pp. 359–372.

—— *The Trail of Black Ulysses.* Indianapolis, 1928.

Johnson, John Williams. *The Epic of Sun-Jara: An Attempt to Define the Model for African Epic Poetry.* Bloomington: Indiana University Press, 1978.

Jones, Reginal, ed. *Black Psychology.* Berkeley: Cobb and Henry, 1991.

Kardiner, Abram, and Lionel Ovesey. *The Mark of Oppression: Explorations in the Personality of the American Negro.* New York: World Publishing Company, 1969.

Kelley, Robin D. G. *Race Rebels: Culture, Politics, and the Black Working Class.* New York: Free Press, 1994.

Kimball, Nell. *Her Life as an American Madam: By Herself.* Edited by Stephen Longstreet. New York: Macmillan, 1970.

King, Ethel M. *Reflections of Reedy: A Biography of William Marion Reedy of Reedy's Mirror.* Brooklyn: Gerald J. Rickard, 1961.

Kittay, Jeffrey, and Wlad Godzich. *The Emergence of Prose: An Essay in Prosaic.* Minneapolis: University of Minnesota Press, 1987.

Klingebiel, Chris. "Metaphor and Moral Accounting." Manuscript, Linguistics Department, University of California at Berkeley, 1993.

Kochman, Thomas. "Toward an Ethnography of Black American Speech Behavior." In *Rappin' and Stylin' Out: Communication in Urban Black American.* Edited by Kochman. Urbana: University of Illinois Press, 1972, pp. 241–264.

Kodish, Debora. *Good Friends and Bad Enemies.* Urbana: University of Illinois Press, 1986.

Kremer, Gary R. *James Milton Turner and the Promise of America: The Public Life of a Post–Civil War Black Leader.* Columbia: University of Missouri Press, 1991.

Lakoff, George. *Cognitive Semantics: Meaning and Mental Representation.* Bloomington: Indiana University Press, 1988.

—— *Master Metaphor List.* Berkeley: Cognitive Linguistics Group, 1991.

—— *Metaphors We Live By.* Chicago: University of Chicago Press, 1989.

Lane, Roger. *Violent Death in the City: Suicide, Accident, and Murder in Nineteenth-Century Philadelphia.* Cambridge, Mass.: Harvard University Press, 1979.

Larson, Mildred Lucille. *The Functions of Reported Speech in Discourse.* Austin: Summer Institute of Linguistics and the University of Texas at Arlington, 1978.

Lawrence, Stanley A., ed. *Rap: The Lyrics.* New York: Penguin, 1992.

Laws, Malcolm G., Jr. *Native American Balladry: A Descriptive Study and a Bibliographical Syllabus.* Philadelphia: American Folklore Society, 1964.

Lévi-Strauss, Claude. "The Structural Study of Myth." In *Structural Anthropology.* New York: Doubleday, 1986.

—— *Tristes Tropiques.* New York: Penguin, 1973.

Levine, Lawrence W. *Black Culture and Black Consciousness.* London: Oxford University Press, 1977.

Lhamon, W. T., Jr. *Raising Cain: Blackface Performance from Jim Crow to Hip Hop.* Cambridge, Mass.: Harvard University Press, 1998.

Lieb, Sandra. *Mother of the Blues: A Study of Ma Rainey.* Amherst: University of Massachusetts Press, 1981.

Lipsitz, George. *Time Passages: Collective Memory and American Popular Culture.* Minnesota: University of Minnesota Press, 1990.

Litwack, Leon. *Been in the Storm So Long: The Aftermath of Slavery.* New York: Vintage, 1980.

—— *Trouble in Mind: Black Southerners in the Age of Jim Crow.* New York: Alfred A. Knopf, 1998.

Locke, Alaine. *The New Negro.* New York: Atheneum, 1992.

Lofaro, Michael A., and Joe Cummings. *Crockett at Two Hundred: New Perspectives on the Man and the Myth.* Knoxville: University of Tennessee Press, 1989.

Lomax, Alan. *Mister Jelly Roll: The Fortunes of Jelly Roll Morton, New Orleans Creole, and "Inventor of Jazz."* New York: Pantheon, 1993.

—— Liner notes. *Prison Songs*. Rounder Records, Cambridge, Mass., 1957.

Lomax, John. *Adventures of a Ballad Hunter*. New York: Macmillan, 1947.

—— "Self-pity in Negro Songs." *Nation*, no. 105 (1917): 141–145.

—— "Sinful Songs of the Southern Negro." *Southwest Quarterly* 19 (1934): 105–131.

Lomax, John, and Alan Lomax. *American Ballads and Folk Songs*. New York: Macmillan, 1934.

Longstreet, Stephen. *Storyville to Harlem: Fifty Years in the Jazz Scene*. New Brunswick, N.J.: Rutgers University Press, 1986.

Lord, Albert B. *The Ballad Hunter*. Parts 1–10. Washington, D.C.: Library of Congress, Recording Laboratory AAFS L53, 1949.

—— *The Singer of Tales*. Cambridge, Mass.: Harvard University Press, 1960.

Lovell, John. *The Forge and Flame: The Story of How the Afro-American Spiritual Was Hammered Out*. New York: Paragon, 1986.

Manning, Frank E. *Black Clubs in Bermuda: Ethnography of a Play World*. Ithaca: Cornell University Press, 1973.

Marcus, Greil. "Sly Stone: The Myth of Staggerlee." In *Mystery Train*. 3d ed. New York: Dutton, 1990, pp. 65–95.

Martin, Richard P. *The Language of the Heroes: Speech and Performance in the Iliad*. Ithaca: Cornell University Press, 1989.

Martin, Sherill, and George R. Keck. *Feel the Spirit: Studies in Nineteenth-Century Afro-American Music*. New York: Greenwood, 1988.

Marx, Karl, and Friedrich Engels. *The Communist Manifesto*. Edited by Frederic L. Benton. New York: W. W. Norton, 1988.

McCulloh, Judith. "Some Child Ballads on Hillbilly Records." In *Folklore and Society: Essays in Honor of Benj. A. Botkin*. Edited by Bruce Jackson. Hatboro, Pa.: Folklore Associates, 1966.

McIlwaine, Shields. *Memphis down in Dixie*. New York: E. P. Dutton, 1948.

McLuhan, Marshall. *The Essential McLuhan*. Edited by Eric McLuhan. New York: Basic Books, 1999.

Milner, Christine. "Black Pimps and Their Prostitutes: Social Organization and Value System of a Ghetto Occupational Subculture." Ph.D. diss., University of California, Berkeley, 1970.

Mitchell-Kernan, Claudia. "Signifying, Loud-talking, and Marking." In *Mother Wit from the Laughing Barrel*. Edited by Alan Dundes. Jackson: University of Mississippi Press, 1972, pp. 310–329.

Montell, William Lynwood. *The Saga of Coe Ridge: A Study in Oral History*. Knoxville: University of Tennessee Press, 1970.

Morris, Pam, ed. *The Bakhtin Reader: Selected Writings of Bakhtin, Medvedev, Voloshinov*. London: Edward Arnold, 1994.

Morrison, Toni. "Folklore and African American Literature." 1987.

Mudimbe, V. Y. *The Invention of Africa: Gnosis, Philosophy, and the Order of Knowledge*. Bloomington: Indiana University Press, 1988.

—— *Parables and Fables: Textuality and Politics in Central Africa*. Madison: University of Wisconsin Press, 1991.

Mumford, Kevin J. *Interzones: Black/White Sex Districts in Chicago and New York in the Early Twentieth Century*. New York: Columbia University Press, 1997.

Neale, Larry. "And Shine Swam On." In *Black Fire: An Anthology of Afro-American Writing*. Edited by Leroi Jones and Larry Neale. New York: Morrow, 1968.

Nielson, David Gordon. *Black Ethos: Northern Urban Negro Life and Thought, 1890–1930.* Westport, Conn.: Greenwood, 1989.

Oakley, Giles. *The Devil's Music.* Milwaukee: Miller Freeman, 1998.

Odum, Howard W. "Down That Lonesome Road." *Country Gentlemen* 91 (May 1926): 18–19.

—— "Folk-Songs and Folk-Poetry as Found in the Secular Songs of the Southern Negroes." *Journal of American Folklore* 24 (1911): 255–294.

—— *Negro Workaday Songs.* Chapel Hill: University of North Carolina Press, 1926.

—— *Rainbow Round My Shoulder: The Blue Trail of Black Ulysses.* Indianapolis: Bobbs-Merrill, 1928.

Odum, Howard W., with Guy B. Johnson. *The Negro and His Songs.* Chapel Hill: University of North Carolina Press, 1925.

Okpewho, Isidore. *The African Epic: Towards a Poetics of the Oral Performance.* New York: Columbia University Press, 1979.

—— *Myth in African: A Study of Its Aesthetic and Cultural Relevance.* Cambridge: Cambridge University Press, 1983.

——, ed. *The Oral Performance in Africa.* Ibadan, Nigeria: Spectrum, 1990.

Oliver, Paul. *The Blues Fell This Morning: The Meaning of the Blues.* Cambridge: Cambridge University Press, 1984.

—— *Screening the Blues.* New York: Da Capo, 1968.

—— *Songsters and Saints: Vocal Tradition on Race Records.* Cambridge: Cambridge University Press, 1984.

Ong, Walter J. *Fighting for Life: Contest, Sexuality, and Consciousness.* Amherst: University of Massachusetts Press, 1981.

—— *Orality and Literacy: The Technologizing of the Word.* London: Routledge, 1982.

Oshinsky, David M. *Worse than Slavery: Parchman Farm and the Ordeal of Jim Crow Justice.* New York: Free Press, 1966.

Ostendorf, Brendt. *Black Literature in White America.* Sussex: Harvester, 1982.

—— "Black Poetry, Blues, and Folklore: Double Consciousness in Afro-American Oral Culture." *Jahrbuch für Amerikastudien* 20 (1975): 210–259.

Oster, Harry. *Angola Prisoner's Blues.* Arhoolie Records, Cerrito, Calif., 1959.

Pareles, Jon. "On Rap, Symbolism, and Fear." *New York Times,* February 2, 1992, p. 23.

Parry, Adam. *The Collected Papers of Milman Parry.* Edited by Adam Parry. Oxford: Clarendon Press, 1971.

Parry, Milman. *L'Epithète traditionelle dans Homère.* Paris: Société Editrice Les Belles Lettres, 1928.

Poussaint, Alvin F. *Why Blacks Kill Blacks.* New York: Emerson Hall, 1972.

Primm, Jamers Neal. *Lion of the Valley: St. Louis, Missouri.* Boulder: Pruett, 1990.

Propp, Vladimir. *Morphology of the Folktale.* Austin: University of Texas Press, 1990.

—— *Theory and History of Folklore.* Minneapolis: University of Minnesota Press, 1984.

Puckett, Newbell N. *Folk Beliefs of the Southern Negro.* 1926; reprint, Chapel Hill: University of North Carolina Press, 1968.

Putzel, Max. *The Man in the Mirror: William Marion Reedy and His Maga-zine.* Cambridge, Mass.: Harvard University Press, 1963.

Rabateau, Albert J. *Slave Religion.* Oxford: Oxford University Press, 1980.

Radin, Paul. "Literary Aspects of North American Mythology." *Canada Geological Survey Museum Bulletin* 16 (1915): 1–51.

Rawich, George P. *The American Slave: A Composite Autobiography.* Vol. 7: *Oklahoma and Mississippi Narrative; North Carolina Narratives,* parts 1 and 2. Westport, Conn.: Greenwood, 1972.

Redman, Eugene. 1971. "The Black American Epic: Its Roots, Its Writers." *Black Scholar* 3 (January): 16–22.

Reynolds, Anthony M. "Urban Negro Toasts: A Hustler's View from L.A." *Western Folklore,* 1974, 267–300.

Riis, Thomas L. *Just before Jazz: Black Musical Theater in New York, 1890–1915.* Washington, D.C.: Smithsonian Institution Press, 1989.

Robert, Randy. *Papa Jack: Jackson and the Era of White Hopes.* New York: Free Press, 1983.

Roberts, John. *From Trickster to Badman.* Philadelphia: University of Pennsylvania Press, 1989.

—— "Stackolee and the Development of a Black Heroic Idea." *Western Folklore* 3, no. 41 (July 1983): 179–189.

Roheim, Geza. *The Gates of the Dream.* New York: International Press, 1952.

Rose, Al. *Storyville, New Orleans.* Tuscaloosa: University of Alabama, 1974.

Rose, Tricia. *Black Noise: Rap Music and Black Culture in Contemporary America.* Hanover, N.H.: University Press of New England for Wesleyan University Press, 1994.

Rosenberg, Bruce. *Folklore and Literature: Rival Siblings.* Knoxville: University of Tennessee Press, 1991.

Rourke, Constance. *American Humor: A Study of the National Character.* New York: Harcourt, Brace, 1931.

Rubin, David C. *Memory in Oral Traditions: The Cognitive Psychology of Epic, Ballads, and Counting-out Rhymes.* Oxford: Oxford University Press, 1995.

Sandburg, Carl. *The American Songbag.* New York: Harcourt, Brace, 1927.

Scheub, H. "Performance of Oral Narrative." In *Frontiers of Folklore.* Washington, D.C.: Westview, 1977, pp. 55–78.

—— "The Technique of the Expansible Image of Xhosa Ntsomi Performances." *Research in African Literatures,* 1970, pp. 119–146.

Scholes, Robert, and Robert Kellogg. *The Nature of the Narrative.* New York: Oxford University Press, 1979.

Seale, Bobby. *A Lonely Rage.* New York: Times Books, 1978.

—— *Seize the Time: The Story of the Black Panther Party and Huey P. Newton.* New York: Random House, 1970.

Seitz, Don C. *Joseph Pulitzer: Liberator of Journalism.* 1924; reprint, New York: AMS Press, 1970.

Seward, Adrienne M. "The Black Pimp as a Folk Hero." Master's thesis, University of California, Berkeley, 1974.

Shapiro, Nat, and Nat Hentoff. *Hear Me Talkin' to Ya: The Story of Jazz as Told by the Men Who Made It.* Toronto: General Publishing, 1955.

Shecter, J. (the Sultan). Interview. *Source: Special Collector's Edition* 3 (January 1990): 12.

Sidran, Ben. *Black Talk.* New York: Holt, Rinehart and Winston, 1971.

Silverman, Kaja. 1983. *The Subject of Semiotics.* Oxford: Oxford University Press.

Simpson, George Eaton. "Cult Music of Trinidad." In *Folkways Ethnic Library Album.* Washington, D.C.: Library of Congress, 1962.

—— "Shango Cult in Nigeria and Trinidad." *American Anthropologist* 64 (1962): 1204–19.

Sithole, Elkin T. "Black Folk Music." In *Rappin' and Stylin' Out.* Edited by Thomas Kochman. Urbana: University of Illinois Press, 1972, pp. 220–240..

Smitherman, Geneva. *Talkin and Testifyin: The Language of Black America.* Boston: Houghton Mifflin, 1977.

Sollors, Werner. *Beyond Ethnicity: Consent and Descent in American Culture.* New York: Oxford University Press, 1986.

Southern, Eileen. *African-American Traditions in Song, Sermon, Tale, and Dance.* New York: Greenwood, 1990.

—— *The Music of Black Americans: A History.* New York: W. W. Norton, 1971.

Spaeth, Sigmund. *Weep Some More My Lady.* Garden City, N.Y.: Doubleday, 1927.

Spencer, Onah L. "Stackalee." *Directions* 4 (Summer 1941): 14–17.

Stafford-Clark, David. *What Freud Really Said.* London: Penguin, 1965.

Stanzel, F. K. *A Theory of Narrative.* Cambridge: Cambridge University Press, 1987.

Starling, Marion Wilson. *The Slave Narrative: Its Place in American History.* Washington, D.C.: Howard University Press, 1988.

Stephanson, Anders. *Manifest Destiny: American Expansion and the Empire of Right.* New York: Hill and Wang, 1995.

Stevens, Walter, B. *St. Louis: History of the Fourth City, 1763–1909.* St. Louis: S. J. Clarke, 1909.

Steward, Douglas U. *The Disguised Guest: Rank, Role, and Identity in the Odyssey.* Lewisburg, Pa.: Bucknell University Press, 1976.

Stuckey, Sterling. *Going through the Storm.* Oxford: Oxford University Press, 1994.

—— *Slave Culture: Nationalist Theory and Foundation of Black.* Oxford: Oxford University Press, 1987.

—— "Through the Prism of Folklore: The Black Ethos in Slavery." In *American Negro Slavery: A Modern Reader.* Edited by Allen Weinstein and Frank Otto Gatell. New York: Oxford University Press, 1973.

Sultan, J. "2 Live Crew Update." *The Source: The Voice of The Rap Music Industry* 3, no. 4 (1990): 16–17.

Swanberg, W. A. *Dreiser.* New York: Charles Scribner, 1965.

Sweeney, Amin. *A Full Hearing: Orality and Literacy in the Malay World.* Berkeley: University of California Press, 1987.

Talley, Thomas W. *Negro Folk Rhymes: Wise and Otherwise.* New York: Macmillan, 1922.

Tannen, Deborah. 1994. *Talking Voices: Repetition, Dialogue, and Imagery in Conversational Discourse.* Cambridge: University of Cambridge Press, 1994.

Tatar, Maria. *LustMord: Sexual Murder in Weimar Germany.* Princeton: Princeton University Press, 1995.

Tester, Keith. *The Flaneur.* London: Routledge, 1994.

Thompson, Robert Farris. *Flash of the Spirit: African and Afro-American Art and Philosophy*. New York: Vintage, 1983.

—— "Kongo Influence on African-American Artistic Culture." In *Africanisms in American Culture*. Edited by Joseph E. Holloway. Bloomington: Indiana University Press, 1991, pp. 148–184.

Thompson, Stith. *The Folktale*. New York: AMS Press, 1979.

Thomson, Elizabeth, and David Gutman. *The Dylan Companion*. New York: Da Capo, 2001.

Thormahlen, Marianne. *T. S. Elliot at the Turn of the Century*. Lund: Lund University Press, 1991.

Toop, David. *The Rap Attack 2*. Bridgend, Wales: Serpent's Tail, 1991.

Troen, Selwyn K., and Glen E. Holt, eds. *St. Louis*. New York: New Viewpoints, 1977.

Turner, Frederick William, III. "Badmen, Black and White: The Continuity of American Folk Traditions." Ph.D. diss., University of Pennsylvania, 1965.

Turner, Victor. *The Anthropology of Performance*. New York: PAJ, 1986.

—— *From Ritual to Theater: The Human Seriousness of Play*. New York: PAJ, 1982.

Vansina, Jan. *Oral Tradition as History*. Madison: University of Wisconsin Press, 1985.

Vincent, Ted. *Keep Cool: The Black Activists Who Built the Jazz Age*. London: Pluto, 1995.

Vivante, Paolo. *The Iliad: Action as Poetry*. Boston: Twayne, 1991.

Vlach, John Michael. *The Afro-American Tradition in Decorative Arts*. Cleveland: Cleveland Museum of Art, 1979.

Volosinov, V. N. *Marxism and the Philosophy of Language.* Edited by Ladislav Matejika and I. R. Titunik. Cambridge, Mass.: Harvard University Press, 1973.

Watkins, Mel. *On the Real Side . . .* New York: Simon and Schuster, 1994.

Watts, Jill. *The Father Divine Story.* Berkeley: University of California Press, 1992.

Wepman, Dennis, Ronald B. Newman, and Murry B. Binderman, eds. *The Life: The Lore and Folk Poetry of the Black Hustler.* Philadelphia: University of Pennsylvania Press, 1974.

Wheeler, Mary. *Steamboatin' Days.* Baton Rouge: Louisiana State University Press, 1944.

White, Shane, and Graham White. *Stylin': African American Expressive Culture from Its Beginnings to the Zoot Suit.* Ithaca: Cornell University Press, 1998.

Wideman, John Edgar. "Charles Chesnutt and the WPA Narratives: The Oral and Literate Roots of AfroAmerican Literature." In *The Slave's Narrative.* Edited by Charles T. Davis and Henry Louis Gates Jr. Oxford: Oxford University Press, 1985, pp. 59–78.

Wiggins, William H., Jr. "Jack Johnson as Bad Nigger: The Folklore of His Life." *Black Scholar* 5 (January 1971): 35–46.

Williams, Brett. *John Henry: A Bio-Bibliography.* Westport, Conn.: Greenwood, 1983.

Wilson, Olly. "Black Music as an Art Form." *Black Music Research Journal,* 1983, pp. 1–21.

Wright, Richard. "Blueprint for Negro Writing." *New Challenge* 2 (Fall 1937): 53–65.

—— "How 'Bigger' Was Born" (1940). In *Early Works of Richard Wright.* Edited by Arnold Rampersad. New York: Library of America, 1991.

—— "The Literature of the Negro in the United States." In *White Man, Listen!* Garden City, N.Y.: Doubleday, 1957, pp. 105–149.

—— *12 Million Black Voices.* New York: Viking, 1941.

Young, Nathan B. "Transgressions: Death, Legends, and Music of Bad Man Stackolee." Manuscript M2, St. Louis University Archives, 1983.

—— "Madam Babe: St. Louis' Golden Bordello Idyll." Manuscript. St. Louis University, 1987.

—— "The Saga of Stackerlee." Manuscript. St. Louis University, n.d.

Ziff, Larzer. *American 1890s: Life and Times of a Lost Generation.* New York: Viking, 1987.

Zumwalt, Rosemary Levy. *American Folklore Scholarship.* Bloomington: Indiana University Press, 1988.

ARCHIVES

Library of Congress, Washington, D.C.

American Life Histories: Manuscripts from the Federal Writers' Project, 1936–1940

Letters of Robert W. Gordon

Lomax Collection, Archives of Folk Song

W. K. Wilgus Collection, Folklore Archives, University of North Carolina at Chapel Hill

Index

Hardy, John, 114
Harlem Renaissance, 197
Harris, Aaron, 97–98, 114
Harris, Jesse, 163–164
Harvey, Judge, 32, 77
Havelock, Eric A., 217–219
Hearn, Lafcadio, 102, 244n11
Hearst, Patty, 209–210
Hell: Jim Crow South as, 199–201. *See also* Devil, the
Henry, John, 13, 134–135
Hillbilly music, 142–143, 189
Hip-hop, 183, 187, 220–225. *See also* Rap music
Hipsters, 99–100
Hoboes, 128, 198–199
Hogan, Ernest, 107
Hood, Walter, 11
Huey Lewis and the News (musical group), 4
Hughes, Langston, 197
Hull, Papa Henry, 151–152, 198–199
Hunt, Bill, 142
Hunter, Robert, 68
Hurston, Zora Neale, 197
Hurt, Mississippi John, 4, 152–157
Hustling, 223–224
Hutchinson, Frank, 142–143, 184, 189

Iceberg Slim (pimp), 224
Ice Cube (rapper), 222
Ice T (rapper), 222
Inversion (in characters and situations), 69, 70
Ireland, Tom, 96
Irwin, May, 107–109
Isley Brothers (musical group), 178
Isobel, Miss, 174

Jackson, Bruce, 166, 168, 254n1
Jackson, Peter, 65
Jagger, Mick, 14

Jazz, 4, 146, 172, 255n9
Jim Crow, 41–42, 119–121, 158, 169, 170–171, 198–203. *See also* Racism
Johnson, Charles P., 84
Johnson, Guy, 215
Johnson, Jack, 13, 149–151
Johnson, Robert, 163
Johnson, Rosamond, 107; "Under the Bamboo Tree," 109
Johnson, Tommy, 14
Jones, Eddy, 114
Jones, Leroi (Imamu Amiri Baraka), 174
Joplin, Scott, 92, 93–94, 95, 96, 98, 105
Joyce, James: *Finnegans Wake*, 247n20

Kelley, Robin D. G., 14–15, 87–88, 99, 176, 221, 236n5
Kelley, Sam, 82
Kelsoe, W. A., 131
Kimball, Nell, 96–97, 103
King, Martin Luther, Jr., 203
King, Rodney, 214
Kittay, Jeffrey, 259n12

Lane, Roger, 234n4
Laws, Malcolm, 111–112
Lawson, Sherman, 142
Lazarus (black desperado), 114
Lee, Peggy, 4
Leeming, David, 207, 208
Lenin, V. I., 204
Levee work camps, 2, 127–129, 186, 198–199
Lévi-Strauss, Claude, 73
Lewis, Martron D., 83
Lhamon, W. T., Jr., 185–186
Lid clubs, 38, 39, 82
Little Richard, 176
Litwack, Leon, 120
Lodi, Calif., 1927 version of "Stagolee" from, 49, 54–55, 57, 59